The Ethics of Catholicism and the Consecration of the Intellectual

Arguing that religious values can account for differences in the role of intellectual elites, André J. Bélanger compares the very distinct traditions of French Catholicism and Anglo-Saxon Protestantism to demonstrate the strong relationship between the Catholic tradition and the emergence of an intellectual elite in secularized Catholic societies.

Using France as the most representative case of a Catholic context, Bélanger argues that as French society became more secularized intellectuals replaced the clergy as arbitrators of justice and enlightenment. Catholic morality was consolidated by the scholastic tradition and confirmed by the Counter-Reformation, providing the foundation that allowed the establishment of a lay elite. Bélanger describes the progressive takeover of positions of influence by the new elite in Catholic society and examines arguments used by thinkers from the seventeenth to the twentieth century to legitimize their positions. In contrast, the Anglo-Saxon Protestant tradition, due to its emphasis on the priesthood of all believers, led to recognition of the individual's conscience as the sole judge of her or his deeds and failed to provide intellectuals with the basis for any claim to serve as moral leaders in political affairs.

Straddling a variety of disciplines, this study will be of interest to students of political science, sociology, philosophy, and history.

ANDRÉ J. BÉLANGER is professor of political science, Université de Montréal.

The Ethics of Catholicism and the Consecration of the Intellectual

ANDRÉ J. BÉLANGER

McGill-Queen's University Press
Montreal & Kingston • London • Buffalo

© McGill-Queen's University Press 1997
ISBN 0-7735-1517-8

Legal deposit first quarter 1997
Bibliothèque nationale du Québec

Printed in Canada on acid-free paper

Published simultaneously in the European Union by
Liverpool University Press.

This book has been published with the help of a
grant from the Humanities and Social Science
Federation of Canada, using funds provided by the
Social Sciences and Humanities Research Council
of Canada. Funding has also been received from the
Université de Montréal.

McGill-Queen's University Press is grateful to the
Canada Council for support of its publishing program.

Canadian Cataloguing in Publication Data

Bélanger, André-J., 1935–
　　The ethics of Catholicism and the consecration of the
　　intellectual
　　Includes bibliographical references and index.
　　ISBN 0-7735-1517-8
　　1. Intellectuals – History.　2. Intellectual life – History.
　　3. Christian ethics – History.　4. Religion and culture –
　　History.　5. Religion and ethics – History.　I. Title.
　　BJ1231.B46 1996　　305.5'52　　C96-900724-8

Typeset in New Baskerville 10/12
by Chris McDonell, Hawkline Graphics.

Contents

Preface vii

Introduction 3

PART I OBJECTIVE JUSTICE AND ITS DEMISE

1 Catholic Ethics 19

2 The British Moralists: The Eclipse of Natural Law 30

3 The American Assessment of Natural Law 50

4 From the Clerisy to a Sparse Intelligentsia 59

PART II THE RISE AND FALL OF THE INTELLECTUAL: THE FRENCH EXPERIENCE

5 The Counter-Reformation and the Impact of Jesuit Pedagogy 75

6 Lay Ethics within the Bounds of the Church 85

7 The *Philosophe*: The Prefiguration of the Intellectual 97

8 The Revolutionary Reading of Justice 124

9 An Anti-Individualist Liberalism 133

10 Positivism: The Path Leading to the Intellectual 145

11 The Emergence of the Intellectual   152
12 The Consecration of the Intellectual   167

Conclusion   180

Appendix   189

Bibliography   203

Index   237

Preface

This book about intellectuals grew out of a more general reflection on the subject of how different interests are mediated from one country to another. In other words, it is a reflection on the many ways that interests may vent their grievances, whether in public or in the sanctorum of governments. Large rallies in Washington, for example, may have little in common with similar demonstrations in Paris, and their meaning and purpose may also be quite different.

Following that questioning, I have tried to investigate more precisely why it is that, in some countries, artists, novelists, philosophers, and even actors intervene in the political arena, whereas in other countries, this would be simply inconceivable. My purpose here is not so much to establish the definitive status and role of an entity called the "intellectual," but rather to understand why certain forms of interest representation are acceptable in one society, but not in another. Why, for example, do the cultural values of some countries induce certain people to act in arenas that are completely outside their particular fields of expertise?

In seeking answers to these questions, I have drawn from the disciplines of both sociology and political science, as well as from the works of many philosophers and thinkers. The exercise is not as such an inquiry into political philosophy, nor does it purport to provide innovative interpretations of the works under discussion.

I have decided to limit myself to a study of the Anglo-Saxon and French ethical traditions because they serve to put in sharp contrast two very distinct traditions arising from differing interpretations of ethics. In order to extend this comparison somewhat, I have included an appendix dealing with Latin America. This account remains sketchy because of my ignorance of both Spanish and Portuguese, which has obliged me to rely on secondary sources and translations.

I wish to thank colleagues from a wide range of disciplines for their comments, advice, and encouragement, especially Marc Angenot, Martin David-Blais, Graziela Ducatenzeiler, the late Louise Lacoste, Jean-Jacques Nattiez, and Paul-André Perron. I am also grateful to Peter Brown for his many suggestions on style, and to the Social Sciences and Humanities Research Council of Canada for its financial support.

The Ethics of Catholicism and the Consecration of the Intellectual

Introduction

Rule-making is a twofold process of representation; there are rulers who act officially as warrants of the interests of the whole, and there are mediators who act in the name of more specific interests. In the contemporary world politics can be understood as the interplay of agents who claim to represent the interests of others. As societies grow more complex, people tend to delegate the task of promoting their interests to those who specialize in representation. These specialists may be lobbyists, pressure groups, or political parties. The highest and most encompassing level of representation is indeed that attained by legislators, who are duly authorized to perform such functions, and who at least pretend to act in the best interests of the whole.

But not all mediators do possess such mandates. A whole spectrum of mediators assumes the responsibility for acting as representatives of the population, in part, or as a whole. Incipient social movements operate in the following fashion: several individuals gather to advocate a cause without having any other initial form of support. The success of their mobilization serves ultimately to legitimize their mediatory role. When these activists succeed in constituting a well-recognized organization – when, in other words, they become entitled, even though not necessarily mandated, to speak for others – they reach a status of admissibility. Feminist movements are a case in point, as are, to a lesser extent, labour movements. Ultimately, there exists a category of agents whose actions are understood to remain autonomous or free from any institutional bounds, but that are still intended to represent the interests of parts or the whole of society. Such agents are self-appointed representatives whose pronouncements are intended, in the long run, to be beneficial to all. They are what I shall call intellectuals.

Now, whatever the society, mediators do not work at random. Depending upon the culture, the institutional rules of the state (at different levels of government), and the laws governing particular interests, mediators are likely to adopt different patterns of intervention. Lobbyists in Washington, for example, do not operate in the same way as they do in London. Some factors induce people to adopt certain modes of behaviour over others in order for their actions to succeed. The inducement comes from interests that in turn furnish values to be promoted and goals to be pursued, and that are themselves influenced by culture and ideology. The pursuit of capitalist objectives, for example, belongs to a rather well-established set of values in the Western world, but the manner in which such interests are put forward varies from one society to the next, depending upon cultural norms. Finally, institutional rules provide different means of accessing the state's rule-making process; groups within the state must adapt their actions to the rules of the game. Business, labour, and agricultural organizations, for example, do not all mobilize in the same fashion. For, although contemporary societies are activated at the political level by the interplay of mediated interests, this interplay is not fortuitous. The political game differs from one society to another because social determinants make it so. And social determinants are made more complex by psychological factors as well as by individual preferences, idiosyncrasies, and differences of socialization. The mediation of interests is thus significantly affected by the cultural or ideological environment and by the channels of access to rule making within a society.

Because intellectuals are interested in influencing politicians via large audiences, they usually resort to using the mass media, and avoid the more intricate tracks of political manoeuvring. In so doing, they tend to escape the institutional constraints of politics. Unlike lobbyists who must conform to the rules of gaining access to governments, intellectuals are relatively free in their mobilizing action, though they enjoy less financial support. As representatives of the whole, or of a large part of it, they are likely to be more influenced by cultural factors than are some other groups.

The main objective of this book is to illustrate the close connection between culture and the status of intellectuals in a given society. While intellectuals can be found almost anywhere, they do not receive the same measure of recognition everywhere. They are more inclined to act politically in some societies than in others. I submit that this difference can be accounted for by considering the values of particular cultures, values that have religious origins.

WHAT IS AN INTELLECTUAL?

Before going any further, I should clarify my terminology. The word "intellectual" has many meanings, though some definitions have become more or less standard. Lipset's definition is commonly used and among the most comprehensive. For him, intellectuals are "all those who create, distribute, and apply *culture*, that is, the symbolic world of man, including art, science and religion"(1963, 333). More recent authors like Brym (1980, 12) and Etzioni-Halevy (1985, 9) use a similar definition, though Brym insists upon the importance of the "production of ideas." We could amplify the definition a bit by saying that intellectuals are producers of signs and symbols, and therefore that the "class" of intellectuals includes artists and performers. Following this line of thought, Shils proposes three types of intellectuals: producers, interpreters and transmitters, and finally consumers (1973, 21). But despite this broad perspective, Shils emphasizes the intellectuals' privileged access to the "central zone" of culture, "the centre of the order of symbols, of values and beliefs that govern the society," adding that this zone "partakes of the nature of sacred" (1970, 1). In this sense, every society has an "official" religion (ibid.). Intellectuals are the interpreters of that religion and thus have a special status which is not shared by all producers of ideas or signs and symbols. Shils is joined by Coser who writes, on the subject of intellectuals, that "[they] consider themselves special custodians of abstract ideas like reason and justice and truth, jealous guardians of moral standards that are too often ignored in the market place and the houses of power" (1965, viii).

It becomes obvious that the word "intellectual" lends itself to a variety of treatments. But my purpose here is not to exhaust the traditional repertoire of definitions, nor even to arrive at a definition that would achieve a consensus. In this respect, some scholars have complained that the literature on intellectuals does not succeed in delineating a concept that allows for rigorous or comparative analysis (Nettl 1970, 60). Lipset and Basu point out that studies on intellectuals have remained at a descriptive level without ever providing interpretations from a "coherent theoretical framework" (1975, 433). With the exception of Gramsci, who did attempt to provide such a framework and several others like Gouldner, who proposed a Hegelian notion of the "flawed universal class," most authors have generally stuck to the simple recognition of a social category (Gouldner 1979, 6).

My intention here is thus not to offer a new definition but to identify a certain type of social relation, or, to be more precise, a sub-type of an already existing type of social relation. I use the term "intellectual" here to signify a mediator or representative. I am thus qualifying, or adding to, the meaning of a word that already exists, much as Shils did when he used "intellectual" to refer to an individual with special access to the "sacred zone" of culture. Such qualifications mean that intellectuals have special attributes that are not shared by all producers of ideas.

In France, where the term "intellectual" was popularized, many authors have used the word in a narrower and more familiar sense. Benda (1928a) noticed, about three decades after the Dreyfus Affair, that modern clerics had given up letting laymen mind the business of politics, and used their own *status* as a way of introducing themselves in the public arena. We could review a series of writers, not necessarily social scientists, who over the years have chosen a similar perspective. From Jean-Paul Sartre (1972) to Maurice Blanchot (1984) and Jean-Francois Lyotard (1984), there is near consensus regarding the general contours of the concept. It is agreed, on the whole, that writers, scholars, artists, or scientists are *not* intellectuals until they use their status to place themselves within a political debate. More recently, Rieffel has summed it up well by identifying an intellectual as the individual who from a competence in matters of cultural creation oversteps his or her initial role in order to become committed in public debates (1993, 16). Thus, he adds, and with reason, the idea of an *"intellectuel engagé"* becomes a tautology since the essential condition for being one is to be *engagé*.

Let us therefore define an intellectual as a person who, from the status of public producer of signs and symbols involves him- or herself in the political arena to express views on the workings of a specific collectivity.

This definition calls for some comments on certain problems of delimitation. First, it refers to public producers of signs and symbols; it therefore includes philosophers, writers, scholars, painters, musicians, scientists, artistic performers, and others who address their works to a diffuse audience. The public aspect is important because such people use their fame – that is, the public's recognition of their proficiency in one abstract field – to *transfer* this proficiency to another field. Simple professionals such as lawyers, physicians, engineers, or teachers are excluded unless they have produced works in their own disciplines which place them in the limelight in one way or another. The same rule of exclusion would apply to a novelist who has never published his fiction. Public recognition is a matter of degree: some disciplines within the arts and sciences are better recognized than others, and the degree of respect accorded to each varies within particular cultures.

Do actors or singers qualify as intellectuals? In France in 1985 Yves Montand was given an hour of prime-time television by the French publicly owned network to vent his opinions about his country's defence policy. In the United States, Jane Fonda went to the hustings to protest against the American involvement in Vietnam. These are indeed borderline cases. On the other hand, Ronald Reagan's entrance into Californian politics, from which he proceeded to the national level, was not legitimized because of his fame on the screen; he did not become involved in politics as an actor. But André Malraux was chosen minister of culture in France because he was considered a prominent thinker.

To a certain extent, intellectuals' involvement in politics, as intellectuals, borders on the usurpation of competence since, most of the time, they move beyond the limits of their competence.

Second, this definition refers to a personal involvement in politics as opposed to one that is collective and organized. Writers who group themselves together to defend their copyrights, painters who petition for state funds in their own favour, or professors who use public pressure to obtain pay raises or better working conditions would not qualify under this definition as intellectuals, because they would not be acting individually. But if these same people signed a petition as individuals in order to pursue a cause that was not immediately theirs, they would be operating as representatives of others' interests on a personal basis, and would therefore be, according to the definition, intellectuals. These act under their own auspices and locate the foundations of their legitimacy in their own values as prominent writers or scientists. But if, for example, they join an organized group such as a political party, they lose a great deal of their autonomy. They become identified with partisanship and severely weaken the independence that characterizes the intellectual.

Third, intellectuals are basically identified by their public involvement. According to the definition, producers of ideas as such are not considered intellectuals until they take a public stance on a political issue. But they do not all reach the same degree of involvement. We can distinguish three levels of commitment: 1) the full-fledged intellectual, who is more or less a professional in the field, espousing many causes (Jean-Paul Sartre stands as the prime example); 2) the defender of a cause, which may sometimes last for a long period of time (those who protested against the Vietnamese war would qualify under this definition); and 3) the individual who takes up an issue, who is often a specialist who applies or extends his or her expertise to a circumscribed point of contention (as did Nelson W. Polsby, scholar of presidential politics when he gave his point of view in the *New York Times* on the press's scrutiny of candidates' private lives after Gary Hart withdrew from the presidential race). These three levels correspond to descending degrees of intensity, with the lowest level indicating a very limited commitment. In fact, the ideal intellectual is one who is fully committed to many causes, whereas the "middle-range" intellectual is the defender of a single cause.

Finally, intellectuals express views on the workings of a specific collectivity. In other words, they raise an issue or debate one. This provision puts aside political philosophers who elaborate general theories or diffuse opinions without specific references to contentious points in a given society. Under this definition, Rousseau's *Social Contract* and Hegel's *Theory of Right* would not qualify as the works of intellectuals. Political philosophy, which is meant to legitimize one form of authority to the exclusion of others, is likely in some instances to be interpreted as an opinion in a public debate. Of course, there is room here for differences of interpretation. But whether or not an author adopts an intellectual stance does not in itself affect the quality of his or her production, just as becoming an intellectual does not entail, from the definition here proposed, any upgrading or downgrading of status. Authors or scholars may derive greater satisfaction by becoming politically involved, but only to the same extent that any person might feel gratified by enlarging his or her own sphere of influence. Certain cultures may, however, provide rewards for producers of ideas who enter public debates. Whether these ideas are traditional or progressive is immaterial: the purpose of the analysis is solely to determine the social conditions that facilitate the emergence and maintenance of a stratum of mediators that I call intellectuals.

Intellectuals can be found in all Western societies, but they do not operate nor are they welcome in the same fashion from one country to another. In some instances, they are induced to become involved, spontaneously receiving the media attention that is necessary to diffuse their actions; in others, their words and deeds do not extend beyond the confines of limited circles or literary journals.

In France, for instance, intellectuals have long been furnished with platforms to express their views. The mass media have faithfully reported their excursions into public life, so that writers such as Sartre and Simone de Beauvoir enjoyed for decades a political following that far exceeded their reading audiences. By comparison, a recognition of that magnitude at the political level is rather rare in countries such as Great Britain, the United States, and Australia, where scholars, novelists, and artists are generally taken for what they are in their respective fields. Their reputations, as great as they may be, do not allow for extension or any spill-over into the political arena. This difference cannot be attributed merely to fantasy or idiosyncrasy.

When we look more closely at such differences of behaviour, we note that they accord with the value attributed to *mediated* opinion. Some cultures seem receptive to mediated opinion, while others are hostile to the idea of granting some individuals the exclusive privilege of expressing certain opinions. What then accounts for the difference? I submit that it arises from different religious world views.

THE INTELLECTUAL'S RELIGIOUS MATRIX

Catholicism and Protestantism oppose each other on the question of the freedom of individual conscience. Catholicism relies on the clergy and its moral authority to maintain the unity of the Church. The clergy is thus vested with the immense responsibility of interpreting the word of God, the revelation of the Almighty. It places itself between God and the faithful, collectively assuming an exclusive mediatory position. Knowledge is vested in an enlightened elite. On the other hand, Protestantism establishes its unity directly on the Bible, which is seen as the basic foundation of the Church.

Luther reckoned that consensus, if not unanimity, would emerge from the general access to the infallibility of the scripture. The Holy Spirit had inspired the Bible, leaving it up to the faithful to rally themselves without the mediation of a clergy being necessary. Things did not turn out exactly as Luther had imagined. The reading of the Bible by the laity opened the way to a diversity of interpretations that led ultimately to a *subjective* conception of ethics. Catholicism, on the other hand, stuck to an *objective* conception and reinforced, as a measure of the Counter-Reformation (the Council of Trent), its trust in the clergy's commitment to the one true justice.

As time has passed, the Catholic Church has lost its grip on lay matters, and societies formerly under its moral ascendancy have freed themselves, and have become completely independent of the Church. Concurrently, Protestant churches have evolved, emphasizing the exercise of free will in the direction of a pluralistic outlook of morality in general. In both cases, the transition has been one of secularization: the churches, whether Catholic or Protestant, have today virtually no say in the direction of the state. This transition has mainly affected the way people are governed, and by whom; it has also established a neat demarcation between faith and reason. But such a profound change has not necessarily modified the attitude toward the way in which values are diffused in society, especially moral values.

In Protestant systems of ethics, the individual conscience has become the ultimate judge of moral matters. Following this principle, people are expected to inform themselves and make up their own minds about moral issues. The first step consists of reviewing and appraising the facts; the second, of making decisions about how to behave. Catholic ethics works differently. There is, at the start, a definite assumption, not to say a conviction, that justice exists, that it has been created by God, and that it can be found in natural law and in Revelation, as these have been interpreted by the tradition of the Church. Until recently, principles of morality were not meant to be discussed by the faithful; they were meant to be followed. The abstract search for moral codes of behaviour was left to an elite, the clergy.

My approach is Weberian in inspiration, but not entirely in rationale. In *The Protestant Ethics and the Spirit of Capitalism*, Max Weber follows the paths determined by his "comprehensive" mode of dealing with social relations: he tries to *understand* the motives behind patterns of social behaviour. His ideal types are constructs that are designed to make us comprehend, for example, the frame of mind that puts a capitalist in action. My purpose here is not actually to uncover in the abstract the agents' intentions or to make presumptions about them. In this sense I depart somewhat from Weber. On the other hand, I believe cultural values are hard to kill and may, under different guises, reappear despite the demise of the social structures that first sustained them. To grasp these values is an insuperable exercise unless one resorts to the heuristic use of analytic constructs. It seems to me safer, as I have elaborated elsewhere (1985, 40–56), to conceive of culture and ideology as useful constructs that are able to account for identifiable behaviours. The recourse to the ideal type is then indicated so long as it remains strictly at the level of social values and patterns of behaviour.

Weber's treatment of Protestantism and its relationship to capitalism is based on the transfer of a teleological ethos from religion to the marketplace, the passage from an ethics to a spirit. A religious drive, the Lutheran *Beruf* or Calvinist calling (as interpreted by Weber), is transposed into a "moral habitus" (Poggi 1983, 49) of entrepreneurship and methodical accumulation of capital. The entire phenomenon remains at the level of deep aspirations and the means by which to realize them. (Weber's work, we know, has given rise to a series of critiques pro and con (see Marshall 1982)). Such, at least, were Weber's manifest intentions, though they may not have always been consistently demonstrated throughout his work, as some commentators have noted.

The religious reality I wish to explore has less to do with a teleological ethos than with the strategic position of actors in the determination of moral values. The advent of the Lutheran protest and the Reformation that followed introduced a political dimension in the conflict against Rome: what became an issue was Rome's exclusive right to interpret revelation and the moral prescriptions that ensued. Protestant ethics asserted the emancipation from this control, whereas the Counter-Reformation was a strategic response to the whittling away of the clergy's power. Protestantism (the term speaks for itself) and the Counter-Reformation arose in mutual conflict. The former asserted the moral and intellectual capacity of the believer to interpret the Book by him- or herself, the latter reaffirmed the moral authority of the Church as expressed by its clergy.

From this absolute antagonism, the two evolved in opposite directions, thereby confirming their mutual incompatibility. Protestants were led to question the foundations of ethics and progressively accepted a secularized form of it. The transition to an acceptance of lay expression of morality proved to be a gradual process. The Catholic societies' passage to the secular state has often been more tumultuous, giving rise to serious tensions and, at times, to the exclusion of particular religious orders. The Protestant transition to liberalism occurred as an extension of the Reformation. In Catholic societies, it represented a break from the past.

Interestingly enough, this break created the condition for the appearance of intellectuals. They appear most fully in previously Catholic societies that have achieved a complete stage of secularization. They do not, of course, emerge suddenly like jacks-in-the-box: their actions depend upon the secularizing process. But their presence as full-fledged mediators is acknowledged only when they have displaced the religious elite. How does this transformation come about? I propose that the explanation is to be found in the cultures of these societies, cultures that furnish both the incentives for certain individuals to become intellectuals and the necessary values that allow for their social acceptance. If there is an *ethos* of the intellectual, it is one of a responsibility felt for the social sphere. But contrary to the Weberian capitalist who experiences inner gratification for accumulating the fruits of his or her labour, the intellectual, if he or she is to act as a *recognized* representative of the whole, depends upon a form of social legitimation. The capitalist operates within the confines of an impersonal market and requires no recognition (except that of the law), but a novelist or philosopher who strongly desires to act as an intellectual, may involve him- or herself in all sorts of public debates, but may still fail to be recognized as an intellectual. The status of the intellectual is achieved through the medium of communication, and it depends upon the audience's acceptance, which is to a large extent determined by cultural values. The Catholic tradition is receptive to mediation by an elite group which, because of the recognized competence of its members, is authorized to express views on moral matters. Whenever the clergy loses its ascendancy through secularization, a vacuum is created that has to be filled. Intellectuals exist to fulfil this same moral function.

Because they must put aside any spiritual consideration in the establishment of their moral authority, intellectuals tend to fall back on rationalist modes of legitimation. On the whole, as we shall see, they usually claim a superior knowledge of what is good for the "masses." These are presumed to be often alienated, submissive to indoctrination, propaganda, or advertising, and thus incapable of objective knowledge. They need the intelligence and the intuitions (since we are still on ethical matters) of a moral elite. At least, this is the intellectuals' side of the story. But, as I have said, there must be an audience to receive the message and to agree with the principle of mediation. The Catholic frame of reference provides for both: an elite and a receptive public.

While the Protestant tradition has evolved toward a secular ethics, the Catholic tradition has stuck to the notion of natural law, which through secularization has been transformed into the belief in an objective justice that has to be discovered and worked out. Depending upon the era, this justice has been located in human nature (but still given by God, the eighteenth-century deist approach), in nature itself (positivism), or in the interrelationship between human beings and their consciences (existentialism). But whatever its foundation, it is understood that justice is objective and that it should be expressed by those who are best disposed morally and mentally to discover and diffuse it.

In order to better understand the emergence of the intellectual within the Catholic tradition, I propose to contrast it with the Protestant tradition. By means of this comparison, the road leading to the consecration of the intellectual should become more visible. Since it is impossible to delve into entire religious traditions, I shall deal with the most representative form of each, namely, the Anglo-Saxon and the French traditions and their divergent evolutions. The former is used here because it embodies to a high degree a tradition that recognizes the individual's ability to determine for him-

or herself what should be considered morally good or desirable for the whole community. My purpose here is not, therefore, to shed any new light on this evolution as such, but to compare one of the most advanced traditions of ethical pluralism with the intellectual mode of representation.

The authors discussed in this work have been selected in order to *illustrate* the evolution of both traditions. My goal is not, therefore, to be particularly innovative in examining their respective contributions to ethics. Their ideas are presented in an abbreviated format that is intended only to illustrate how they are associated with either the Anglo-Saxon trend, which evolves toward a dissolution of transcendental justice, or the French trend, which progresses toward the recognition of an intellectual elite.

The argument adopted here favours the religious factor as one major determinant to the presence or absence of intellectuals. It does not follow that it is the only one. For instance, the political structure may or may not be propitious to their emergence. Members of aristocratic societies are more likely to be suspicious of public opinion and to expect wisdom to be found among the few. By contrast, egalitarian societies share the view that one person is as good as another in making ethical judgments. What interests me here is the extent to which the religious dimension contributed to sustaining this state of political organization. But at no time can I claim that the religious factor is an exclusive determinant. In other words, the purpose of the book is to show *the extent* to which the religious factor has operated within a given society, making *likely*, after secularisation takes place, a replication of the relationship that formerly existed between the clergy and the faithful.

I wish to draw exclusively on the case of France because, compared to other countries of Catholic tradition, the role of the intellectual emerged early on and has flourished most fully there. I do not intend, however, to recount the history of intellectuals in France or in any other countries to which I shall refer.

Political and social factors can certainly encourage or discourage intellectuals in the expression of their views. Intellectual expression differs from other forms of interest articulation, which use the channels of formal representation, social movements, interest groups, or mass media. In the case of France, persistent ideological divisiveness has helped to foster the intervention of intellectuals as privileged representatives of social interests. Recurrent regime crises in the recent past have probably prompted this intellectual involvement. The Great Depression, the German occupation, the trauma of decolonization, and the uprising of May 1968 have successively shaken the regime's stability and have thus elicited solutions from outside the immediate political arena. Different times, of course, provoke different forms of intellectual intervention. Émile Zola's action during the Dreyfus Affair, for example, was quite distinct in nature and in style from Jean-Paul Sartre's political engagement more than half a century later. Historical circumstances make each intellectual's involvement a unique event.

Despite this historical contingency, I would argue that a common appeal to transcendental values of one sort or another always serves to legitimate the political involvement and the recognition of intellectuals in general. With this argument I do not wish to define exhaustively the meaning of, or the rationale behind, intellectuals' commitments. Instead, by presenting some of the representative figures among twentieth century intellectuals from the time of the Dreyfus Affair down to the present, I intend to bring to light the particular form of public representation that intellectual involvement entails.

Throughout this analysis, we shall keep in mind that mediation remains the point of reference; in other words, mediation is the basic social relation to be explored. But since intellectuals are self-appointed mediators, much emphasis will be placed upon the way these people, depending on their religious backgrounds, actually justify their action.

The book is set in two parts. Part One establishes how from orthodoxy as posited by the Catholic Church through the teachings of Thomas Aquinas (chapter 1), the criteria used to legitimize an elite from the recognition of natural law and the existence of an objective justice have been later put into question by the British moralists (chapter 2), and how Americans made a very different reading of that same natural law (chapter 3). This situation led in Anglo-Saxon countries to a very limited range of political activity on the part of intellectuals (chapter 4).

Part Two follows the opposite trend which, from the Counter-Reformation up to very recently, magnifies the role of an elite whose legitimacy lies in its exclusive ability to extract the components of an objective justice. The persistence of the Jesuit educational system has helped to sustain that pretension through a good part of that period (chapter 5), while successive generations of thinkers have attributed to reason the sole access to an understanding of ethics. Renaissance skepticism was short-lived and soon gave way to a rationalist perspective that set the trend (chapter 6). When eighteenth-century *philosophes* took over, it was to strengthen that pretension and project it into the political arena (chapter 7). Despite its occasional claims to individual rights, the French Revolution that followed was largely carried by principles that remained faithful to the rationalist paradigm in the interpretation of justice (chapter 8). And people who claimed to be liberals in the nineteenth century espoused nonetheless a strong anti-individualism in favour of a communitarian conception, if not a populism that ironically was meant to bolster the expression of the happy few (chapter 9). In the meantime, positivism was establishing itself as an almost official philosophy, thus conferring on the scholar the ultimate moral power over society (chapter 10). With the secularization process that occurred at the turn of the century, the ground was set for the recognition of the intellectual, as the Dreyfus Affair illustrated (chapter 11). The ultimate consecration of the intellectual was to coincide with the post-war period and Jean-Paul Sartre's flamboyant interventions, though it was succeeded by a liberal era that has since contributed in the demise of the same intellectual (chapter 12).

PART I

Objective Justice and Its Demise

1 Catholic Ethics

There may be different ways of contrasting the Catholic and Protestant traditions. Discussing Catholic ethics first allows us to respect the chronological order in which the two appeared, and to underline the Protestant departure from orthodoxy. Since my purpose here is merely to demonstrate the opposing characteristics of the two traditions, I prefer to steer clear of any considerations of precedence. Instead I will emphasize the political consequences that can be derived from their contrary positions. I shall treat the Catholic perspective first in order to delineate a basic paradigm that will subsequently be used as a point of reference for the remainder of the work. I will try to show that the Protestant tradition serves as a counterpoint to this, which led to a different direction and subsequently to a reconsideration of the very foundations of Christian ethics. I have also chosen to discuss Catholicism first because it is a more or less unified entity. It is easier to show how it became diversified than to trace the reverse process. The Catholic paradigm will therefore be submitted in the form of a reduction that I shall call the Catholic ethics. However, both traditions, Catholic and Protestant, will be presented in a simplified format since my intention is to show only the effects of moral systems on subsequent social structures, not to examine the fine nuances within or between the Catholic and Protestant traditions. With this in mind, I shall draw from some authoritative authors whose works are representative within their respective cultures.

THE CATHOLIC VISTA THROUGH THE OUTLOOK OF THOMAS AQUINAS

The Catholic ethos envisages the ecclesiastical life as unfolding under the strict guidance of an "upper" clergy that, through a hierarchy, ensures that the Church will remain united, stable, and infallible. Indeed, most churches attempt to achieve such attributes, but few rely on the same internal discipline. Until very recently, the Catholic clergy has been vested with the exclusive function of setting moral standards for its faithful. Based upon the Bible and tradition (which is largely what the hierarchy set in the past), the Catholic ethic is interpreted and determined by an elite, which exercises an almost exclusive right in this matter. The Scriptures are considered to be inspired, and thus the source of revelation, but are inaccessible to the common people. Only established theologians are considered to be in a position to understand the exact meaning and import of such an obscure and unsystematic text. Theologians, therefore, serve as both moral and sacramental mediators between God and the believers.

Thomas Aquinas is one of the figures who, due to the extent and insight of his works, exemplifies the Catholic ethics. The Church readily recognized him as the best representative of its approach toward theological and secular matters. One of his pivotal achievements was his unification of worldly and celestial considerations into a cohesive teleological perspective. In contrast to Augustine, who had a vision of two cities, one of God and the other of Satan, Aquinas endowed a meaning to the whole of nature, whose ultimate purpose was the glorification of God. In this scheme, the Church, with the Pope at its head, became the sacred intermediary between God and the world.

God's most valued attribute in the philosophy of Aquinas is unmistakably reason. This is not to say that Aquinas ascribed only one attribute to God, far from it. But throughout Aquinas's discourse on nature and humanity, God's role remains fundamentally one of rationality. The argument unfolds from the premise that nature is a pure product of divine reason. Nature responds to the imperatives of rational organization, which involves different levels of perfection; from the inanimate, those things that are deprived of intelligence, to the divinity, which is *the* intelligence. Creation as a whole is therefore understood in terms of a hierarchy whereby species are unalterable natures with their own distinct beings: the natural order of things is at the same time a rational order of "is right reason about things to be done" (1947, pt I, II, Q65, 1).[1] It involves the objective application of universal principles to practical situations. Prudence is therefore operative in acquiring the knowledge of both *universal* and *singular* aspects of action. Its primary function is "to regulate the means" to the achievement of ends (ibid., Q47, 6). Prudence permits a person to understand first as well as secondary universal principles. As with speculative science, secondary universal principles of practical reason are not acquired from nature but are discovered through experience or study (ibid., Q47, 15). Even though all human beings might possess the ability to discover individually the basic rules of natural law, they do not equally enjoy sufficient prudence to derive the logical consequences from these basic rules. It is, of course, demanded that all people, since they are rational animals, search prudently for morality, but some are better equipped than others to do so. Human beings are far from equal when it comes to interpreting and expressing the law. Some have been created to rule, and others to be ruled. Following Aristotle, Aquinas reminds his reader that "prudence is in the ruler *after the manner of a mastercraft*, but in the subjects, after the manner *of a handicraft*" (ibid., 12). The respective roles stem from a difference of ability that obligates the ruled to remain docile: "Man has a natural aptitude for docility ... He must carefully, frequently, and reverently apply his mind to the teachings of the learned, neither neglecting them through laziness, or despising them through pride" (ibid., Q49,3).

The whole Thomist structure is built on the notion of a hierarchy that operates between and within species. Thus the precedence of brute animals over plants is explained by animals' capacity to reach some sort of knowledge. In turn, brute animals are "subjected" to human beings by the latter's use of intelligence. Similarly, there is said to exist an analogous order among people. Those of outstanding intelligence are naturally required to exercise command over the less intelligent. These natural authorities are the wise (1947, pt I, II, Q100,1).

---

1 It is inspired by Aristotle's prudence, *phronesis*, or practical wisdom, a "disposition with true reason and ability for *actions* concerning human goods," (*Nicomachean Ethics*, bk z, 1140b, 20–5). Goerner (1979; 1983) suggests that Aquinas is much closer to Aristotle than is usually acknowledged. Following Goerner, Aquinas's ethics are derived from Aristotle's notion of virtue in which prudence is to be found. Natural law plays there a subordinate role. Goerner claims that the popularity of Thomas's natural law teaching is a consequence of the legalistic move adopted by the Counter-Reformation.

De Regimine Principum broaches the question of authority in terms of guidance. In order to attain their individual ends, human beings are in need of some form of guidance; society itself exists so that individuals may achieve their ultimate end, "the enjoyment of God" (Aquinas 1954, ch. xiv). This guidance is dual: it is exercised by the political authority, which translates natural law into "human laws," laws governing temporal affairs; and it is exercised at a higher level by the priest or *sacerdos*, who works out the rules that govern the spiritual sphere. Over the authority of the state lies the authority of the Church. Both govern, but in different spheres, the spiritual matters taking precedence over the temporal ones. The buck stops at the Church: "Kings must be subjects to priests" (ibid.). As Passerin d'Entrèves notes (ibid., ch. xx), Aquinas stopped short of a systematic account of the problem of state and Church. The reason for such an omission might reside in the status that Aquinas attributed to the clergy. If "the secular power is subject to the spiritual even as the body is subject to the soul" (1947, pt ii, ii, Q60,6), just as philosophy is to theology, it does not follow that the temporal power falls under the *immediate* authority of the Church. Instead, the latter is expected to exercise a power which will be later associated with the *potestas indirecta* (indirect power or authority) after the Council of Trent.

In Aquinas's time the term "secular power" itself connoted a type of authority confined to non-ideological matters. The world of ideas or opinion was largely left to the clergy to judge. Political authorities contented themselves with managing the material aspects of life and furnishing through incentives and deterrents the opportunity of achieving the virtuous life. It was expected to bolster the beneficial action of the Church while remaining aloof from debates over doctrine.

Combining the Platonic and Aristotelian traditions with the Christian tradition, Aquinas, in sum, argues that the elaboration of ethics should be left to the wise; from the Church's perspective, this largely amounts to entrusting this function to the clergy.

Having determined *who* is entitled to speak on matters of morality, we are left to examine the character of the natural law as expounded by Aquinas and as subsequently endorsed by the Church. Natural law participates of an external and objective justice and is conceived of as a transcendental entity, very different in nature from the utilitarian ethics which will be developed later by British moralists. The utilitarian ethics is seen as immanent and rests upon the individual's perception of moral values.

Aquinas's recognition of natural law as the one true justice of God did not imply any acceptance of individual rights. On the contrary, the Thomist approach stressed the compulsory aspect of law. Natural law as understood by Aquinas is not one of rights but one of duties: duties of individuals between themselves, between themselves and the state, and even more emphatically, duties of the state in general. The entire approach considers first the *cosmos* from which is derived an ordered conception of law (Passerin d'Entrèves 1951, 46). The argument focuses on the common good: since the ends of community and those of the individual are united, they are, in fact, identical. The individual's fusion with the whole is considered a condition for his or her self-development. To the extent that a person conforms to laws of the organic whole, that person fulfills his or her own true nature, which is inherently social.

Just as the ancient Greek philosophers were often blind to the notion of equal rights, which would have appeared to them unjust, so Aquinas considers the best organization of society one that takes into account unequal capacities. The intellectual fiction of a hypothetical 'state of nature' outside society is alien to him (in any case, the 'state of nature' appeared much later in the history of political thought). The right to hold property, for instance, is recognized by him only as a part of human as opposed to natural law.[2]

Aquinas's argument is consistent throughout. The world is construed as abiding by rational laws set in a teleological perspective. Ethics functions in the same way, and one cannot make precise distinctions between politics and ethics, since both obey the same global imperatives. The world is composed of species and beings that occupy different levels of perfection. The situation is therefore one of basic inequality. This being so, it is not surprising that those who are better gifted should hold positions which conform to their abilities. Ethics, being a strictly a matter of *rationality*, should be explained by those best suited to do so, the *wise*.

Aquinas's system of morality provides us with a paradigm of the Catholic ethics; it is, for this reason, worth retaining. He is not, of course, the only one to have elaborated an ethics within the complex context of Church doctrine. Others, for instance, have relied more heavily on will, especially as a distinct faculty of the intellect. (Such was, much later, Suarez's position, as we shall see.) But despite periodic differences of emphasis, the Church, through the centuries, has stuck with the Thomist tradition, recognizing in Aquinas's

---

2 As Tuck (1979, 20) comments about Aquinas's understanding of natural law: "It is not designed to attribute rights to people in a state of nature ... The *ius naturale* is neutral in the areas of personal servitude and private property, and that cuts both ways. There is no *prima facie* right to either servitude *or* liberty, either private property *or* common possession."

works the *philosophia perennis*, the moral system that is most representative of the Catholic conception of salvation. This is not to say though that Aquinas's contribution was solely his, for in addition to the ancient Greeks, he relied upon the immense tradition of the Church itself, whose Fathers had drawn even from the Roman legists. Whatever its predecessors and successors, the Thomist system synthesizes the Catholic outlook on morality. This stands exclusively as a matter of reason, enjoying an absolute status of *objectivity* and *universality* in time and space, which can only be satisfactorily explicated by the prudent and the *knowledgeable*, that is, by the priests.

The authority of the clerical hierarchy in determining moral affairs is, in this scheme, legitimized by the claim that the majority of individuals are not in a position to entirely grasp the rules of morality. Protestantism will hasten to undermine the clergy's legitimacy.

SUAREZ'S NATURAL LAW

The Reformation posed a direct challenge to the interpretation of ethics and progressively led to modifications which were followed by a dissolution of natural law. True, the Thomist school had to weather attacks from the Scotists and the Nominalists as early as the turn of the fourteenth century. Just as, a century later, natural law was developed within the boundaries of Thomism.

Some authors come to mind who while pursuing Thomist goals, brought new light to the original conception of natural law. The Dominicans of the renowned sixteenth-century school of Salamanca greatly expanded the external consequences of natural law as it applied, for example, to international law. Such was the contribution of Francisco de Vitoria. The Spanish Jesuits, including Fernando Vasquez, continued this innovative trend. But the most revolutionary of the Spanish theologians, at least from hindsight, was undoubtedly Francisco Suarez (1548–1617).

If I turn momentarily to Suarez, it is because the liberal position frequently attributed to him can be seen as a forerunner of the modern natural school that followed. There is also no denying the importance of his bold strategy for secularizing the kingly authority and making it inferior to that of the Pope. However, I think one should avoid making rapid conclusions about Suarez's position on natural law.

First, Suarez did not intend to introduce a new way of thinking in general. As a Jesuit he was entirely devoted to the congregation's mission of defending the Pope's ascendancy against the current onslaught of the Reformation. His contribution must then be

Protestant movements. All of creation is seen to be governed by the sovereign reason of God, whose laws permeate both the natural and the supernatural worlds.

Aquinas is indeed aware of the epistemological problem raised by his recognition of human beings' natural understanding of first moral precepts. How, he asks himself, can the mind arrive independently at such knowledge? To answer this question, Aquinas draws a parallel between pure rationality and what we might call ethical rationality. Since the rules of ethics abide by the principles of reason, they must, like logical truths, be discoverable by the same intellectual process. So, just as speculative reason is capable of deducing self-evident principles – principles of understanding (*intellectus principiorum*) such as the principles of identity and contradiction – so is practical reason able to extract through a natural tendency (*inclinatio naturalis*) the idea of the good as distinguished from the bad, and through deduction, some other moral precepts. The mental dispositions toward speculative and ethical knowledge belong to what is called by Aquinas a *habitus*; the moral *habitus* is termed *synderesis* and is the disposition to know spontaneously the fundamentals of ethics, but, as we shall see, not the whole of ethics. *Synderesis*, which is sometimes called conscience, is expected to furnish the first principles of practical reason. It is a natural habit that induces us toward the good only, and it belongs to natural law.

This entire operation remains one of the mind. Natural law manifests itself through natural reason, which is able to grasp at least the basic components of morality, as these pertain to the natural order of things. According to Aquinas, human beings, from their inner nature as intelligent beings, are capable of recognizing to some extent their true end, and they can act accordingly. The process originates from an act of reason, which is nothing exceptional in Aquinas's mind since it simply flows from human nature's power of understanding: "Man's good or evil is something in reference to reason: wherefore the passions, considered in themselves, are referable both to good and evil, for as much as they may accord or disaccord with reason" (1947, pt I, II, Q59, 1).

All this trust in reason is nonetheless qualified by other considerations that have to do with the unequal ability of human beings to acquire a satisfactory knowledge of ethics: some people are more apt to attain it than others.

There exists in Thomas Aquinas's philosophy an intellectual virtue known as prudence, which, though it is cognitive in nature, is applied to action. Prudence operates at the level of practical reason; it things. In a nutshell, nature is order, and is thus understood in terms of hierarchy, since all beings are not granted the same degree of perfection.

Any reference to order implies a reference to law; not law in the strict legal sense of the term, but law in a broad sense, one that covers ethics. As Aquinas writes: "Law is nothing but a rational plan of operation" and a "rational plan of any kind of work is derived from the end" (1955, *Summa,* bk III, ch. 114, 5). In his mind, there exists first the eternal law, which is the expression of divine governance over all beings. This law is the work of perfect intelligence, not basically of will; for commanding is supposed to be the ordering of a movement toward an end. After eternal law comes natural law, which nevertheless participates in eternal law. Natural law, which is merely the tip of the iceberg, is accessible to humanity.

Natural law determines which actions are good in the fulfilment of the ends that God has determined for human beings. For Aquinas, it derives from the true nature of things. It is by definition an objective justice characterized by both universality and immutability; that is, it is applicable in all times and places. Natural law is related to *recta ratio,* which is right reason. But how does this law manifest itself? How, in other words, can one discover it?

Since natural law is derived from eternal law, which is *in se* the expression of rationality, it follows that it can be discovered solely through an act of reason. It has nothing to do with feeling, sentiment, or the senses. Thanks to a divine light within ourselves, the light of natural reason, which is "an imprint on us of the Divine light" (1947, pt I, II, Q91, 2), we are capable of grasping the premises of the true law, which says that one must do good and avoid evil, and from which other precepts follow, such as, for instance, "Thou shalt not kill." Such an operation of the mind is performed by the intuition; only after the initial insight do the rules of deductive logic play a role. The argument makes no empirical claims. On the contrary, it relies solely on reason's ability to partake of the divine reason, of which the former is but a pale expression. "Man's good or evil is something in the reference to reason," writes Aquinas (ibid., Q59, 1). Ethics is a matter of understanding.

Aquinas sees no contradiction between faith and reason, for the revealed truth of Christianity is there to complement the acquisition of the truth already reached by natural means. Nature is perfected by grace, and from this conjunction nature attains a state of harmony. In this respect, Thomist philosophy is much more optimistic than that of both the preceding Augustinian school and the subsequent understood within this framework. His work might be interpreted as containing a strategy that was geared toward breaking the claims of divine authority, especially those of James I, such claims meant, in effect, that the monarch demanded equal status with that of the Pope.

On the one hand, Suarez's intention is to remain obedient to the teachings of the Church and to the orthodoxy of the Thomist school. His perception of human beings remains largely consistent with that of Aquinas; namely, Suarez believes that it is in human beings' nature as "social animals" to form into communities. And he sees the formation of society as abiding by the rules of natural law. Throughout his works, Suarez employs collectivist notions for society, which he views as belonging, together with its ecclesiastical counterpart, to a "mystical community."

Suarez's central argument does depart from orthodoxy, but only to ensure that orthodoxy is better confirmed. He starts with the notion of agreement or *"consensus"* which, as an act of will, legitimates the original constitution of society. The idea of some kind of consent was already common among the Scholastics. What Suarez adds is the distinction between the emergence of society and the establishment of political authority. Suarez claims that people first agree in principle to form a community, and then agree as *one* community acting with one will to delegate authority to a representative. The *"populus"* is *prior* to the *"res publica"* (Jarlot 1949, 81). In other words, the social contract is anterior to the political contract. Suarez intends to demonstrate that temporal power is authorized, so to speak, by the people, though, indirectly it comes from God, and, that the monarch (i.e., James I) therefore cannot claim any divine right to rule. Such a claim could only be invoked by the Pope.

Now, this mode of popular legitimation, which amounts, in reality, to a mode of delegitimation for the divine rights of kings, needs some qualification. Suarez's notion of consent is to be thought of as a construct, not, I would think, as a description of reality. The term "consensus" is itself meant to include the idea of tacit consent. The whole process can be considered as hypothetical. To this effect, the passage from society to the state as it is conceived underlines the fact that the power to rule springs from below, and that society is not a product of some political will from outside. The precedence of the civil contract over the political contract remains a theoretical construct, and is not necessarily a description of temporal sequence. Through the political contract the community as a whole surrenders its jurisdiction over itself: it is a transfer, not a delegation, of sovereignty (Jarlot 1949, 84; Skinner 1978, II: 183). It is interesting to note two aspects of Suarez's thought which show his intimate connection with other non-liberal conceptions of society. First, he considers society to be a corporate body (Figgis 1956, 155) that is an entity in itself; it is *one*, not a composite. Second, the legitimate political authority, the monarch, exercises thereafter an "*imperium*" (dominion) which admits neither the sharing of power nor the intervention of control over it; it is absolute sovereignty, a concept which was gaining recognition at the time, and which contributed to a Christianized adaptation of the Roman idea of the sovereignty of the people (Hamilton 1963, 4,36).

Suarez nevertheless still recognizes the universal and eternal validity of natural law. As a matter of fact, the very existence of society is to be understood as the result of the working of natural law. Suarez insists upon the distinction between morality, or objective justice, and law, since legislating is an act of both reason and will. He seems, indeed, more modern than his Scholastic predecessors because he acknowledges the consecration of will through the notion of "*imperium*" or sovereignty. William of Occam, a Franciscan, had also discussed the role of will, but to a lesser extent. Nevertheless, Suarez remains a rationalist (Jarlot 1949, 98), and he assesses the value of law by its conformity with an objective justice, which can only be discovered by reason. An idea rampant at the time claimed that the rudiments of natural law were written in our minds by the hand of God (Skinner 1978, II: 151). Law is therefore law only if it is just. But what is just law? The whole of Suarez's discourse revolves around his notion of the common good (*commune bonum* or *felicitas publica*), which is consistent with his understanding of society as *one* community. If, at this time and even previously, there was a notion of international rights for societies, there was no question of individual rights, as such, within these same societies. Suarez couches his discussion of interests in collective terms, but by doing so develops a secular reading of the community as an entity.

Suarez and the Jesuits in general are readily identified as defenders of the right to resist. This is true for Suarez but only under very particular conditions, those extreme situations in which brutal violence is exerted on the community as a whole and thus puts the latter in real jeopardy. In such rare cases, it is up to the community, acting as the collective authority, to adopt a policy of resistance; it is not and should not be the action of individuals who feel oppressed as individuals. We are here still quite far from a liberal conception of society. In any event, in 1610 the Jesuits were forbidden by their general, Father Aquaviva, to make any comments that could have been interpreted as encouraging or sanctioning tyrannicide.

The writings of Suarez show little interest for what we could call liberal values, though, by opposing the pretensions of James I, he indirectly clears the way for the recognition of a wholly secular sphere of politics, which centred on the state. At the same time, he foreshadows the type of thought that will become common among eighteenth-century French authors. In the writings of these authors we shall find a concern for society as a whole, a rationalist reading of objective justice and an account of absolute authority, which relies on a form of tacit consent. By introducing the duality of reason and will into his discussion of the exercise of authority, Suarez makes it possible for future thinkers to leave rationality to those most suited to it, and to restrict the expression of will to the legitimate authority.

Interestingly enough, even before the Council of Trent, that is, before the Counter-Reformation, the Dominicans were moving from a strictly organic notion of natural law toward the recognition of a law among nations (*ius gentium*), which might have progressed toward an identical conception of a natural law applicable to individuals. In this scheme, nations were treated as individual units within an international arena; the next step would have been to apply the same principles to the national arena, human beings thus becoming the individual units. This progression was, however, thwarted by the Counter-Reformation. Suarez, like some other Thomists, had argued that human beings were born free; this justified his opposition to the idea of natural subordination (Skinner 1978, II: 154–6). But the principle would know little extension within the political community. It was left to Protestant ethicists to develop a theory of individual rights and, ultimately, to help to dissolve the notion of natural law.

2 The British Moralists: The Eclipse of Natural Law

This chapter focuses on the social consequences that emerged from the Protestant conception of moral authority. My intention here is not, therefore, to make any original contribution to the scholarship on Protestantism, nor to explore extensively the religious foundations of the movement, but to view the Protestant tradition as a foil for the Catholic tradition. The Protestant tradition, as carried by the Anglo-Saxon world, is interesting to observe because of the social consequences of such a break, especially when it is compared to the Catholic societies, which took a different course.

THE PROTESTANT ONSLAUGHT

By breaking with the Catholic orthodoxy, Protestants sought to put an end to the long tradition of clerical authority. Catholicism banked and still banks to some extent on the role of intermediaries, who are deemed to be indispensable to the salvation of the whole.

In Protestantism, the Bible becomes the main, if not the only, source of authority. The Bible, to use Troeltsch's word, is itself canonized (1931, 486). All the elements of moral law are there to be found and to be understood by the faithful. Following Luther, every person is deemed to be able to receive salvation through a state of faith granted to him or her as a gift from God. The relationship with God is not one of freedom, but of submission, with an emphasis placed on the person's internal faith and individual commitment. The shared condition of the faithful makes them equal before the

Almighty. As Luther argues, the consecration of baptism makes them all priests. Hence the famous expression "the priesthood of all believers," which is derived from the principle of inwardness. In direct contrast to Catholicism, which at the time put little trust in the common people's capacity to discern the divine message, all believers are seen as both able and duty-bound to reach the light emanating from the Bible. This direct contact with the Bible, and especially with the Gospel, excludes any interference from outside intermediaries.[1]

Protestantism is an attempt to rediscover, by going back to the congregation, the absolute truth, which is deemed to have been corrupted by the Catholic hierarchy. Ascetic life is thus brought to the laity, which makes Protestantism a movement toward laicism.

John Calvin's contribution to Protestantism was to accentuate the trend toward a "deep spiritual isolation" (Weber 1952, 104), which excluded the Church and the sacraments as institutionalized means of salvation. These were aspects of Christian life that the Lutherans did not, to the same extent, forgo. Moreover, in ethical matters, the Calvinists, though they recognized the existence of divine calling, claimed that the individual was responsible for its identification. This ethic also placed an importance on the realization of more wordly objectives.

It is usually recognized that the Reformation generated the emancipation of the individual (Laski 1936, 30; Troeltsch 1931, 328) even though this was not necessarily the intention of the reformers. The consequences of the Reformation widened the gap between Catholicism and Protestantism; self-examination gained ever more advocates, which led in turn to the proliferation of sects within the Protestant fold, and ultimately to the recognition of pluralism in the realm of moral preference.

The development of individualism was aided by another equally important factor. Protestantism was not indifferent to the adherence of the believers. It stressed a very specific method of uniting the flock. In Luther's case, this method lay in the notion of faith. The appeal was to belief, an inner feeling which was expected to put the individual will into motion. In the Puritan tradition, the will of God and that of the pilgrims came together by means of the covenant. As Walzer observes in *The Revolution of the Saints*: "God's command

---

1 As George and George comment: "The Roman Catholic conception of the priest was seen as a denial both of a privilege and a responsibility which rightfully belonged to the whole Christian community. As no man could achieve salvation for another, so no man could presume, by virtue of an office, to intervene between the salvation-seeking soul and its Creator. Each Christian individual must be his own Priest." (1961, 29).

sought out not only pious acquiescence, but a kind of eager consent, a response registered, so to speak, not in the mind or the heart so much as in the conscience and the will. Men must make themselves 'serviceable'; God's willfulness required human willingness" (1965, 67). Obviously, correct conscience should not be confused with reason, which throughout the Protestant tradition plays almost no part in matters of belief.

The discrepancy between Protestantism and Catholicism suggests that the former is more likely to accept opinions based on personal belief, whereas the latter relies exclusively on doctrinal truth. Opinion depends upon the individual conscience, whereas truth requires gnostics, those who know, to discover and transmit it. Herein lies the difference between the two approaches as they relate to whether, and how, people can discover the nature of morality.

Laicism, which is a product of Protestantism, progressively evolved toward a state of complete secularism. At first it merely meant that the individual attempted to emancipate him- or herself from the mediating role of the clergy. Later it came to mean a state of total disassociation with any reference to the sacred. This left morality in need of a new formulation.

By allowing the individual to discover the truths of the Bible by him- or herself, Protestantism led to a re-evaluation of morality itself. Ultimately, it was left to the faithful to determine the nature of the moral game, to ask "What is the status of ethics in this world?" In other words, what is morality's nature, its origins, its foundations and authority, and at the same time, what is the ability of believers to grasp this set of moral principles? By the logic of its momentum, the Protestant movement was conducive to calling into question basic principles themselves. Stephen notes that "as the intellect freed itself from the old authority, the mere stress of the argument forced Protestants gradually to fall back upon first principles" (1962, 1: 64).

In different societies the development of laicism has probably been accelerated or delayed depending upon other cultural factors and especially upon the orientations taken by certain congregations. In this respect, Calvinism has probably left more traces in its wake than Lutheranism.

In Britain the process can be traced from its beginning in the middle of the seventeenth century, when ethical studies began to depart from strictly theological considerations.[2] Of course, some eminent

---

2 I intentionally put aside the modern natural law school of Grotius, Pufendorf, Barbeyrac, and Burlamaqui in order to limit the discussion on Protestantism to a simple illustration based upon the Ango-Saxon experience, with the risk of occasional oversimplifications.

authors, like Hooker, had somewhat anticipated the trend by pointing out the role of reason in assessing "what is good to be done" (1977, bk I, ch. VIII, sec. 8), and, as a matter of fact, it was through the door of rationalism that new developments on ethics were to be introduced. The argument from reason, however, belonged to the Catholic tradition and tended to wane as time went by.

NATURAL LAW, A STUMBLING BLOCK: HOBBES AND LOCKE

Thomas Hobbes epitomizes, virtually in a single book, the process of secularization that would take more than a century to fully realize itself.

Hobbes's innovation lies in the role he attributed to the intellect. He arrived at his conception of the intellect by reasoning from a perspective that had originated toward the end of the Middle Ages (Oakeshott, n.d., xxvii). *The Leviathan* opens with a blast at the approach to knowledge taken by Aristotle, the Scholastics, and the essentialists. He quickly establishes science as distinct from morality: "Science is the knowledge of Consequences, and dependence of one fact upon another" (1965, pt I, ch. v) Reasoning is reserved to two processes: scientific reasoning, which is the investigation of the relationships between various facts and events, and practical reasoning, which is the determination of the means of achieving an end whose virtue is already established. In contrast to Bacon, Hobbes identifies science as an *a priori* method of deduction similar to geometry and mathematics. Hobbes sees inner experiences as scientific facts, and, in an extension of Galilean physics, he argues from the direct observation of internal passions to political facts. He goes even further and deduces moral standards from empirical observation based upon the notion of self-interest taken as an observable phenomenon (Macpherson 1962, 13, 73).

Even if reason is put to the fore as an instrument of investigation, desire and will – "the last appetites in deliberating" – remain the moving forces of human beings. Contrary to Descartes's "*cogito ergo sum,*" Hobbes's motto could be "*volo ergo sum,*" (I will, therefore I am). For Hobbes the individual finds his or her identity in *will* rather than in self-consciousness. Reason becomes instrumental in shedding light on self-interest, but no more; it has no means of explaining the ultimate ends being pursued. It is content to state, for instance, that peace offers greater utility than war, or that cooperation is worth more than anarchy.

From these assumptions, Hobbes creates a revolution in the understanding of natural law. He first posits the existence of a right of nature (*jus naturale*), which is considered to be a simple fact: each individual in the state of nature is said to enjoy an absolute liberty in the expression of will in order to ensure his or her own preservation, the means used being, as we know, power. Again Hobbes depends upon a psychological factor as *the* moving force; reason enters the equation secondarily and serves as a means of recognizing the laws of nature (*lex naturalis*). The first two laws are prescriptive; they determine what human beings should do in the pursuit of their own interests. They are maxims of rational prudence of each individual's political expediency. The first claims that "every man ought to endeavour Peace, as far as he has hope of obtaining it"; the second that "a man be willing, when others are so too, as far-forth, as for Peace ... to lay down this right to all things" (1965, pt I, ch. XIV). The third law, which states that people should keep their covenants, can also be interpreted as consistent with an enlightened self-interest (Raphael 1977, 56), this law establishes, in the long run, the benefit of each individual from the rational obligation of all; it is a rule based on universal prudence (Gauthier 1969).

It is not my intent here to reopen the debate over this contentious part of Hobbes's *Leviathan*. Some authors like A.E. Taylor (1965) and Warrender (1957) argue that a distinction should be made between Hobbes's egotistical psychology and his ethical doctrine, the latter conforming, to some extent, to the traditional understanding of natural law. Other authors such as Watkins see Hobbes as the philosopher who wanted to "reduce morality to rational self-interest "(1965, 84). Perhaps, as comments Plamenatz, Hobbes would have been wiser to limit political obedience to a derivation of self-interest and fear, rather than making reference to divine laws (1963, I: 147). But since this is not the case, we may surmise that the distinctions which appear clear-cut to our contemporary minds were not so at the time. This consideration may provide little consolation; but it may show to what extent a materialistic approach to morality and politics had to make at least implicit concessions to the still pervasive categories of moral scholarship. Or, as Oakeshott suggests, it may illustrate the extent to which the message had to be coded in order to reach only the initiated (1974, 287–8).

Whatever the interpretation of Hobbes's principles of morality, in this scheme the sovereign remains, in legal matters, the sole source of justice, which is said to exist only within the confines of a political entity outside of which justice has no status at all. For, as Oakeshott writes in his famous introduction to the *Leviathan*: "The Sovereign is the product of will ... Sovereignty is the Right to make Laws by willing. The Sovereign, therefore, is not himself subject to Law, because Law creates Obligation, not Right. Nor is he subject to Reason because

Hobbes, who proposed a secular morality, Locke, Dunn argues, conceived of morality as religious and derived from God's will. Senses and desires, planted in the mind by the Creator, together with reason, God's voice in man, join in expressing the law of nature. Nevertheless there persists a tension in Locke's ethics between, a type of voluntarism, on the one hand, in which morality is founded upon the will of God, who is the supreme legislator, and a kind of rationalism on the other, in which morality is a matter of logical deduction, similar to mathematics (Locke 1954, 56).

The theocentric understanding of Locke also runs counter to more conventional readings of his works, particularly those which claim that Locke's versions of the state of nature and the social contract set up a contractual situation without any reference to either society or any other social reality. The fiction of the compact can be interpreted as an expression of Locke's atomistic preferences: individual interests take priority over any social commitment. Gough finds this interpretation too reductionist, since the first and fundamental law of nature proposed by Locke provides for the preservation of society, and also, one must admit, of every person in it (1948, *Second Treatise*, sec. 134). Locke's perspective would, in this case, be more social then is usually admitted (Gough 1973, 22).

Whatever social interpretations can be drawn from Locke, many of his basic propositions are unambiguous. Statements like the following from a *Letter concerning Toleration* are quite explicit: "The commonwealth seems to me to be a society of men constituted only for the procuring, preserving, and advancing their own civil interests" (1948, 126). These interests are for him life, health, "indolency of body," and material possessions. The same logic of exposition is followed in *The Second Treatise of Civil Government* where the initial emphasis on individual property extends to the preservation of people's lives, liberties, and estates (sec. 123). Grotius and Pufendorf had already grounded rights in what they considered to be essentially one's own (*suum*): life and body, liberty, and actions (Tully 1980, 80, 86). Natural rights are here equated with individual possession. In this sense, Locke's conception of natural law indicates a break, not only with the Scholastic tradition, but also with the ancient Roman tradition which focused on the citizen rather than on the individual as such. Locke's notion of natural law introduces a conception of individual rights from which the duties of others follow, whereas the Scholastic view of natural law claimed that rights were a consequence of duties which preceded them.

Authors like Simmons (1992) have tried to attenuate this understanding of Locke by arguing for a comprehensive view whereby the preservation of society as a whole would confer in many instances a priority of duties over rights. This interpretation reinforces the ambiguity surrounding Locke's conception of natural law.

In Locke the liberal notion of property includes the property of or right to one's own conscience; as the oft-quoted sentence goes: "The care of every man's soul belongs unto himself" (1948, 137). Whether these rights partake of an overall theocentric framework, as John Dunn suggests, does not in itself alter the original impact of Locke's contributions. Even though he may not have intended freedom of conscience to be an absolute right, for example, it was offered as a means of pursuing religious truth, of discovering one's duties to God (Dunn 1969b, 264). It was therefore denied to atheists who, in any case, had annihilated their contractual reliability. The right remains a principle which will be subsequently developed by Locke's successors into an absolute right.

Locke combines the secular and the sacred while at the same time sanctioning their separateness in society. Individual rights are a consequence of this combination; his Puritan background influences his conception of the secular. Similarly, Locke, being well acquainted with the Cambridge Platonists and the Cartesian system, developed a rationalist ethics which also had to be reconciled with a hedonist legitimation of morals. It is significant to note that Locke performed intellectual acrobatics precisely on the question of natural law. He is particularly interesting as a figure who is representative of contradictions or dilemmas that were resolved or transcended only by the generations that followed him.

After Hobbes and Locke the discussion of the status and origin of morality as well as of the means and ability through which human beings are likely to interpret it, continued. The eighteenth century is a prolific period in this respect. Authors of different hues were involved in heated debates over aspects of ethics that had already raised some problems for Hobbes and Locke. As we have already seen, natural law had been a stumbling block for both of them, and even today, interpreters continue to assess its importance in the works of these authors. People's minds, at that time, were far from being made up on the subject of the exact nature of ethics.

THE MORALISTS' PROGRESSIVE DEPARTURE FROM OBJECTIVE LAW

The Protestant approach to the reading of the Bible brought about a general agreement as to the capacity of ordinary people at least to arrive at a satisfactory understanding of morality. There was already somewhat of a consensus to the effect that nobody was entitled to interfere or mediate in the relationship of the faithful to the Book. This reasoning provided an incentive for the inquisition into the foundations of morality. Individual contact with the Bible and the obligation to make up one's own mind naturally led to the following questions: What is morality? Where does it come from? How do we perceive it? Through the senses? Through reason?

The discussion among British moralists of the eighteenth century revolves around the nature, origin, and perception of ethics. And two almost irreconcilable tendencies dominate the period: advocates of an objective justice apprehended through reason pit themselves against those who defend the senses as the true source of morals. Though interesting in itself, this controversy is discussed here only in light of the consequences it had in dissolving any right an intellectual elite could later claim within the Protestant tradition.

The rationalist contenders had as immediate predecessors the Cambridge Platonists, a school about whom Cassirer disparagingly wrote that, in the seventeenth century, it already looked outmoded in its content as well as in its literary forms of expression (1953, 157). A prominent figure of the group was Cudworth (1667–88) who opposed Hobbes and averred that morality was objective, real, and was based upon rules as imperative and inflexible as those governing mathematics. To his mind, there existed justice as an essential reality that was both prior to, and independent of, God's will, the role of the Creator being to transmit this knowledge to human minds. Cudworth's position was inherited by Samuel Clarke (1675–1729) who equated justice with truth. Arguing against Hobbes, as Cudworth had done, Clarke wished to develop a theory of ethics that would be equivalent to Newton's *Principia* in astronomy: a work of science. For Clarke there existed an "eternal Rule of Equity," universal and everlasting, antecedent to God's command, "founded on the eternal Reason of Things, as absolutely unalterable as Arithmetic Truths "(Selby-Bigge 1964, II: 29, 31). As Stephen comments, for Clarke, "things are not holy and good because commanded by God, but are commanded by God because holy and good" (1962, I: 104).

This theological position marks a significant departure from the traditional teachings of the Catholic Church and opens new avenues in the secularization of morality. Aquinas, as we have seen, saw justice as an emanation of God's eternal law, and some thinkers after him, such as Duns Scotus, William of Occam, and much later, Suarez, envisioned morality as a product of God's will. In both cases, God was recognized as the author of law, but in different ways. Locke too, following Puritan ethics, paid respect to this theocentric framework of thought. Even Hobbes felt obliged to recognize the right of nature as derived from God's "irresistible power" (1965, pt 2, xxxi). (Whether or not Hobbes actually believed this, I cannot say.)

The emancipation of ethics from God's command brought about by Clarke and his predecessors opened the door to the complete autonomy of morals. This was not their intention; far from it, for being idealists, they were engaged in a battle royal against the subversion of ethics by the nascent naturalism found in Hobbes. Clarke's goal was to demonstrate the certainty of revelation. Nevertheless, even the title of his work indicates new forms to come: *A Discourse Concerning the Unchangeable Obligations of Natural Religion* (1706). The idea of natural religion is amenable to treatments which, in the future, will have little to do with his rationalism.

Despite his idealist conception of ethics, Clarke remains democratic, I would say, when it comes to deciding who is sufficiently competent to understand morality. For him, the rules of morality are accessible to all because of the "faculties of reason" given to each person by God, so that everybody, or almost everybody, is able to discover the rules of equity: "The mind of man naturally and necessarily assents to the eternal law of righteousness" (Raphael 1969, 1: 204) (exception is made for depraved or corrupted minds). Later idealists of the eighteenth century such as John Balguy and Richard Price, who reacted against Hutcheson's moral sense, still insisted upon both the necessary truth of morality and the capacity of any human being to grasp it, whether through intuition (Price) or through reason, aided by affection (Balguy). Even though this mode of thought had much in common with the Platonist approach to moral values, its advocates refrained from utopian elitism. To this extent, these authors followed the Protestant tradition of accessibility to the faithful of the true source of justice, the Bible. But, at the same time they opened the way for a secular ethics.

Secularization was further accelerated by the inductivist thinkers who probably best illustrated the originality of British ethical thought. The goal they pursued remained the same as that pursued by the rationalists and it conformed to the overall Protestant quest for the foundation of morals. As their rationalist vis-à-vis, the inductivists longed for the systematic knowledge of morals; ethics remained an object of science but it was to be perceived from a different perspective which entailed significant consequences.

Two traits mark the difference between the two schools. First, the new school relies on the gathering of facts; the approach is deliberately empirical, and keeps metaphysical speculation to a minimum. Second, it substitutes senses for reason as the explanatory element; reason is reduced to a secondary function. Except for Hume, this epistemological position led to very few efforts being made to establish any connection between knowledge and morality. These authors wished to be scientific and empirical but failed to evaluate their own instruments of knowledge. Whatever the real weight of their legacy, they did contribute significantly to the demise of Scholastic ethics.

The first of these authors was Lord Shaftesbury (1671–1713). Considering himself a moral realist, he proposes to observe the human soul by documenting how people actually behave. Hostile to any metaphysics and fairly optimistic in temperament, Shaftesbury places much confidence in every person's ability to discover, or better, to verify by him- or herself the nature of his or her own appetites. Referring to his work as a "plain home-spun philosophy," he makes no claims to be anything but a practical, no-nonsense moralist (Norton 1966, 24, from *Characteristics*, I, 31). At the same time, Shaftesbury proposes no less than a scientific endeavour, but one that would have for its first laboratory our own experience. Like some of his contemporaries, his ambitions are as far-reaching as those of his rationalist opponents: "If there be no article exceptionable in this scheme of moral arithmetic; the subject treated may be said to have an evidence as great as that which is found in numbers, or mathematics" (Raphael 1969, I: 187).

The entire framework is naturalistic in tone, and absolutely secular in its consequences. The basic principle of Shaftesbury's discourse is that the universe is orderly, well organized, and, therefore, harmonious in its working and congruous with the laws governing it. For him, human beings are naturally sociable in the sense that they are endowed with social impulses proper to their condition. They are provided with an internal faculty of discriminating right from wrong that Shaftesbury associates with a "natural affection" toward equity, or a moral sense. He seems to be among the first to have introduced the idea of a moral sense which, in his case, is defined in a rather loose manner (Raphael 1947, 2). Following a naturalist teleology, our individual inclinations are geared in such a way as to contribute to the improvement of the social whole. Self-interest is thought to be basically consistent with the interests of the collectivity, that is, with the interests of the species. Virtue is reconciled with self-interest, as are, consequently, private interests with the public good. This approach, as we can see, is as functionalist as biology can be: private and public concerns are organically related to each other.

There are many interesting and significant aspects to be found in Shaftesbury's work. First, reason loses its former pre-eminence in favour of sense, though the former is still expected to "secure a right application of the Affections" (Shaftesbury, from Willey 1949, 71).

In order to be truly virtuous, an action must derive from the acquiescence of reason toward the appropriate feeling, for, as Basil Willey writes," Reluctant or merely dutiful well-being is (in Shaftesbury's mind) not genuine virtue" (1949, 71). Nevertheless, reason is relegated to the background. *Exeunt* the abstract rational principles which were the backbone of Thomist morality. By being somewhat freed from reason, ethics is more spontaneously projected toward aesthetics, the realm of feelings and emotions, to which it is easily related. Shaftesbury's numerous attempts to specify the nature of moral sense lead him to make constant reference to such opposites as regularity/irregularity and harmony/dissonance. Virtue, he writes in the *Inquiry Concerning Virtue*, is "no other than the Love of Order and Beauty in Society" (from Willey 1949, 72). Second, with Shaftesbury begins the era of empirical psychology that will serve as a foundation for further developments in British moral philosophy. Third, his invariable preoccupation with the social whole should not obscure his basic individualistic perspective. Shaftesbury's ethics are based upon individual impulses and experience. Society is the result of a "sense of fellowship" that is ingrained in human nature, through which self-interest meets the public good (probably considered to be the communal self-interests. Human beings "are *naturally* and *necessarily* united for each other's Happiness and Support" (Shaftesbury, from Arieli 1964, 102). Fourth, Shaftesbury's thought frees ethics from authority in general and religion in particular, since morals come from our inner nature and not from external abstract principles. Here we find united in one framework all the components of an anti-Catholic and anti-intellectualist position.

Joseph Butler (1692–1752), Bishop of Durham, attempted to supplement Shaftesbury's moral sense with a stronger cognitive aspect that would account for both the direct intervention of God in the construction of our nature and the presence of an imperative authority within us. In keeping with Shaftesbury's aversion for speculative reasoning, Butler discusses morality using an empirical and introspective approach to human nature. But instead of attributing to human perception an instinctual quality, Butler grants it a more reflective ability. There is, according to him, a natural faculty within each human being that is superior to all others, and that acts as an absolute and infallible authority; this faculty is God-given and, therefore, reliable, and it acts as an internal tribunal which monitors our actions. Human beings become laws unto themselves. Conscience is, for all of us, the internal legislator. It is "the voice of God within us" but it is independent of the external world, and it dictates, on an individual basis, what each of us must do (Butler, from Stephen

Reason creates nothing, neither Right nor Obligation" (lii).

Hobbes's departed from the Scholastic school in a number of ways: the individual is given priority over society, for even though he bases an "unlimited political authority on unlimited individualism" (Gauthier 1969, vi), reason is reduced to the role of computing one's own interests. Hobbes's entirely secular approach to ethics would take a long time to be widely assimilated. In fact, John Locke, one of Hobbes's successors, exhibits significant hesitation about this matter.

Locke is not always easy to follow, since he seems to modify his perspectives as problems arise. In the past, commentators have not always been patient with him. Stephen, for instance, was particularly stern when he abruptly concluded a discussion of Locke by writing: "Locke's teaching is palpably inconsistent, and the attempt to deduce a coherent doctrine would be waste of labour" (1962, II: 72). We do not have to abide by such strictures and, in any case, many authors today would probably not agree with him. The coherence usually found today in Locke's works is not necessarily obvious, and it requires an understanding of the whole before the parts can be explained. Interestingly enough, the contradictions or misunderstandings about Locke's philosophy have usually had much to do with the nature of his ethics and particularly with his conception of natural law.

Early in life, Locke recorded his views on natural law. The *Essays on the Law of Nature*, written in Latin around 1660, were not published during his lifetime. They serve as a prolegomenon to his later works and should have opened the way for a more elaborate disquisition on those works. For all sorts of reasons, Locke never provided a systematic treatment of natural law. Many commentators have surmised that he had put himself in an epistemological predicament that prevented him from proceeding any further. Whatever the exact cause of this symptomatic want of precision, it becomes obvious when reading Locke that he was prey to contradictory tensions.

At the very beginning of the *Essays*, Locke betrays an elitist bias by entrusting "those who are more rational and perceptive than the rest" with the task of finding "the secret and hidden laws of nature" (1954, I, 115). In keeping with the rationalist side of his thought which, at times, resembles the thought of Aquinas, he designates these laws as eternal and immutable. Like Aquinas, he proposes a deductive approach to morality in the *Essay concerning Human Understanding*. There, morality is understood to be a product of reason that is apprehended through intuition and demonstration. His trust in perfect knowledge of morals expresses a confidence in the speculative intellect. Such is the rationalist aspect of Locke's thought, which assigns to reason the function of finding what is good, and even points toward the foundation of an exact science of morals.

There is in Locke a quest for moral truth typical of seventeenth-century rationalism. Morality, like mathematics, is presented as amenable to systematic demonstrations, "since the precise real essence of the things moral words stand for may be perfectly known" (1963, bk III, ch. XI, sec. 16). Locke furnishes as an example the right to property, stating tersely that "Where there is no property, there is no injustice, is a proposition as certain as any demonstration in Euclid" (ibid., bk IV, ch. III, sec. 18).

But there is also in Locke's philosophy a hedonist aspect, in which goodness is defined in terms of pleasure. No innate practical principles exist in the human mind, instead there is simply a "desire of happiness and an aversion to misery" (1963, bk I, ch III, sec. 3). Gough (1973, 14, 19) sees here a complex whereby Locke could be neither entirely rationalistic nor entirely hedonistic, his hedonism having in any case to conform to his religious faith. This hedonism could therefore refer to moral good as affording pleasures "intelligently appointed" (Aaron 1971, 259) which do not have to be pleasant in themselves but are so in their consequences. These become "delayed gratifications" (Dunn 1969b, 195), often for another world. Some authors (Dunn 1969b, Colman 1983, 236) claim that Locke's rationalism relies on sensory data that are furnished by experience; this conforms to his rejection of innate ideas. Indeed, as early as his *Essays* (IV), Locke understands natural law as deriving from the "light of nature." Here he portrays natural law as alien to both innate ideas and tradition, since it is discovered through the harmonious interplay of two faculties: reason and perception, the latter being deemed as indispensable as the former. From this happy combination, Locke takes an optimistic tack, though at the risk of being self-contradictory: "If man makes use properly of his reason and of the inborn faculties with which nature has equipped him, he can attain to the knowledge of this law without any teacher instructing him in his duties, any monitor reminding him of them" (1954, II, 127). The reliance on sensory perception as a full partner in the recognition of morality (1963, bk II, ch. XX, 1) automatically opens ethics to interpretation by a larger audience. It contributes to a naturalization of ethics.

In considering Locke's entire works, Dunn provides them with an explanatory framework: Locke's own religious belief. According to Dunn, Locke's perspective is fundamentally theocentric (1985, 55), in conformity with the harmonious conception of a God-given world, and his ethics are demonstrative, based on natural theology (1969b, 190). This holistic reading of Locke provides a more consistent explanation of his entire work. In opposition to his predecessor

1962, II: 40). As Stephen comments, "To Butler the individual is the centre of interest" (ibid., I: 248). But, like Shaftesbury, Butler recognizes a natural benevolence in human beings.

He makes duty and self-interest coincide: "Conscience and self-love, if we understand our true happiness, always lead us the same way" (Raphael, 1969, I: 360). The harmony between self-interest and duty, and self-love and conscience is achieved within the individual. (It should be pointed out that "self-love" is not synonymous with "self-indulgence.") We are here faced again with a natural religion: we can conclude that we can dispense with clergy, since our intuitive moral judgment is reliable. As Stephen writes: "The God whom Butler worships is, in fact, the human conscience deified" (1962, I: 248).

Unlike Butler, Francis Hutcheson (1694–1746), who was one of Hume's ethical forerunners, establishes the distinct roles of both reason and the moral sense in the determination of morality. Hutcheson wished to clarify and elaborate on Shaftesbury's moral sense. He systematically employs the inductive method in his study of morals and bases his analysis on the careful observation of human nature. Hostile to complex and *a priori* reasoning, Hutcheson discards metaphysical speculation of any sort in favour of a more modest form of inquiry. Morality is not to be discovered through deductive proof or learned discussions but by the plain study and understanding of our own natural dispositions. His approach is, therefore, inductive and introspective at the same time, since our own individual, personal experience serves as a testing ground. Hutcheson, though, does not intend to advocate moral subjectivism and non-cognitivism, but rather moral objectivism (Norton 1982, 92), which sustains the existence of morality in opposition to the skepticism exemplified by writers such as Bernard Mandeville. Instead, the goal is to locate morality in the right way and at the right place, an exercise which can be made simple since we have only to pay "a little attention to what passes in our own hearts" (Norton 1966, 102).

Hutcheson posits that reason cannot be at the origin of action. Instead, human beings are endowed with inner senses, such as a sense of beauty and harmony, a sense of honour, or of decency, which produce a certain "determination of the will" (Stephen 1962, II: 49). Among these is the moral sense, a distinct faculty independent of feeling, with which we perceive what is good and what is not in our own conduct as well as in that of others. Hutcheson insists that the moral sense has nothing to do with innate ideas; it is rather a disposition of the mind, foreign to any form of socialization; it is, he says, "originally implanted in our nature by its great author"

(Selby-Bigge 1964, 1: 55). It is God-given and is a part of our inner nature, but possesses no speculative function. It remains a reliable *sense* which stays outside any prior knowledge. Just as the mind spontaneously takes aesthetic satisfaction from the observation of regular forms and harmonious constructs, so too does it take a kind of moral satisfaction from the perception of proper morality. Both the aesthetic and the moral senses are determined by our nature. Moral sense is, for Hutcheson, the seat of moral approbation, since it has a monitoring function, as it does in Butler. Now, where the natural determination comes from remains a mystery: it is, Hutcheson, writes, "an occult quality" (Raphael 1969, 1: 295).

One thing we do know is that this moral sense is absolutely distinct from reason which on ethical matters is confined to an instrumental function; reason is simply a means of achieving particular ends. It may, in some instances, shed light on the consequences or effects of actions upon which the moral sense is to judge. For Hutcheson, reason itself should not be trusted on moral questions even if its aspirations appear noble, since speculation is all too vulnerable to selfishness. Though commentators agree on this aspect of Hutcheson's thought, David F. Norton assigns conceptual features to Hutcheson's moral sense and argues that it implies two aspects: one cognitive, involving the perception of objective moral qualities, and the other affective, involving subjective feelings of approval or disapproval toward these same qualities. "Our moral sense," adds Norton, "constitutes us not only to perceive right and wrong, but to react to them" (1966, 111)

Nonetheless Hutcheson searched for a "*universal rule* to compute the morality of any actions," having already argued that "*that action* is *best*, which produces the *greatest happiness* for the *greatest numbers*" (Raphael 1969, 1: 285, 284). The search for a systematic understanding of morals is obvious here. But still, the subordination of private to public good comes from the moral sense rather than from reason. Hutcheson hoped to attain the object of his quest, a specific conception of ethics, without having to posit any abstract sources of moral cognition.

Even though Hutcheson looks eagerly for an objective measure of morality, he reverts nevertheless to a highly subjective and naturalist mode of inquiry, putting aside any transcendental considerations and advocating the internal approach that David Hume would develop more extensively. We are again moving progressively toward a complete secularization of morality. Ethics is freed from any interpretation drawn from outside our inner nature.

ABSENCE OF NATURAL LAW: HUME AND BENTHAM

Before going into Hume, it is well to reiterate the fact that this discussion is not intended to provide a novel interpretation of the moralists of a given period, but to illustrate the unfolding of a vanishing process whereby ethics was interpreted by an elite group. In this respect, Hume embodies the most eloquent expression of this progression, which finds some sort of resolution in Bentham and Mill.

Despite the manner in which his contemporaries viewed him and his work, Hume was neither a skeptic nor a relativist on ethical matters. On the contrary, he was committed to establishing the scientific foundations of morality. We should not forget the subtitle of the *Treatise of Human Nature*: "Being an Attempt to introduce the experimental Method of Reasoning into Moral Subjects." His search was, therefore, rational and empirical, while also being introspective, as it was for some of his predecessors. But the difference between Hume and his contemporaries lies in the acuteness with which Hume's inquiry is rigorously conducted, an acuteness that disregards any ontological or teleological considerations.

For Hume, both sentiment and reason have significant roles to play in moral matters; however he grants passion a definite priority over reason, the latter being the servant of the former. This argument is not foreign to previous authors, such Hutcheson, for instance. According to them, reason cannot produce any ethical rules; the good, just like the beautiful, can only be felt.

Hume distinguishes two types of virtues: those that are natural and those that are artificial. The first are considered invariable and are directly connected to natural impulses. They are, according to him, inherent in our constitution, whereas the second derive largely from convention and tradition. The natural virtues are based solely on the sentiments felt by the mind regarding actions which involve external objects. Such sentiments translate into degrees of utility, arousing feelings of pleasure or pain for actions of benevolence (generosity, compassion, gratitude), or malevolence. Hume considers morality to be a matter of passion and volition which cannot be subjected to demonstration. Will cannot be influenced by reason. Therefore, the major sources of action are external to reason. He also assumes (without actually saying so) a stability in human nature: he presumes that all people are endowed with the same faculties, which should engender the same feelings. Hume appeals to uniform standards of utility, which come from the common experience of humankind as it is reliably expressed by common sentiment.

Artificial virtues, or what is more commonly called justice, are, on the other hand, rational contrivances; reason informs the natural virtues in order to create further utility (which is originally perceived by the sentiments), that is, to project utility into the long term. Because of the benefits they can enjoy *in common*, human beings agree upon rules of behaviour, such as the keeping of promises and the respect of property, which secure life and its preservation. These conventions, originating in an enlightened self-interest, introduce restraints that amount more or less to what society is made of: "Public utility is the *sole* origin of Justice" (*Inquiry concerning the Principles of Morals*, sec. III, pt I.). They correspond to rules of prudence, no more. Left entirely to themselves, people would destroy society, since, according to Hume, individual avidity is insatiable, perpetual, and universal.

The state is essentially a social convenience. Subjects obey it because it is in their long-term interests to do so. In the state, private and public interests meet. Afterward, habit makes the acceptance of social rules seem natural. The sense of duty is then substituted for by discipline and education. Here, Hume joins Hobbes in ascribing to reason a part in channelling passions into an appropriate collective goal. For both of them, society is based on functional rules.

For Hume, reason is purely instrumental, but nonetheless indispensable. He is adamant: "Reason is perfectly inert, and can never either prevent or produce any action or affection" (1896, bk III, part I, sec. I) So actions cannot be deemed reasonable or unreasonable. Though reason is excluded from the perception of morality, it can inform and therefore excite or temper passion. More specifically, reason establishes the relationship between causes and effects as they relate to the satisfaction of pleasure. As Stephen notes, in Hume there is, strictly speaking, no question of a struggle between reason and passion (1962, II: 74).

Hume states that reason, left to itself, may be dangerous, since it can be found among "fanatics," for instance who "may suppose that dominion is founded on grace, and that saints alone inherit earth," or among people like the Levellers, against whose position he argues that "a rule, which in speculation may seem the most advantageous to society, may yet be found in practice totally pernicious and destructive" (*Enquiry*, sec III, pt II). Just as passion left to itself would lead to social destruction, so too would unbridled reason, though for other reasons.

From this analytical position Hume occasionally shifts to a more normative one, confusing as some commentators have noted, the "is" with the "ought." It leads him to adopt a posture of moderation and incrementalism, which is the trademark of pragmatic anti-intellectualism as can still be found today. If Hume allows a guiding role for philosophers or the "wise" who, by their profession, are more apt to express new rules for society, it is in order to have these rules and their consequences better explicated by these thinkers who can never pretend to comprehend exhaustively moral artifices.

The whole of Hume's discourse rests upon individualistic and naturalistic premises which, when developed by reason, evolve toward a sociological account of human society. His form of utilitarianism leads to a strictly anthropocentric reading of culture; culture exists to satisfy human needs and progresses with the addition of further conventions. This, as we shall see, is opposite to the Catholic tradition of an abstract true justice. Throughout his discourse, Hume discards the terms of a religious and clerical understanding of society. In particular, he delivers to natural law its final blow, which opens the way for Jeremy Bentham's utilitarian calculus.

Bentham joins the debate about ethics in order to change its basic nature. His purpose is to reform the "moral world" through a rational and political operation. More specifically, he wishes to re-establish jurisprudence on scientific foundations. Intending to proceed methodically, Bentham first dismisses inherent values attributed to action and, therefore, natural law; second, he excludes any reference to custom or moral sense. He wants to arrive at a new objective standard of morality by making a strictly factual reading of the effects which particular actions have on human happiness. It is at this stage of the discussion that he professes his notion that the greatest moral good arises from "the greatest happiness of the greatest number." Bentham may have considered this saying to be a useful fiction which served to emphasize the importance of the individual in the legislative process. It indicates the path to be followed by legislators.

Bentham pairs "discovery" and "information" under the informative action of reason, which gauges and calculates units of utility. Reason is solicited in the name of efficiency, just as liberty is considered a *sine qua non,* but only for the sake of reaching a higher level of pleasure. Both reason and liberty are used as means of securing greater happiness, although in different fashions. They are more or less combined in his elaboration of toleration, which is a conscious recognition of the utility to be secured from a certain amount of freedom. Utility is not found in liberty itself, but in the completion of acts that produce pleasure.

The act of legislating becomes one of efficiency by setting the appropriate liberties and constraints that govern individuals in their pursuit of maximum pleasure. In practice, Bentham felt that it was not the government's business to provide happiness directly but it should remove any obstacles in the individuals' quest for it. He even feared governmental abuses, and recommended constant vigilance over the government.

Bentham's uniqueness lies in his attempt to equate the common interest of the collectivity with the greatest possible sum of individual interests. As he writes, "Individual interests are the only real interests" (1843, 321) and the interest of a community, simply the sum of its members' interests. Otherwise, as Bentham says, the community as a whole amounts only to a fiction. This idea brings us close to the end of the journey leading to individualism. Rights, duties and liberties are thought of as products of imagination. With Bentham all transcendence is completely absent from moral values, and ethics, though important in practice, is reduced to the accumulation of individual interests, having no existence outside themselves. In other words, any individual's testimony of the interests of the whole is attributed the same value. At this point, all the components that led to the formation and the maintenance of an elite are dissolved. In this respect, Bentham stands in direct opposition to Aquinas.

In our reading of British moral thought from Hobbes to Bentham (including many prominent Scots), we have overlooked numerous authors. The moralists, discussed were chosen, not to exhaust the topic, but merely to indicate and delineate some of the most characteristic lines of inquiry. Not considered, for example, were the proponents of the theological utilitarian tradition, as illustrated by William Paley, John Gay, and John Brown (Crimmins 1983).

On the other hand, the trend was not only on the utilitarians' side; the opposition to Hume and his followers by thinkers like Thomas Reid (1710–96) serves as a reminder to this fact. Reid, who considered himself a realist, wished to reinstate reason into the determination of morality. In Reid's work, reason is set up as a regulator of the passions, and morals are thought to be objective realities which, through moral sense, can be intuitively grasped by all. The last phrase is significant, for even if reason is somewhat rehabilitated, the individual remains the primary concern: "In order to know what is right and what is wrong in human conduct, we need only listen to the dictates of conscience when mind is calm and unruffled" (From Sidgwick 1962, 230).

Apart from a few exceptions, the British Enlightenment led to the eradication of any reference to an objective justice that could be discovered and maintained by reason, and which would be entrusted to an elite of moral scholars. For Aquinas's deductive reasoning, the

British moralists substituted an inductive approach. Reason is put to work, but in an entirely different fashion: it is bent to the examination of observable facts, usually of a psychological nature. In the quest for an empiricism inspired by science, ethics is submitted to an analytical treatment that purports to uncover the springs of human action, particularly human desires, which are considered to be given, uniform, predictable, and easily observable. It is of little importance here if, in reality, this type of inquiry sometimes amounted to a rudimentary form of introspection inspired by common sense.

An immanent notion of justice, in which justice is within each human being, is put in the place of a transcendental conception of justice in which ethics and morality lie outside human beings. For Aquinas, who followed in the wake of Aristotle, the human being is part of a universe that imposes upon the individual a finality and thus a set of values. The universe is, so to speak, sacred. In the British Enlightenment, metaphysics is jettisoned, and the human condition is looked at from the inside; this process generates a naturalist explanation of morality. That ethics underwent such a transformation is not insignificant. We shall see that such was not the case in French thought of the same period. But this should not come as a surprise, since Protestant ethics puts the individual in a situation of defining his or her position with others and with the outside world in general; whereas the Thomist tradition recognizes the cosmos as a primary entity, of which the individual is a secondary part.

The American revolutionaries followed the lead of the British ethicists, and made adaptations imposed by the political imperatives of the time. From the lofty heights of theological and philosophical speculations, we now move on to the grounds of political contingency.

3 The American Assessment of Natural Law

The revolutionary features of the American understanding of natural law are intimately linked to the colonies' Protestant tradition, particularly that of Puritanism. Puritans conceived of salvation in individualistic and juridical terms. Their religious universe was one of law derived from God's will, and the relationship of human beings to God was governed by a covenant or compact. Each individual stood alone in a direct relationship to God: the covenant of grace with God allowed no intermediaries. So it is not surprising that natural law was translated into individual rights.

THE REVOLUTIONARIES' CONCEPTION

Locke had already asserted that there were a number of basic rights, such as life, liberty, and estate. Commentators noting the continuity from Locke to American liberalism have ascribed to American culture an internal Lockean logic. Hartz (1955), for one, described American culture in this way, and Pangle (1988), Dworetz (1990), and Zuckert (1994) have tried to keep alive a Lockean reading of American revolutionary thought. Nonetheless, the general trend has been to move away from this interpretation. Rossiter, in the early 1950s, argued that there are few explicit references to Locke in the works of the revolutionary authors (1963, 69). Whatever the degree of Locke's influence, it is obvious that some aspects of his writings were retained (although they may have come from secondary sources), just as the Swiss jurist Jean-Jacques Burlamaqui is said to have had a following among the founding fathers. The English legal scholar Sir William Blackstone may also have been a vehicle of influence.

The call for natural rights, first principles, or rules of justice is omnipresent in American revolutionary discourse, and, probably because there is such a significant consensus on these ideas, little pain is taken to explicate them. The revolutionary period was one of political rather than speculative involvement, and few felt the need to develop or elaborate crucial concepts. "The men of the Revolution," as Rossiter writes, "were consumers rather than producers of ideas"(1963, 65). The revolutionaries' purpose was practical; they wished to redress specific abuses. Their goal was not to produce an elaborate conception of ethics, but to arrive at a legal arrangement that would respect the degree of autonomy they had already enjoyed in the past. In this respect, their claim was conservative. But it was innovative to the extent that, contrary to the tenets of the British constitution, it proclaimed that a set of laws had priority over laws made by Parliament. The recourse to natural law as a basic principle antecedent to any others served, at the time, to legitimize the defiance of British authority and, subsequently, to establish rules that would respect a sort of common law of mankind (Barker 1948, 307–8). The intent of their action was certainly sincere, even though natural law was falling into disrepute among British utilitarians.

At that time, natural law was, as a rule, equated with, and therefore confused with, natural rights. It is significant that there was little concern expressed for natural law as such; the idea of natural law is absorbed into the discourse of natural rights. Most pronouncements were directly made in the name of natural rights that were spontaneously expressed as specific rights. These were usually life, liberty, property, conscience, and happiness. In turn, civil rights such as freedom of speech, freedom of the press, freedom of assembly, and so forth were derived from, or confused with, the natural rights. Civil rights were considered absolute and were thought to partake of justice itself. As to their origins, they were believed to be God-given and, at times, natural, nature here signifying a simple, ultimate reference. On the whole, the terminology used was secular. However, people were not irreligious. The pulpit in the early stages of the War of Independence served as an efficient means of mobilization. But as we approach the revolutionary period, it becomes obvious that politicians and laymen in general had taken over from the clerics. So the discourse on rights was couched in worldly terms, even if legitimacy was searched for in the Creator.

Because natural law was used as an ideological instrument in the immediate challenge to British colonial policy, it was largely among politicians, by chance rather gifted ones, that the argument in favour of natural rights was developed. Thomas Jefferson comes spontaneously to mind as a champion of natural rights, if only because of his major contribution to the Declaration of Independence. But, like many of the founding fathers, he espoused natural rights largely because of his moral beliefs. As we have seen, such beliefs have little to do with the rationalistic approach that is typical of the natural law school.

Despite his strong belief in natural rights, Jefferson does not found morality on reason, but on moral sense, which is a moral instinct that he attributes to almost all human beings. He sees all people as endowed with social dispositions, an innate sense of right and wrong, which, he says, is "submitted, indeed, in some degree to the guidance of reason"(letter to Peter Carr, 10 August 1787). But he hastens to add that very little of the latter is needed. In moral matters, Jefferson relies on the spontaneity of nature as opposed to the contrivances of abstract reasoning: "State a moral case to a ploughman and a professor. The former will decide it as well, and often better than the latter, because he has not been led astray by artificial rules" (ibid.).

It would be incomprehensible to Jefferson to suppose that the Creator had vested morality in the hands of the knowledgeable few. For outside the field of science, which he thinks is the preserve of reason, Jefferson is suspicious of any extension of reason into morality. In his famous dialogue between Head and Heart, he expresses fear about the "uncertain combinations of the mind," and apprehends "errors of reasoning or of speculation" that might lead us morally astray (to Mrs Cosway, 12 October 1786, and to T. Law, 13 June 1814). Morality, unlike science, is everybody's business, since it is commonly shared by all. Jefferson's stance is at once pro-scientific and anti-intellectual (according to the definition we have adopted for the term "intellectual"). Science does not extend into the realm of morality as it does in the work of Auguste Comte, for instance. The emphasis that Jefferson puts on moral sense locates him closer to the Scottish thinkers such as Hutcheson than to Locke. Furthermore, this stance probably led him to adopt a more egalitarian posture than did Locke (Wills 1978, 238).

In order to link natural rights and common sense, Jefferson attempts a compromise in which moral sense and reason are reconciled: "Questions of natural rights are triable by their conformity with moral sense and reason of man" (1944, III: 228–9, 235). This is no solution, indeed, but it shows that he probably did not take into account the rationalist costs for defending his cause by appeals to natural law.

For Jefferson, as for those of his contemporaries who defended natural rights, there exists a natural social order that is thought to be antecedent to political society. In other words, he makes the presumption that there is a natural justice that is detectable by the *individual*, whatever his or her station. This natural justice is like that of Locke. While in the Virginia Declaration of Rights, George Mason proclaims the right to life, liberty, and property, Jefferson, several days later in the draft of the Declaration of Independence, opts for the right to "Life, liberty and pursuit of happiness," the right to property being considered a civil rather than a natural right. (Jefferson is said to have struck out a similar reference to property from Lafayette's draft of the French Declaration of the Rights of Man; it is not the place here to discuss the meaning attributed to "pursuit of happiness," a term that was used frequently in the eighteenth century.)

Whatever the influences, whether pure or mixed, the consensus to defend inalienable rights constituted the thrust of the revolutionaries' message and belief. Natural rights stand resolutely in the way of any authority's claim to absolute sovereignty, even if it is duly elected. In a sermon preached at Cambridge in 1770, Samuel Cooke had already stated that "all the great rights which man never mean, nor ever ought, to lose should be *guaranteed*, not *granted*, by the constitution" (from Bailyn 1967, 183). Government had the right to infringe upon individual liberty only so far as was necessary for its own functioning. If there is a general acceptance of Blackstone's recognition of natural rights, there is also an implicit rejection of his rather paradoxical vindication of Parliament's sovereignty. As is often underlined by scholars, the Preamble to the Declaration of Independence is not an appeal to British constitutional law or to the rights of Englishmen, but to God's nature, and the rights derived from it. The Blackstonian notion of legal sovereignty is shifted from Parliament to the people as a whole (Wood 1969, 599), and is thus established on new foundations of legitimation. It is with this in mind that the revolutionaries became the founding fathers of the new republic.

THE FOUNDERS' CONCEPTION

The founders contemplated the creation of a polity whose essential function was to compensate for the imperfections of society. Society was considered primarily to be composed of individuals who had needs that society could not always satisfy. From this observation the polity was introduced as a secondary entity that assumed a complementary, albeit a necessary, function. This conception of politics is opposite to that of the French political theorists who, several years later, claimed that the individual was primarily a citizen who was part of the nation-state. The Americans, instead, came out with a sort of social contract, the Constitution, which takes the form of an official agreement between the government and the people, whereby the latter merely delegates certain offices to the former. Though contradictory in its terms, the notion of limited sovereignty best illustrates the founders' intentions. The constitution delineates the respective powers delegated to the executive and the legislative branches of government by supplying a system of checks and balances. The simple enunciation of these commonly used terms by the founders evokes an anti-hierarchical and anti-organic view of governance.

James Madison proposed a justification for both the notion of equal rights, including the right to vote, and a means of countering sheer majority rule. Indeed, his position indicates a departure from the Whiggish optimism of the 1770s. On the one hand, justice and natural rights, referred to frequently in his essays in *The Federalist* (nos 10, 51), are acknowledged as being among the primary goals of government, even if the meanings of these terms are not completely spelled out, as was often the case at the time. In the *Memorial and Remonstrance against Religious Assessments* (1785), Madison recognizes freedom of conscience as a "fundamental and undeniable truth," a right to which every human being is entitled. He furthermore spells out some of the conditions of the social contract: "If 'all men are by nature equally free and independent'[1] all men are to be considered as entering into Society on equal conditions; as relinquishing no more, and therefore retaining no less, one than another, of their natural rights" (1953, 301).

On the other hand, while accepting the rationalistic aspects of natural law, the authors of *The Federalist* were basically empiricists in their approach to politics (White 1987, 38). Madison's Essay No. 10 calls for the sophisticated construction of instruments that could thwart the expression of an "interested and overbearing majority" which does not act according "to the rules of justice and the rights of the minor party" (*Federalist*, nos. 10, 54).

Madison's argument begins from the premise (reminiscent of Hobbes) that, right from the start, human beings, because of their nature, generate factions ("rival parties"); politics is, in fact, made up of these factions. But inspired by Hume's "Of Parties in General," from the *Essays* (an influence noted by Adair 1974), Madison identifies three types of factions: those that arise from differences of

---

[1] From the Virginia Declaration of Rights, art. 1.

opinions regarding religion, government, and "many other points"; those that arise from the passion for various types of leaders; and the most persistent factions, those that result from the "different and unequal faculties of acquiring property" (*Federalist*, nos 10, 55)

So far as opinions are concerned, and this is the aspect in which we are most interested here, Madison is adamant: we can always imagine "giving to every citizen the same opinions, the same passions, and the same interests" (*Federalist*, nos 10, 55). But he adds, as the reader can imagine, this is simply impracticable: "As long as the reason of man continues fallible, and he is at liberty to exercise it, different opinions will be formed. As long as the connection subsists between his reason and his self-love, his opinions and his passions will have a reciprocal influence on each other; and the former will be objects to which the latter will attach themselves" (ibid.). We are here deeply submerged in politics but far away from the organically ordered world of the Thomism.

For Madison because the causes of factions remain constant (i.e., immutable), we are left with the problem of accommodating ourselves to the regulation of their effects. And we cannot rely on the presence of "enlightened statesmen" at the helm: there must be some kind of mechanism which can solve the problems created by the factional nature of politics. Here is a Hobbesian challenge to imagination and rationality in the harnessing of passions and interests. The problem is therefore stated as follows: "To secure the public good and private rights against the danger of such a faction, and at the same time to preserve the spirit and the form of popular government" (*Federalist*, no 10).

To solve this problem, Madison proposes two conditions of political life: first, the size of the political community must be large in order to be less vulnerable to the emergence of oppressive majorities; second, institutions must be so established as to provide mutual checks within as well as without the government. Summing up the situation several years later, he writes: "In all political societies, different interests and parties arise out of the nature of things, and the great art of politicians lies in making them checks and balances to each other" (1953, 35).

Concluding his disquisition on *The Federalist*, White (1987, 227) calls it a "philosophical hybrid," one that draws from both Locke and Hume, depending upon the goals being pursued. We can conclude that Madison was rationalistic to the extent that he accepted moral rights as self-evident truths, and that he was empirical to the extent that he believed that the public good could be discovered through experimental reasoning. It is not incidental that Madison's natural rights are not put to work in the organization of governance. In fact, he seems to have distinguished between justice, which expresses itself through natural rights, and the common good of a society, which is known through utilitarian considerations. Whereas Madison accepted the right to vote as an equal right as such, he resorted to the notion of utility to explain the rule of the majority as binding on the minority: "It does not result, I conceive, from a law of nature, but from compact founded on utility" (Letter to Jefferson, 4 February 1790, Madison 1953, 31)

Even though Madison's purpose and arguments may have been inspired by the intention to preserve the "minorities of wealth, status and power," (interests as Dahl (1956, 30) calls them), the discourse reflects, at least in its references to natural rights and its apology for checks and balances, the major preoccupation of many of his contemporaries. Few at that time would have followed the radicalism of Benjamin Hichborn, who had proclaimed, in 1777, that "civil liberty" was not to be "a government of laws, made agreeable to charters, bills of rights, or compacts, but a power existing in the people at large ... (for) their own sovereign pleasure" (in Niles 1822, quoted in Dietze 1965, 60–1). If there was any opposition, it came from those who feared the lack of real checks and balances. Such was Patrick Henry's position, for instance, at the Virginia Convention called to ratify the Constitution.

The ideology of the Anti-Federalists was not very different from that of the Federalists. Of course, the two groups did not defend the same interests. The Anti-Federalists were concerned with yeomanry, and its protection within the confines of the states. The yeomanry was considered to be politically moderate and morally superior; because it was in the middle, neither too wealthy nor too poor, neither too educated nor too ignorant, its interests were said to conform with the interests of the whole. Communitarian in attitude, the Anti-Federalists pleaded for the respect of cultural diversity among the thirteen states while claiming at the same time a similarity of manners, sentiments, and interests within each of them.

Labelled as "men of little faith" (Kenyon 1955), they were especially skeptical of the institutions that claimed to represent the people (Wood 1969, 520). Hence their demands for protection and safeguards. But despite their insistence upon autonomy for the states and for a bill of rights, the Anti-Federalists held the same basic political beliefs as their Federalist opponents. The arguments the Anti-Federalists employed were often informed by the same values as those of the Federalists, even though they were not meant to defend the same interests. But we are more concerned here with the values being defended than with the interests that lay behind them.

The Anti-Federalists felt that the safeguards were not satisfactory; their action was, therefore, defensive, and this position was shared by the Federalists who were also concerned to protect against government's propensity to concentrate powers in its own hands.

Unlike Madison, the Anti-Federalists were convinced that greater freedom could be secured if more autonomy were vested in the states. They thought that freedom was linked to size, and small republics were seen as both schools of citizenship and a model of government (Storing 1981, 21). They believed that small republics were bound to keep closer links to the people and that consequently they were less likely to allow the emergence of an aristocracy. State powers are here defended in the name of individual liberty. Madison's argument runs counter to this view, but it shares the same preoccupation: greater freedom for the individual. The threat of oppression is felt by both sides, Federalist and Anti-Federalist, but for different reasons – since they did not have the same interests in mind. Both were concerned with the fundamental fact of *representation*. Representation should not provide the opportunity for any majority to gain ascendancy.

The Anti-Federalists also argued for a bill of rights, which they ultimately received in the form of the first ten amendments, but only, as we know, after the adoption of the Constitution. For them, a bill of rights was considered indispensable, if only to circumscribe more neatly the amount of liberty relinquished for the necessary functioning of government.

Agrippa (perhaps James Winthrop(1752–1821)) made a point which few of his opponents could counter when he wrote in a public letter (1788) to the Massachusetts convention, that "unbridled passions produce the same effect, whether in a king, nobility, or a mob;" a bill of rights was therefore considered necessary "to secure the minority against the usurpation and tyranny of the majority" (in Kenyon 1966, 154). Natural rights serve as bulwarks against intervention of the public sphere into the private.

Ironically, the Bill of Rights, which was meant to circumscribe the powers of the national government and particularly the Congress, became an instrument used much later to thwart the states' infringements on individual rights (Berns 1987, 126–7).

Whether Federalist or Anti-Federalist, the quest was for individual rights that would be protected against any form of imposed uniformity, and against any concentration in representation. No room was left for other agencies of representation. Madison, who would have been happy to leave government in the hands of the enlightened, resigned himself to admitting that such could not be the case in the usual course of politics. Instead, sophisticated mechanisms of checks and balances had to be designed and implemented.

There is here almost nothing left of the medieval conception of natural law as it had been elaborated by Thomas Aquinas. Having travelled through the ethical tradition of Protestantism, natural law emerges as completely transformed. First, very little, if anything, is now said of natural law as such; the concept emerges from a political conflict and is immediately used to this effect. The whole revolutionary discourse uses the language of specific natural rights and even political rights that are said to enjoy an existence of their own. They are obvious to all and therefore require no further explanation. They are immediately defined in concrete terms and are spontaneously enumerated. Second, natural rights, not requiring any further abstract elaboration, did not have to be entrusted to an intellectual elite. Third, having been conceived of originally in organic, communitarian, and hierarchical terms, natural law becomes, in its American form, an instrument to defend the individual from the authority of the whole, whatever the regime. The institutional apparatus designed to secure the respect of natural rights depends on ambition counteracting ambition (to use Madison's terms), and this mutual checking springs from a totally secularized conception of politics; it assumes the proper functioning of a mechanism which, in itself, is alien to any specific notion of justice.

Whether they developed forms of utilitarianism, as did the British moralists of the eighteenth century, or created innovations on the notion of natural law, as did the American revolutionaries, the moral theorists of these Protestant societies created an ethical vocabulary that allowed for the complete absence of a moral elite whose function was to formulate social and political values. These values were progressively thought to be everybody's business, and everybody was considered able to evaluate and decide upon ethical matters by themselves, without the mediation of more learned people.

4 From the Clerisy to a Sparse Intelligentsia

Even if Enlightenment in Britain brought about the downfall of natural law and organic conceptions of governance in general, it nonetheless privileged an elite of thinkers who were expected to act as beacons for the "vulgars," as Hume called them. The era was individualistic in its articulation of morality, but still depended upon philosophers to express them. The liberal democratic conception of ethics was to develop through the two following centuries before the need for a learned elite vanished entirely.

THE CLERISY: COLERIDGE AND JOHN STUART MILL

As a counterpoint to the eighteenth century's progressive liberation from a clerical approach to social life, some nineteenth-century authors in Britain remained nostalgic for the existence of a specific group of individuals whose responsibility would be to diffuse, maintain, and expand the Western heritage of values. Samuel Coleridge stands as one the most prominent persons who still believed in a moral mission that would be vested in a group within each national community; he called this type of group a *clerisy*.

Coleridge's clerisy constitutes an organic and functional apparatus integrated with the state and having as its official objective the safeguarding of the country's culture. Just as in Elizabethan times there is said to have existed a third estate "in whom the reserved nationalty was vested" (Coleridge 1976, 42), so, Coleridge believed, should there be one in his own time, whose assignment would be to preserve and diffuse both knowledge and "moral science." Here Coleridge proposes the establishment of an intellectual elite that serves as the custodian of essential values accumulated in the course of history, and, further, attempts to bind the present with the future. The basic aim is one of education: training people to become real citizens of the country as well as free subjects. To this effect, Coleridge provides for different levels of social intervention. Those at the bottom, the lower rank of clergy, would aid in the general socialization of people, while those at the top would make up a moral establishment in its own right.

It is interesting to note that Coleridge's national clerisy is considered to be distinct from, without being opposed to, the Church of Christ and is ascribed a definitely secularized function: keeping society together by sustaining its basic values. This approach is relativistic and reminiscent of Edmund Burke; it refers neither to natural law nor to any kind of objective justice. The purpose remains astonishingly secular; Coleridge assigns no religious function *per se* to the clerisy. For him, the theologians of the past, members of the national church, stood apart from the masses, not because of their sacerdotal status, but because of the importance attributed to the science of theology which, at the time, was the "root and trunk of the knowledges that civilized man" (1976, 47). For Coleridge, this consecration of the learned is ultimately linked to the imperatives of the state of which they are part. Their role is indeed functional, defined within the confines of law, which is set by the political power (ibid., 54). But the role of the clerisy is not, it seems, to represent other people's values or interests, but rather to provide every individual, as an *individual*, with the ability to be "the free subject of a civilized realm" (ibid., 74).

The emancipation of Catholics in Britain forced Coleridge to reconsider the respective functions of society and the secular state, and to determine what was specific to them. Coleridge's Protestant perspective inclines him to emphasize the national character of societies as opposed to the universality implied by Catholicism, and prohibits him from trespassing the frontiers of individual conscience.

John Stuart Mill who, like many of his generation, had been much impressed by Coleridge, shares with him a profound concern for the enlightened direction of society. While it is founded on very individualistic grounds, Mill's conception of social life always refers to the unequal distribution of the capacity for abstract reasoning. Whether it is on matters of scientific knowledge, arts, morals, or politics, his thought persists in recording the same obdurate fact: few are proficient enough to make pronouncements on these matters. Being a strong believer in progress, Mill expands upon the condition of its achievement, which can only result from the activity of the few. But the few must enjoy a freedom of expression and, at the same time, must be protected from the "tyranny of the majority."

The reader may be familiar with Mill's generous pronouncements on human beings as progressive beings and on the primacy of "free development of individuality" (*On Liberty*, CW, XVIII: 261). But when situated in their proper context, it becomes apparent that these propositions may acquire a different sense. My purpose here is not to attempt to gauge the degree of Mill's liberalism. Cowling (1963), for one, may have gone too far by conferring merely an instrumental value to Mill's notion of individual liberty. Nonetheless, Mill's conception of utility and progress are often called upon to legitimize individual freedom.

Mill may well have entertained deep convictions concerning the "rights of individuality," but it is noteworthy to underline their functionality. He is much concerned with the interest of truth, as he calls it, and with the advantages it provides for society. Absolute certainty being inaccessible, we are obliged to accept the free circulation of opinions and ideas for the sake of obtaining better knowledge. The tyranny of the majority through the prevailing opinion is tantamount to "social tyranny." But worse, he sees it as a guarantee of stagnation in the pursuit of knowledge, it is, therefore, dysfunctional. Human progress is, in the long run, likely to be hindered by any attempts to curb the free circulation of ideas. The enlightened few may hold views that are frowned upon by the many. Mill's emphasis on progress even applies to individual rights since, for him, the individual's boldness and originality are a source of progress. Interestingly enough, Mill's thought seems individualistic in its approach to progress but ultimately quite holistic when the results are evaluated. Mill's prescriptions on liberty are derived, to some extent, from social necessities. Opinions must compete in the market place of ideas, and the best shall survive and provide for the interest of the community.

But the best opinions or ideas, it seems, are those likely to be held by the few. For Mill, there exists a hierarchy of pleasures; some feelings are more noble than others, and "cultivated minds" will have more intellectual, that is more noble, tastes. In this universe of inequality, some will be expected to lead, others to follow.

If the best are to be efficient, they must not disperse their energies. At one time Mill showed little concern for the involvement of the enlightened minority in the day-to-day management of politics, that is, three decades before he served as an MP (from 1865–68): "Great talents are not needed for carrying on, in ordinary times, the government of an already well-ordered society" (*De Tocqueville on Democracy in America*, CW, XVIII: 76). The problem, as we shall see, is that, at that time, English society was not, to Mill's mind, a well-ordered society. "The mere everyday business of politics," as he says, "is an occupation little worthy of any mind of first-rate powers" (ibid.), (gentlemen politicians please take note!). In normal times the "commanding intellects" are better utilized to pursue their studies and leave the "mechanical details of government to mechanical minds" (ibid.).

Mill's social world is one built in tiers and upon a division of labour in accordance with each person's abilities. Though Mill looked down on and was cynical of politicians, he, nonetheless desired that the ablest be at the helm, but under certain conditions: "The people ought to be the masters ... who must employ servants more skillful than themselves" (*De Tocqueville*, XVIII: 72). The conception underlying such a statement is one of full representation rather than mere delegation. While he did not share Coleridge's conservative views, Mill always recognized the relevance of Coleridge's views on the necessity of providing, within any society, room for that society's best minds. Mill's argument proceeds from the postulate that a natural state of society exists: "That state in which the opinions and feelings of the people are, with their voluntary acquiescence, formed *for* them, by the most cultivated minds which the intelligence and morality of the times call into existence" (*The Spirit of the Age*, CW, XXII: 304).

The Spirit of the Age was an early work published in 1831. Mill argues here that England is in a transitory stage; it is a society in which old doctrines have fallen into desuetude but have not been entirely replaced by new ones. Humankind has outgrown its religion, says Mill; the Catholic clergy, which in the Middle Ages was well adapted to its time, is of little relevance today. Nonetheless, people cannot be left entirely on their own; they are in need of guidance. Mill understands the religious aspects of the discussion. His purpose is to reintroduce a social body, which, in his eyes, is indispensable for the well functioning of any society. Here again (and this is quite early in his life), he reveals an implicitly functionalist approach. A substitute for the Catholic clergy must be found which also suits the particular necessities of his times. And these times, as Mill often states, have been indelibly marked with the stamp of Protestantism. There is no question, in his mind, of reverting to the former state of society in which "the Catholics received the priest from God, and their religion from the priest" (*Spirit*, CW, XXII: 312). Protestantism has irremediably broken this way of thinking and has instead "resorted to the teacher"(ibid.), who, to some extent, one *chooses*. The ultimate condition is to be found in the Calvinist tradition: "Every head of a family ... in Scotland, is a theologian; he discusses points of doctrine with his neighbours and expounds the scripture to his family. He defers, indeed, though with no slavish deference, to the opinion of his minister; but in what capacity? only as a man whom his understanding owns as being at least more versed in the particular subject – as being probably a wiser, and possibly, a better man than himself ... It is not the ascendancy of a priest: it is the combined authority of a professor of religion, and an esteemed private friend" (ibid., 312–3).

Mill is very sensitive to the need for the learned and the virtuous, and is much concerned about "the weakening of the influence of superior minds over the multitude" (*Civilization*, CW, XVIII: 135), but, throughout his work, he opposes any systematic institutionalization of a clerisy. On matters of education, he opposes an exclusively national system, especially one under state control, but he remains agreeable to a certain amount of state intervention, particularly in order to allow the lower classes to become better educated (*On Liberty*, CW, XVIII: 302). Here again, competition is expected to give the best results. For Mill, any monopoly is conducive to authoritarianism of one form or another. In this respect, he diverges noticeably from Coleridge.

Mill's connections with the Saint-Simonians and later with Auguste Comte makes his position even more explicit. He objects to any organization of the Saint-Simonians' "spiritual power"; this power becomes admissible only if it functions as an "insensible influence of mind over mind "(To Gustave d'Eichtal, 1829, CW, XII: 41), the proper setting of such an influence being private conversation, the pulpit, or the press. For Mill, no actual institution is necessary, since the ascendancy of the thinkers, if there is to be any, will come naturally from the convincing power of their arguments. Their legitimacy should arise from their own intellectual ability. Any formal authority given to them would, for Mill, amount to a "spiritual despotism" (*Essays on Ethics*, CW X: 314). He relies on individuals' capacity to discern what is in their own best interests. Mill is critical of Comte's inability to place any confidence in individuals. Comte, Mill writes: "looks on them with as great jealousy as any Scholastic pedagogue, or ecclesiastical director of consciences" (ibid., 327). Mill notes the religious nature of Comte's work and emphatically expands on Comte's misunderstandings of Protestantism. In Mill's eyes, Comte failed to perceive the primary distinction between Protestantism and Catholicism, and the role played by the individual believer's conscience and intelligence: "[Protestantism] makes a demand on the intelligence; the mind is expected to be active, not passive, in the reception of it.

The feeling of a direct responsibility of the individual immediately to God, is almost wholly a creation of Protestantism" (ibid., 321)

And no one coming out of the Protestant tradition would relinquish this legacy. Mill's refusal to follow Comte springs most obviously from their incompatible religious backgrounds, even though both men had abandoned their respective faiths early in their lives.

Throughout Mill's writings, the right of the individual to make up his or her mind, despite pressures exerted by society (*On Liberty*, CW, XVIII: 222), is clearly derived from Protestant theology. At times though, Mill seems rather reluctant to accept the consequences of individualism, as when, for example, he agrees that the Reformation marked the "dawn of the government of public opinion" (*De Tocqueville*, CW, XVIII: 12).

Even the qualified elitism of Coleridge and Mill, demonstrates some typical Protestant safeguards against the imposition of authority over the mind of individuals.

THE BRITISH INTELLECTUALS

Even though the cultural environment is not propitious to either the emergence or recognition of intellectuals in British public life, writers and artists have occasionally made their appearance on the public scene; some have even achieved a certain degree of fame. When discussing J. S. Mill, one cannot ignore his role among the Philosophic Radicals who publicized their views through such instruments as the London Debating Society, the *Westminster Review*, and for some, Parliament.

As a mutation and outgrowth of liberal utilitarianism, the work of the Fabian Society toward the end of the nineteenth century might be considered a type of intellectual endeavour. Their purpose was to reshape British society by suggesting changes to social legislation that would help regulate the economy. The Society acted as a group but never sought power for itself or its members. Their strategy was to "permeate," as they called it, centres of decision making. The Fabians identified themselves as a learned elite. After the foundation of the Labour party, they became intimately identified with it but never merged with it. Sidney and Beatrice Webb were among the most influential members of the group. They saw their actions as an exclusively political mission. In so doing, they are disqualified from being intellectuals, in the sense that I have defined the term. Throughout their lives the Webbs remained militants, albeit enlightened ones; they never looked for recognition as philosophers or *littérateurs*. In conformity with the Protestant tradition, the Fabians were basically teachers, their role being one to convince others by rational argumentation. The London School of Economics was therefore a natural offshoot of their ambitions. Even after he left the Fabians, H.G. Wells still claimed to be a teacher and insisted upon being called one for the rest of his life (Smith 1986, 245).

On the other hand, George Bernard Shaw, who was active in the Fabian Society in its early days, could be considered to some extent an intellectual, though he did not at that time enjoy the degree of celebrity he would achieve later. Initially associated with the Liberal party, Shaw subsequently made more adventurous commitments, such as making statements in support of Stalin and, at times, Mussolini. In these latter pronouncements he was undoubtedly acting as an intellectual; he was able to assert his point of view because of the status he had acquired as a famous writer and dramatist.

If British society was not particularly friendly to intellectuals in general, it did foster various exclusive literary or discussion clubs, such as the "Souls" group, Churchill's "Other Club," and the "Co-Efficients," of whom Bertrand Russell and H.G. Wells were members. The Bloomsbury group was mainly preoccupied with aesthetics, even though some of its members were occasionally active in politics. The group included Virginia and Leonard Woolf, E.M. Forster, John Maynard Keynes, Vanessa and Clive Bell, Duncan Grant, and Roger Fry.

The political significance of intellectuals within a society is often most apparent when the social and political stakes are high. In the case of the Britain, for instance, the General Strike of 1926 is usually considered to be one of the most, if not *the* most, significant domestic event between the two world wars. Interestingly enough, the strike does not appear to have roused an impressive public desire to hear the views of intellectuals, at least not in its decisive stage. Moral intervention came rather from church officials who set the course others would follow or react against. The call by the Archbishop of Canterbury together with Anglican and Free Church leaders for a negotiated settlement put the BBC in a quandary when it was asked to broadcast the message; the BBC waited four days before complying. A petition was circulated to support the episcopal initiative; as Virginia Woolf reports in her diary, "We are getting up a petition" (1980, 81). Her husband Leonard mentions briefly that indeed R.H. Tawney had circulated a petition among well-known people that called upon the government "to see that there was no victimization when the strike was over"(Woolf 1967, 217). In any case Leonard Woolf was skeptical of his own and others' efficacy, for he writes,

"There was, of course, really nothing one could do, and one watched appalled the incompetence of those who called and were conducting the strike" (ibid.). Beatrice Webb had a similar point of view; in her diary, she refers to the strike as a "grotesque tragedy" (1985, 82), which she expected to fail. She was against it, in any case, and argued that the success of any general strike depended upon an activist minority coercing the majority to conform to its will, a situation that would mean the end of democracy (ibid., 76). Though very responsible, these reactions are not those usual reactions one might expect from intellectuals in countries such as France, who, in such tense situations usually take the opportunity to act publicly as mediators who can sort out exceptional conflicts.

Media reports of the General Strike made very little room, if any, for the intervention of intellectuals at the time. The strike was covered as a struggle between economic and political agents, and journalists acted only as observers and commentators.

In the 1930s there were more open commitments from intellectuals in Britain. True, the economic depression, the growth of fascism in continental Europe, and the Spanish civil war provided incentives for intellectual activism. This was also the case in France. The war in Spain served as an intellectual and moral litmus test: it forced people to make up their minds about their political beliefs and compelled even the most idealistic intellectuals to open their eyes.

In the early 1930s, the universities at Oxford, Cambridge, and London proved to be fertile soil for intellectuals who sought some kind of political involvement. The new poets surrounding W.H. Auden and Stephen Spender openly displayed Marxist or near-Marxist leanings, or so they thought. "Marxists of the heart" as they were then called, they expressed their concerns largely through poetry; they had no intention of influencing specific political events. Many of them made the trip to Spain between 1936 and 1939, which has led the Spanish civil war to be labelled the "poets' war" (Ford 1965). Some were killed, like John Cornford who died at the age of twenty-one. Auden and Spender later withdrew from public life. Even at the height of their involvement in public affairs, they remained what they essentially were, poets, who wrote mainly "engagé" pieces. Both joined forces with Louis Aragon in France and many other authors to compose and send out a brief questionnaire on the subject of the war, from which they received back over 140 responses from writers in many countries. *Authors Take Side – on the Spanish War* (1937) served as an instrument of consciousness raising, and the idea was revived thirty years later by Cecil Woolf and John Bagguley in *Authors Take Sides on Vietnam* (1967). The questionnaire was sponsored by the International Association of Writers for the Defence of Culture, a group which published the *Left Review*. The association members (while keeping their association alive) joined For Intellectual Liberty (FIL), a motley group of fifty left-wing intellectuals, which was founded in 1936 and which included Leonard Woolf, Kingsley Martin, E. M. Forster, C.P. Snow, Henry Moore, and Aldous Huxley, who was its president. The role of these organizations was rather loose; nonetheless, they initiated the practice of sending collective statements to newspapers, statements which were frequently signed by numerous prominent people. Their manifestos dealt mostly with international matters and were especially devoted to the defence of peace.

These activities were often influenced and even monitored by the Communist party which, at the time, exerted a strong moral attraction for left-leaning intellectuals. Orwell (1940, 163) wrote about the period (1935–39) that "for about three years, in fact, the central stream of English literature was more or less directly under communist control." Many young intellectuals spontaneously joined the party. The honeymoon did not last long, however. People were soon disillusioned with the USSR as well as with the Spanish civil war, and when Russia and Germany signed a non-aggression pact in 1939, much hope and faith was destroyed.

Some intellectuals like George Orwell, who almost died when he sustained a bullet wound to the neck during the war, joined the Independent Labour Party contingent, most of whose members were strongly anti-Communist even before they left Britain for Spain (Crick 1980, 219). Orwell, for one, had been literally repulsed by the Moscow Trials. Summing up the whole experience, he commented dryly, "On the whole the literary history of the thirties seems to justify the opinion that a writer does well to keep out of politics" (1940, 172). So much for intellectuals who sell their souls to party politics.

In the meantime, other authors had taken the opposite political position. Ezra Pound went to extremes in his support of Mussolini and even Hitler, giving free rein to his anti-Semitism and his hatred of both England and the United States. Evelyn Waugh favored Italy's intervention in Abyssinia.

All in all, intellectuals in Britain were not entirely inactive during the tormented thirties, but their voices were far from omnipresent; moreover, their political commitments seem to have focused on international rather than domestic affairs. In these undertakings, British intellectuals were attracted largely by international organizations whose headquarters were often located in France. This did not forbid the emergence of the Left Book Club, whose range of activities fanned out, spreading to theatre, poetry, music, and cinema. Yet, we may still ask how many full-fledged intellectuals were actually involved in this popular operation.

The 1960s brought many expressions of public commitment but these came from students, and the student movement was worldwide. True, the *New Left Review* was well known, and it provided a focal point for a number of people, but it never achieved the popularity that similar movements achieved in the mid-1930s. One must, however, recognize the influence of the Institute of Economic Affairs (IEA) which, from the end of the 1950s onward, assigned itself the task of *educating* the British people on the nature of economic problems and their solutions (Swingewood 1987, 97). Embodying the philosophy of the New Right it had access to different centres of influence: the universities, the newspapers, the civil service, and ultimately the Conservative party. In some respects, the IEA is not unlike the sort of association the Fabians had in mind when they had the ear of the newly formed Labour party.

In Britain, the network of intellectual influence has seldom been entirely visible. As Annan (1955) suggests, from the nineteenth century there has been a well-rooted "aristocracy of the intellect" which has worked through relationships built along family ties, public school, and Oxbridge connections and which has managed to gain access to established institutions that ensured a form of stability. Even though this situation has probably changed somewhat with the establishment of new institutions such as the British Council, the Arts Council, and the BBC, people with intellectual propensities are still bound to operate within the confines of the old order. Discussions unfold within institutionalized groups, and these debates can be at times as stimulating as any public debates, which are more vulnerable to the concessions or compromises demanded by the audience. My point here is not to evaluate the different arenas, public or private, but simply to acknowledge the preference for one type over another. With an intellectual life that is integrated in this manner, there is little incentive for what I call the free-floating intellectual or the intellectual *tout court*. Of course this does not forbid exceptions to the rule.

Bertrand Russell was such an exception. He ran for Parliament three times, once specifically on the suffragist platform, and was involved in numerous campaigns, almost all of them having to do with international relations. His consecration as an intellectual is obvious when one reads a front-page headline in the *New York Times* which reports the open letter Russell sent to President Woodrow Wilson through indirect channels in 1916: "Famous English Philosopher and Mathematician Asks Wilson to Stop War Ere Europe Perishes" (in Clark 1976, 316). Russell took political and moral positions that some people would consider typical of an intellectual. He welcomed the Russian revolution but soon recanted after a disillusioning visit to the Soviet Union. In *Which Way to Peace* (1936), he argued that resisting Hitler's Germany would bring worse horrors than German occupation – a position he was not very happy with in later life. Before the USSR had developed the atomic bomb, he advocated a pre-emptive strike by the Americans, and afterward, he fought for nuclear disarmament and rallied scientists to the cause; one result of this activity was the Russell-Einstein manifesto of 1955. He even became involved in civil disobedience, was tried with Lady Russell and was sentenced to two month's imprisonment, which was shortened, after doctors' testimony, to a week in prison hospitals. Ultimately, he led a famous tribunal with Jean-Paul Sartre and others over moral responsibilities in the Vietnam War.[1] From the early days of his intellectual career, Russell largely abstained from domestic politics, and this is symptomatic; recognized visionaries generally act on all fronts, posing as sages in every sphere of political life. Russell's selection of a specific field *outside* the immediacy of domestic politics already shows an attenuation of his role as intellectual.

THE AMERICAN INTELLECTUALS

Hofstadter's (1963) classic on American anti-intellectualism roots its argument in religious antecedents that, Hofstadter claims, allowed for the exclusion of intellectuals from the mainstream of social life. He suggests that very early in the history of the colony, there appeared a preference for evangelicalism over formal religion, and that many of America's early inhabitants desired to return to the spirit of the primitive church which, they believed, relied on the wisdom provided by intuition – a natural gift from God – rather than on artificial reasoning. This mixture of evangelicalism and primitivism, according to Hofstadter, is the main ingredient of American religious culture (ibid., 55): "Religion was the first arena for American intellectual life, and thus the first arena for an anti-intellectual impulse. Anything that seriously diminished the role of rationality

---

1 Incidentally, in 1937, John Dewey, the American philosopher, who was seventy-eight years old at the time, led the Dewey Commission of Inquiry into the charges against Leon Trotsky in the Moscow Trial. Holding a sort of court of world opinion, as Russell did later on Vietnam, the Commission spent eight days in Coyoacan, Mexico, and came out with a verdict of innocent.

and learning in early American religion would later diminish its role in secular culture. The feeling that ideas should above all be made to work, the disdain for doctrine and for refinements in ideas, the subordination of men of ideas to men of emotional power or manipulative skill are hardly innovations of the twentieth century" (ibid.). Such is supposed to have been the inheritance of American Protestantism, which from the choices between mind and heart, intellect and emotion, opted for the non-rational, thus conforming to Jefferson's solution to the same predicament. Hofstadter emphasizes the part played by religious reformers who felt that the Reformation had not gone far enough, and, by emphasizing intuition as well as inspiration, combated any learned leadership and rejected the authority of any clergy. This has contributed, he claims, to the alienation intellectuals have felt in the United States; American intellectuals often seem deeply at odds with their own society. Hofstadter's discussion encompasses a wider spectrum of symbolic activities than the definition with which we have been working here, but the argument loses nothing of its explanatory power.

Intellectuals, in the broad sense of the term, are, in the United States, generally identified as a sort of a sub-culture. The New York intellectuals are often singled out as prototypical of such sub-cultures, that is, they are thought to form an almost exclusive species. On the whole, the New York intellectuals have consisted of loose associations which, through time, have revolved around journals like the *Partisan Review, Dissent, Commentary*, and others; occasionally one of these journals, like the *New York Review of Books*, becomes a real forum and source of reference while enjoying a high circulation. Analysts have hastened to note the high proportion of Jews involved, and the same comment is made regarding Jewish representation among American intellectuals as a whole. Indeed, this observation reinforces the role played by religious factors in determining the intensity of intellectuals' presence in different societies.

Even though American intellectuals have seldom made the headlines, they have in certain times made their views known as Lipset and Dobson (1972) note. They were particularly active in the late 1920s and in the 1930s, when they opposed the conviction of Sacco and Vanzetti, and flirted with communism.

By contrast, intellectuals were relatively silent during the 1950s, and the massive public debates of the 1960s were more the result of the mobilization of the universities, where faculty members and students united against the war in Vietnam, than the result of appeals made by intellectuals. Student activism – students being first concerned with conscription – seems to have been the spearhead of the anti-war movement, which was simultaneous with the student and youth movements of the time. Nevertheless, there is one person who stands out from the period and who embodies features of the classic intellectual, as I have defined the term. Noam Chomsky is a professor who, having acquired prominence in linguistics, inserted himself into the political scene in order to defend a cause. According to a survey by Kadushin (1974, 188), designed to establish the reputations of various intellectuals, the most influential intellectual on the Vietnam war was Chomsky, followed by Hans Morgenthau, whose proficiency in international relations gave him obvious credentials. Of the two, Chomsky qualifies best as an intellectual: nothing except his recognized capacities of abstraction as a professor served to legitimize the status of his opinions, whereas Morgenthau was already identified as a specialist in the field.

Even today Chomsky is very active in making his views known, especially on American foreign policy, whether that policy relates to Indochina, Latin America, or the Middle East. (1974, Chomsky and Hermans 1979, 1982, 1983, 1987). Although his influence is now quite limited, he follows in the tradition that was Bertrand Russell's.

It is, therefore, possible to identify in Great Britain and the United States particular public issues in which intellectuals were involved. But, as we have seen, there are relatively few intellectuals in these countries, and their influence remains, on the whole, fairly circumscribed. Jacoby (1987) deplores that those he identifies as intellectuals in the United States are nowadays working within the boundaries of institutions such as universities

Religious positions, which have often evolved into ideological tenets, make it difficult if not impossible for producers of symbols in these societies to become spokespersons for the entire community or for significant segments of it. The United States and Britain lack an intellectual tradition that would be conducive to charismatic leaders (Molnar 1961, 266, Lamont 1987a, 173), such as that which exists in France.

PART II

The Rise and Fall of the Intellectual: The French Experience

5 The Counter-Reformation and the Impact of Jesuit Pedagogy

With the mentality of a besieged city (Delumeau 1971, 44), the Council of Trent (1545–63) convened to counteract the growing influence of Protestant Reformers. Its sessions focused on doctrinal and administrative aspects of the growing Reformation. The Council first reiterated the teaching mission of the Church, which consisted of safeguarding the integrity of the two sources of faith, the Holy Scriptures and tradition. To this effect, the only version of the Bible that was to be recognized was the *Vulgate*, written in Latin, and attributed to Saint Jerome. Soon after, reading of the Book in vernacular languages was prohibited. In order to ensure unity of faith and practice, the Church assumed the exclusive right to interpret matters of faith and morality; thus the Council called for uniformity in most aspects of religious life. This translated into providing only one catechism for the entire laity, one breviary for the clergy, and one missal for the Mass rites. The dispensation of the sacraments was also precisely defined: Latin was to be the sole language of the liturgy, an exclusive code to be used in the administration of rites and the expression of official discourse. In order to guarantee a uniform understanding of theology and philosophy, Thomas Aquinas's *Summa* was recognized as the official interpretation of Church teaching.[1] In

---

1 It does not follow that Thomism subsequently enjoyed a monopoly in the Church over all other philosophical teachings. Actually it had to be rehabilitated and reinstituted in the nineteenth century as official Church teaching.

the meantime, Popes Paul III and Paul IV introduced the *Index Librorum Prohibitorum*, a publication that listed the books considered dangerous to faith and morality, and that were forbidden to the faithful.

After the emergence of Protestantism, which grew by progressively splitting into sects, the Catholic Church, in opposition, reacted strongly by affirming its deep concern for the unity of faith and morality. The Council of Trent left its mark on the Church right up until the early 1960s. when the Council of Vatican II was convened. In order to counter Protestant influence, the Catholic clergy strengthened its authority as the sole interpreter of matters of faith and morality.

THE JESUITS' PEDAGOGY

The Jesuits were one of the groups entrusted with a mission of spiritual redress. This religious order was founded by Saint Ignatius of Loyola in 1534 and was construed as a religious army ready to combat the Protestant heretics.

Over time, the Jesuits came to exert an impressive influence on the education of generations of Catholics. In France, as well as in most Catholic countries, the Jesuits established a pedagogical method which, in many instances, outlasted their own presence. The *Ratio Studiorum*, which served as the book of reference, was officially adopted by the Jesuit order in 1599, and it remained almost untouched for centuries.[2] It was designed for education at the secondary level, where influence over the elite was most likely to be long-lasting. One must take into consideration that, at the time, very few people pursued their studies beyond this level. The Jesuits' method set the terms for thinking, communicating, and acting, terms which, as we shall see, were reproduced by laymen when they took control of education, and which were transposed into secular life long after the Jesuits had lost their immediate influence.

The *Ratio Studiorum* defined a pedagogical system that worked through emulation. By employing a variety of incentives, the Jesuits maintained an atmosphere of constant competition among their students; the distribution of various honours at all times celebrated the glory of the brightest. *Concertatio* (quarrel) was instituted whereby

---

2 The *Ratio Studiorum* comes in a direct line from the *Modus Parisiensis* which was quite widespread in different scholarly centres in Europe (Bernoville 1934, 265); the *Modus Parisiensis* emphasized disputations and contests as well as providing an education geared toward the humanities (McGucken 1932). The importance accorded to rhetoric came from Quintilian.

the class was divided into two competing armies, usually the Romans and the Carthaginians, and each camp had officers of different ranks and distinctions. The battles were exclusively intellectual, submitting each individual to the continuous strain of excellence in performance. The term "performance" is not fortuitous here, for students were expected to impress their teachers and peers by their brilliance, especially their brilliance in style, the art of the ancient rhetoric being considered the ultimate means of expression. Emphasis was put on form. The orator was judged by his power to persuade (as opposed to his power to prove), that is, he was judged by his ability to charm others with his fluency, elegance, rhythm, judicious use of stylistic devices, and by his recourse to rhetorical effects. The rules as specified in the *Ratio*, of how to evaluate Greek and Latin compositions are illustrative of this aspect of Jesuit education; they stipulate that preference should be given to those compositions written in the *best style*: "*cujus melior erit orationis forma ... anteferatur*" ("*Leges praemiorum*," art. 9); *orationis forma* (literally "stylistic form") overrides all other concerns.

Rhetoric, which stood as the ultimate goal at the secondary level, is not in itself a device primarily geared to the discovery of truth. It is more concerned with effects upon the audience than with the accuracy and validity of facts. The Jesuits developed an art of communicating which acted on the psychology of the auditor and had little to do with the detached discourse of rational arguments.

This entire educational process took place in an imaginary world, for all major activities were performed exclusively in Latin and referred to an idealized construct of ancient Rome.

If the Middle Ages adopted Latin as the international language of scholarship, it was for the purpose of facilitating the exchange of ideas. Latin was used in a simplified form in order to make the language accessible to a greater number of people, and content definitely took precedence over form, which was considered secondary. The Jesuits inverted this process: in their educational system, form was pre-eminent, and classical Latin, particularly Latin in the style of Cicero, was imitated with much splendour and proficiency.

The Jesuits were truly products of the Renaissance in that they desired to return to the ancient world. Their strategy amounted to a bold enterprise that consisted of using Roman paganism as an instrument for the glorification of God and the propagation of Christian ethics. To this effect, they envisaged a reconstituted Roman world, purged of all of its pagan aspects and rendered compatible with Christian morality. The Jesuits' major achievement was to create a cultural entity that was completely dissociated from the real world around them. Through the linguistic barrier of Latin, they managed to create a purely pedagogical and immutable universe which was perfectly enclosed. The gap between this fictional world and the real one was, nevertheless, present in the educators' minds; education was thought to be outside the real world, which was considered corrupt (Snyders 1965, 350).

This idealized setting served to inculcate a conception of morality as *immutable*. Human nature and the morality that governs it are both defined in absolute terms; they are invariable through space and time, always identical to themselves, and, therefore, not subject to change. Figures from antiquity were used as more or less mythical characters to illustrate situations where virtues, vices, and passions interacted within a fictitious universe. They were emblematic figures, and were thus very unlike their real or historical counterparts. These personages were removed from their respective contexts, were attributed passions, frequently inferred from real or legendary details of their lives, and were then put to work in order to exemplify abstract values. They acted in the same fashion as did gods in Greek mythology. They personified excesses or excellence that served as pedagogical examples. These examples were chosen to illustrate a *moral* purpose, since they showed how all human beings encounter prototypical problems and situations. Students were called upon to *imagine*, by ascribing intentions to illustrious figures, how they had behaved in given situations; students might be asked to show, for example, Demosthenes's strength of character or Augustus's clemency toward Cinna. They were expected to expound rhetorically on these situations, and actual facts were of little concern. What counted was the ability to elaborate in the abstract, and more precisely, the virtuosity that accompanied it. Ciceronan notions of eloquence still provided the measuring rod; the closer one got to that style, the closer one was to perfection. Imitation was extolled because it relied on perennial aesthetic values. The strength of the Jesuit conception of the world rested on the timelessness of its criteria for truth, ethics and aesthetics as well as its ability to avoid any form of verification. The whole dynamic functioned in the abstract and the plausibility of its references was immaterial. Despite its pretensions to humanism and its constant invocations of the Latin world, the Jesuit system of education was far away from any real knowledge of that world.

The Jesuit outlook on ancient Rome was one furnished by truncated and expurgated texts; these selected extracts severely restricted the serious study of Roman authors and were chosen only for their moral exemplariness. Thus a fictitious world was constructed, one that provided continuous moral lessons illustrated through maxims drawn from the works of the great men of antiquity.

Significantly, Jesuit education allocated very little time for religious study as such. There were, of course, numerous ceremonies in which students participated: masses, prayers, and confessions, but little concern was shown for the doctrinal aspect of religion. In fact, religious teaching was confined to recitation and memorization of the catechism, which took no longer than one-half to one hour per week. When compared with the educational system of the Protestant schools, which at that time emphasized religious instruction, the difference is striking (Boehmer 1910, 228–9). As spearheads of the Counter-Reformation, the Jesuits did not wish to extend religious discussions to the uninitiated; such discussions were left, on the whole, to the clergy. Modern devotion, as the Jesuits understood it, meant the opening up of the inner life to the layman, whereas in the Middle Ages it had been restricted to the contemplatives; moreover, devotion did not entail discussing doctrine which was considered to be inaccessible to the layman (Guillermou 1961, 17–18).

We can, therefore, point to a Jesuit form of socialization that, through generations, developed a culture of its own. This culture was aristocratic in nature; studiousness was spurred by the promise of honour and the fear of shame. This sort of education was most appealing to status-climbers, those who wanted jobs belonging to the *noblesse de robe* and its affiliates. Such was unmistakably the case in France, where a Jesuit education was sought for this very purpose, thus progressively swelling the ranks of the "*gens de chicane*" (pettifoggers). Attendance at Jesuit schools by French aristocrats, for instance, was minimal when compared with that of the other classes (Dainville 1978, 159). This situation allowed the emergence of a class that was located socially between the bourgeoisie and the nobility, and which strove for some recognition in its own right. Wittingly or not, the Jesuits, because of their educational system, encouraged the formation of such a class. Students were educated in such a way that all they knew (and this they knew well) was how to speak and debate profusely. Such circumstances created fertile conditions for the emergence of intellectuals.

The culture that Jesuit education produced was one that favoured intuitive abstractions derived from the generalization of a severely simplified reality. It promoted a form of reductionist rationalism that was completely alien to the verification of facts. Facts mattered little because the Jesuits thought that one should be concerned only with those values that have stood the test of time. Such was the nature of the Jesuits' humanist education, at least that education provided to students at the secondary level.[3]

The Jesuit method of socialization extended to almost all the countries of Catholic heritage. The Jesuits, who considered themselves leaders of the Counter-Reformation, felt obligated to spread their educational mission as far as possible. They made their presence felt in France, Italy, Spain, Germany, Austria, Latin America, and other countries. But it is usually admitted that it was in France that the experience of Jesuitism has been the most far-reaching, in so far as the educational aspect is concerned. (The Jesuits were more politically involved in Latin American countries, for which see the Appendix.)

From 1762, the year of the Jesuits' dissolution in France, until the end of the nineteenth century, the educational program in that country remained relatively faithful to the principles and practices of the Jesuits. (The re-emergence of the Jesuits in 1814 may have contributed to this phenomenon until they were again excluded by political means in 1901.) Nineteenth-century education at the *collège* level was entirely consistent with Jesuit principles; isolation from the external world was achieved through the widespread boarding-school system, and oratory remained *the* ultimate goal. Students were placed in situations in which they were still expected to impersonate illustrious figures – this time figures from seventeenth-century France, classical French figures moulded by Jesuits themselves – and they were expected to live in a "moral, artificial and ideal world" (Prost 1968, 53). As Prost notes, commentaries on ancient texts (that is excerpts of ancient texts) were not analytical but merely laudatory, attention being paid to the wording and structure of the texts rather than the realities to which they referred (ibid., 54). Bréal (1881, 246) complains that oratory led to pleading causes instead of searching for truth. Students, as he says, were required to speak on facts about which they knew little; he explains how one day the topic would be the struggle between Mary Stuart and Queen

---

3 The sciences and mathematics, together with Thomist philosophy, were taught after the secondary level proper, and were designed to balance the weight of previous years' humanist teachings. In fact, the Jesuits developed an expertise in science that is increasingly recognized among scholars. Their eighteenth-century teaching was progressively diffused in vernacular languages; it led to history and geography, which then led to the sweeping spirit of nationalism.

Elizabeth, and the next, the debate between the Gracchi and the patricians (ibid., 248). The whole exercise unfolded in an atmosphere of intense competition for ranks, marks, and lists of merits.

Toward the turn of the century in France, the dissertation took the place of the famous discourse (which had long been a written exercise), but this did not prevent educators from imposing such "narrow" topics and questions as the following: "Demonstrate the superiority of prose over poetry in nineteenth-century French literature and give the reasons" (Mr Jourdain would have failed) or "Has the Renaissance impeded the spontaneous development of French literature?" (Prost 1968, 247–8).

This educational system had opponents who called for immediate reforms. As early as the eighteenth century, the Encyclopedists were looking for a method of teaching that would educate students through observation and experimentation. The lay system of the *École centrale*, inherited from the Revolution and introduced in 1795, provided a break in the literary and rhetorical tradition, but was short-lived, being halted in 1802. At different times throughout the nineteenth century, attempts were made in France to introduce science at an earlier stage in secondary school education. In 1852, a special curriculum to this effect was instituted and later on reinforced (1865), but was always considered as a Cinderella option. Many discussions took place from 1880 to 1902 over the status that should be allocated to sciences. Actually, the Reform of 1902 confirmed it but was nevertheless much attenuated in 1923 and reconfirmed soon later. Although these reforms provoked heated discussions, the superiority of classic studies was still taken for granted, and teachers continued to pursue the application of a speculative approach. Up to the 1920s, the spirit and intentions were remaining largely in conformity with the principles first applied by the Jesuits.

At least up to very recently, French education seems to have remained faithful to its formalist and literary propensities.

Bourdieu and Passeron (1977, 143, 155–6) comment on the inherited aptitude for a literary virtuosity whereby the pedagogical action would be still reduced to a verbal incantation from the part of the teacher: an exercise in professorial charisma. Clear and sweeping thinking could serve therefore as a substitute for scholarly demonstration from factual references. Though Crozier (1964) imputes these same attitudes to the bureaucratic spirit, he notes the strong propensities in the French *lycées* (which took over from the *collèges*) to stress individual competition which tested the pupils' presentational panache and neglected logical rigour in general.

Aron's *Mémoires* (1983) furnishes a vivid account of the importance accorded to the rank one did or did not receive and to the brilliancy of one's academic performance. Though of Jewish origin, he had internalized the scholarly manners of French culture. Referring to his *agrégation* from *l'Ecole normale supérieure* in 1928, he recounts how, in that year, Jean-Paul Sartre failed (for having been, it seems, too personal in answering the questions) whereas he, Aron, placed first and, as he relates more than fifty years later, "with an important advantage over the next one, Emmanuel Mounier (about 10 marks on a total of 110)" (ibid., 37). Aron admits in the next paragraph that Sartre's setback was redressed when he placed first the following year with a higher mark than Aron had received. These recollections express great sensitivity to the position a student held among his peers. Further on in the book (ibid., 348), Aron tells how Alain Touraine asked him to be his thesis director. Since Touraine's thesis was completed, it either meant, in Aron's mind, that Touraine considered him outstanding, or that he thought that Aron would add some lustre to the ceremony. In any event, the ceremony, as Aron recounts it, did not turn to Touraine's advantage. Apparently Touraine presented his thesis with an "élan de conquistador" and he concluded it with a Spanish poem. (One might interpret that the spirit of Loyola was not far from his thoughts.) Aron's comments were, by his own account, devastating, and the rest of the examiners followed suit. Disconcerted, Touraine is reported to have almost given up defending himself, which would have created an unbearable situation. Aron claims in his *Mémoires* that for weeks, Touraine relived this terrible experience. Here is a clear example of how, in order to achieve a brilliant performance, one has to display glory and pride.

The Jesuits definitely left their mark on the manner in which academic matters were treated; importance was placed on abstractness as well as on form and style.

THE CATHOLIC ETHICAL PARADIGM AND THE IDEAL TYPE OF INTELLECTUAL

We have seen, from the outset of this work, the importance attributed to a clerical hierarchy as the sole interpreter of the Bible, and the status of objectivity assigned to natural law. The upper clergy, as a knowledgeable elite, enjoyed the exclusive right to expound on the origins, existence, and prescriptions of an objective justice. The Counter-Reformation undertaken by the Council of Trent was meant to strengthen clerical authority over the definition and understanding of ethics, leading to one faith, one truth, and one Church. The Jesuits contributed a means and a style to the acquisition and distribution of knowledge. This, in a nutshell, sums up what could be called the paradigm of the Catholic ethics under the stress of the Reformation. The Jesuits provide us with magnified traits which become even more obvious in periods of high tensions.

On the other hand, the secularization process was triggered at the time of the Reformation. (Some may consider Protestantism to be a transient mode of secularization but this is beyond the range of our discussion.) Whatever the circumstances, the Church developed a defensive reaction to Protestantism and stuck to it. The Church put in place a vast system of socialization whose function was to diffuse and maintain a system of ethics, and of which the Jesuits were merely a part. It was under these conditions that the Catholic ethics became as strong as if not stronger than the Protestant ethics, because the Catholic Church was able to keep alive and strong an entire way of thinking about morality as a whole; so much so that the frame of reference was to remain intact despite secularization. In other words, the *secular* culture of former Catholic societies still retains elite groups which function as *mediators*.

This leads me to propose an ideal type of the secularized cleric: the intellectual. The purpose of an ideal type is not to define reality in its exact form but to embody values that are integrated in the abstract. (In any case, culture and ideology, as I once stated, can only be grasped as useful mental constructs (1985, 45–6)). The intellectual, as the reader may remember, is the individual who, as a producer of signs and symbols transcends her or his particular or professional sphere of competence and becomes actively involved in the political arena.

The intellectual declares him- or herself to be acting on behalf of others, and therefore assumes the role of an elite possessor of ethical knowledge. He or she claims to be able to determine what is good or bad for the whole, that is, what constitutes the moral interests of the whole.

The Catholic tradition was not only conducive to this type of mediation but it also furnished the ethical foundations that legitimized it. Objective justice, at one time understood as natural law, could be expected to evolve through secularization, but we shall see how the idea of an *objective* morality managed to survive despite the great changes in philosophical thought. Discussions over morality as such, its nature, origins and the means of grasping it, were and still are largely avoided in cultures of Catholic heritage. There are indeed exceptions, but on the whole there is, as we shall see, a strong tendency to take morality as given, and as not very amenable to questioning. This is in direct opposition to the Protestant tradition.

For purposes of illustration, the French experience approaches the ideal type and it therefore serves as a good point of reference. It exhibits the full process of secularization, which evolved from a deeply entrenched Catholicism.

6 Lay Ethics within the Bounds of the Church

France does indeed have a long tradition of *moralistes,* as they are called, but they are more often than not *littérateurs* who are concerned with the harmonious adaptation of human beings to life in society. Their discourse pertains to the overall human condition and to the manner in which a well-educated reader should conduct him- or herself. Their prescriptions usually take the form of short considerations that are several paragraphs in length, that is, when they are not summed up in maxims or aphorisms. The *moralistes* in the French tradition are, therefore, judged by their qualities as persons of letters, and are remembered for their contribution to literature. They did not usually question the very foundations of morality or seek to establish its relevancy. Throughout French history, we can find defenders of the Catholic faith who, through different means, have fought Protestantism, deism and atheism, from François Véron who attacked the Calvinist claims to interpret from the Scriptures, to Bossuet who criticized Protestantism in general, to the Jesuits who argued against Voltaire, and so on. But these groups and individuals added nothing to the orthodox moral teachings of the Church. However, whenever a movement such as Jansenism, progressed toward developing a new conception of ethics, it would be immediately thwarted. Catholic ethics was simply not open to a diversity of interpretations, or at least, not in theory. In practice, it was amenable to a form of casuistry, as the Jesuits revealed. But the principles, foundations, and rules remained intact.

The Catholic tradition, for obvious reasons, has not been at all concerned with any sort of epistemology of morality. Very few Catholic thinkers tried their hands at it, and many of those who did were often condemned by the *Index*. It is, nonetheless, interesting to examine the extent to which they went. In most cases, as we shall see, they did not go very far.

For purposes of exposition, it is useful to group authors within schools and periods. The end of the Renaissance marks the beginning of the Counter-Reformation, an era when philosophical hesitancy was still apparent, whereas the seventeenth century in France witnesses rationalism at its apex. Throughout this discussion of the emergence of the role of the intellectual, the reader will be able to recognize the more obvious evolution from the eighteenth century to the present.

THE BEGINNINGS OF SKEPTICISM

Montaigne lived at a time when the Renaissance's self-assurance had been dimmed by a series of events that, each in its own way, had introduced a deep sense of relativism into humanity's relationship with this world. Doctrinal dissent was tearing Christianity asunder, the geocentric interpretation of the universe was being disputed, and discoveries of other continents were testing widely accepted moral principles. In the meantime, an alliance developed between Counter-Reformers and "Nouveaux Pyrrhoniens" in order to counter the growing influence of Calvinism (Popkin 1979, 67); skepticism, whose ancient forms were being diffused could serve to shatter any attempts, by rational argument, to attack or reform the Church.

Montaigne was far from being the sole *moraliste* of his time, but he stands out as the most prominent and as the first in a line of writers that succeeded him. His form, the *essai* has remained unsurpassed in French, and well suited his purpose. Montaigne's goal was not to neatly elaborate any one theory, but to consider the means by which he, as an individual, could cope with the world of his time. His *Essais* were presented as personal investigations of attitudes, people, and events. In many respects, Montaigne's approach is one of self-withdrawal. Chapter xii of Book ii, entitled "Apologie de Raimond Sebond" serves him as an opportunity for him to expound his views on perceptions of knowledge and morality for almost two hundred pages.

The "Apologie" advocates skepticism regarding earthly matters and confidence, from faith, in the existence of God. Without grace the human being cannot reach any certainty, and skepticism is, for Montaigne, the philosophical attitude that best predisposes one to have faith. For, he says, Christians are mistaken when they try to establish their faith on rational grounds, since faith comes from the supernatural world. As he proceeds, considerations of faith are somewhat put aside, so on the whole, he recommends skepticism as the position to adopt.

Montaigne's skepticism is one that is designed for peace of mind. Any *"persuasion"* (conviction), he says, is conducive to dogmatism and ultimately to dissension and sedition. This is true because nothing in this world can be conclusively verified. *"Que sais-je?"* What can I know? First, I cannot rely on my own senses. Second, my reason is unable to grasp the essential aspect of things. Human beings often change their minds and become involved in unending discussions. They have no measuring rod to establish definitely and rationally what is a satisfactory judgment. Science is uncertain and subject to change. No absolute certainty is possible from our own faculties. Montaigne thus recommends a suspension of judgment, *"dubitation"* having the edge over *"assurance."* This position leads him to deny the possibility of ever discovering the nature of justice through human faculties. As for natural laws, Montaigne argues that there has never been universal agreement on what they might be; customs and opinions have always been diverse.

Montaigne acts like a realist; human beings should not overestimate their ability to change the course of events. The wise person is aware of human limits and conforms to them. The influence of stoicism is obvious here: "To philosophize is to learn how to die." Montaigne's skepticism allows him to introduce doubt as means of achieving speculative freedom within the bounds of moderation.

Nevertheless, Montaigne is faithful to Catholic attitudes toward ethics. Even though he discards natural law as a reality accessible to human minds, he places trust in God and makes no attempt to examine the nature of morality which he seems to consider as given. Montaigne's moralism can be placed within the tradition of psychological inquiry into the attitudes and behaviour of human beings as they achieve wisdom; his moralism advocates a harmony with our environment, an art of living. With Montaigne the traditional understanding of ethics remains intact since it is never put into question. This was a common stance of skeptics.

Though Montaigne himself might have been indifferent about synthesizing his opinions, Pierre Charron (1541–1603), one of Montaigne's followers, did try to bring together many strands of his thinking. He took much both from his master and from other sources such as Guilaume du Vair, his contemporary, who attempted to reconcile stoicism with Christianity (whereas Aquinas, centuries earlier, had integrated Aristotle into Christian tradition). Charron's most significant contribution was to separate secular from religious morality. He is more of a moralist than Montaigne in that he shows greater interest in the nature of morality as such and in the ways of discovering it. Calling it "*Preud'hommie,*" Charron describes and analyses a secular morality, which exists prior to the religious morality that completes it, just as, he writes, philosophy precedes theology, and nature, grace (1970, Preface). According to Charron, God, through nature, provides a sense of equity and universal reason that enlightens the minds of human beings. Wisdom demands that one live according to the rules of nature, since "men are naturally good" (ibid., 37). But Charron claims that to live wisely, one must utilize reason, because true "*Preud'hommie*" consists in a "firm disposition of will to follow the advises of reason" (ibid., 40). Charron's *De La Sagesse* refers to *sapiens,* the antique ideal of the virtuous, and through three books he expounds on the doctrinal and practical aspects of this ideal. He is one of the few Catholic philosophers (he was a priest) who dared to elaborate on morality. But Charron still belongs to the transitional period when the Counter-Reformation had not yet achieved the socializing power it would later on. This may explain the relative freedom he had to express his ideas. Because morality based upon religion had led to intolerance and fanaticism, Charron probably felt that separating them was the best solution.

Montaigne and Charron are considered to be the forerunners of the libertine movement in seventeenth-century France. The term "libertine," at the time, had no pejorative connotation; Mme de Sévigné, a well-respected person, could say, "I am so libertine when I write." The *libertins érudits* desired freedom of thought, thought emancipated from religious teachings. Atheism could not be openly displayed at the time, yet it seems that deism was acceptable (Busson 1933, 89). Proclaiming oneself to be a libertine might have been, in some cases, equivalent to flaunting a rather dissolute life. But, libertinism, whatever the brand, was not conducive to any considerable developments in ethics, except perhaps in the case of Gassendi who, because he was primarily interested in science, ventured into the realm of ethics.

In a move, that was quite bold for his time, Pierre Gassendi (1592–1655) examined ethics scientifically. Like science, and more specifically physics, which established the truth about things, ethics could discover objective criteria of the good and bad in human conduct. Wisdom is acquired by inquiring into both fields, science and ethics, using a strictly observational approach. Gassendi opposed the metaphysical and deductive methods of the Aristotelian school. Influenced by the scientific thought of the time, he considered experience to be the only scientific foundation for real knowledge. His purpose was to set a firm basis on which morality could be established.

Gassendi drew much from the works of Epicurus, which he viewed from a detached and unprejudiced perspective. He tried to reconcile these writings with those of Aristotle and the Stoics while remaining within the orthodoxy of the Church. (Though a *libertin,* Gassendi remained a priest throughout his life.) This led him to a form of eclecticism that was quite common at the time. The Ancients still exercised a heavy influence on philosophers, especially ethicists. Gassendi's boldness came from his Epicurean assertion, which he defended by an appeal to evidence derived from experience, that human beings strive for happiness, and that happiness is the ultimate end of life. In other words, things and events are gauged by the pleasure or pain they produce. Now, in this scheme, all pleasures do not have the same quality; human happiness on earth remains, for Gassendi, only a relative felicity, and the pleasures of the mind are superior to those of the body. Reason is used to enable human beings to look for pleasures that transcend the merely physical. For Gassendi, supreme happiness (*voluptas*) is attained when one has achieved tranquillity of mind, which should not be confused with passivity. Like Epicurus, Gassendi claims that human beings *naturally* aspire to this state of being. Virtues, like prudence and wisdom, concur, but only as instruments whose utility is evaluated according to their usefulness in attaining *voluptas*. In sum, Gassendi's ethic aims at rehabilitating Epicurus by promoting a rather austere conception of morality, austere in spite of its naturalistic foundations.

Gassendi is one of the few exceptions we shall find along the way. Some later *philosophes* made reference to him but without ever attempting to elaborate an ethics of their own. Yet, despite his boldness, Gassendi went no further than Epicurus, and simultaneously attempted to reconcile Epicurean thought with the orthodox teaching of the Church. He did not succeed in this reconciliation, and neither did he provide a legacy for succeeding generations.

THE RATIONALIST ERA

The seventeenth century in France was a period of extreme religiosity which at times approached intense mysticism. This encouraged the foundation of new religious orders and the reformation of existing ones, both for men and for women. Male orders included the Feuillants, the Trappe, the Jacobins (Dominicans), the Eudistes, and female orders, the Carmel, the Visitation, the Ursulines, Port Royal des Champs, the Dames du Bon Pasteur, and the Filles du Calvaire. The secular clergy (priests as opposed to monks) also underwent important change; the Oratory of Jesus was established by

Pierre de Bérulle (a significant figure of his time), as was the Messieurs de Saint-Sulpice (who held missions in Canada) by Jean-Jacques Olier. At the same time, the *curé* Adrien Bourdoise became prominent for educating parish priests at Saint-Nicolas du Chardonnet in Paris (in our own time, the rendezvous for reactionaries). Sacred orators abounded, such as Bossuet, Bourdaloue, Fénelon, Fléchier, Massillon, and Mascaron, all of whom are still remembered today. These are only a few of the examples that bespeak the profound religious commitment of this era of French history.

This deep mystic movement entailed a greater diversity in conceptions of spirituality. It introduced new modes of devotion as well, some of which were more adapted to the worldly condition of certain numbers of the faithful. François de Sales's *Introduction à la vie dévote* is a case in point; the book is intended for members of the aristocracy and proposes a spirituality adapted to their social situation. Confronted by Protestant theology, which proclaimed the priesthood of all believers, the Catholic Church adopted a more democratic stance than it had in the past and tried to show that salvation could be achieved in the secular world, that is, without retreating to monasteries or convents. This did not, however, rule out the expansion of cloisters, as I previously mentioned.

The diversity of means of achieving salvation led to some severe strains which, more often than not, involved the Jesuits. They held fast to Aristotelianism whereas, for instance, de Bérulle's Oratorians were more inclined toward Platonism. The rather long conflict between the Jesuits and the Jansenists became increasingly important. It revolved around the notion of human nature after the Fall, and whether human beings could improve themselves. According to the Jansenists, goodness can come only from outside; since the Fall, human nature is corrupt. Goodness, called grace, is a privilege which God bestows upon a select few by predestination. From this, the Jansenists developed a very stern morality of their own, discarding along the way the long-accepted notion of natural law. The Jansenist conception of morality was too much at odds with orthodox theology to be acceptable to the Church; it annihilated human freedom in favour of an implacable determinism in which reason and the natural law it discovers took no part. Though it was condemned by the Church, Jansenism survived for quite a long period of time. Because the Church feared that Jansenism, like other novel ethical systems, would develop into an actual religion or institutionalized church, it was severely quashed.

It is remarkable that, despite the intense religious activity of a period plagued by severe opposition within and without the Church (Protestantism still was the primary enemy), morality remained untouched, stable in its foundations as well as in its content. Catholic morality was not to be questioned except by very few individuals who were, in any case, marginalized.

The tradition of the *moralistes* in France, as I have already stated, has nothing to do with the Anglo-Saxon moralists that we have examined. The French thinkers belong to a literary tradition that is concerned either with the psychology of sometimes virtuous, but usually vicious, characters, such as the egotist, the hypocrite, and the miser, or with one's personal adaptation to the disappointing or deceptive nature of social life. These are the types of considerations one encounters when reading French authors such as La Rochefoucauld, La Fontaine, and La Bruyère. Molière's plays, particularly *Le Misanthrope, L'Avare,* and *Le Bourgeois gentilhomme,* fit into this tradition.

Pascal is a case apart. Much influenced by Jansenism, Pascal planned to write an apology for Christianity that would have shown his strong sympathies with Jansenist theology. (His scattered writings on the subject have been published in his *Pensées*, and are available in different arrangements, depending on the edition.) On the whole, his ethical thought conforms to the Jansenist reading of the Fall. From the fragments, we can conclude that he shares their pessimism, and their belief that human nature and reason were irremediably corrupted by sin. There are natural laws, he writes, but our corrupt nature can no longer perceive them (1960, no. 294). Moral science and religion, which belong to the supernatural realm, are to be grasped by intuition, "*esprit de finesse*", as opposed to reason, "*esprit de géométrie.*" But since we are blinded by our own interests, we are, therefore, incapable of discovering either justice or truth (no. 82). We can only speculate about how Pascal would have developed a cohesive work. It is not obvious whether *Les Pensées* was meant to be an elaborate essay on morality or a treatise of a more mystical nature.

In fact, only two philosophers of the period really attempted to deal with ethical questions: René Descartes and Nicolas Malebranche. Descartes never brought himself to write a full treatise on morality; Malebranche came closer. Each author, in his own way, contributed to strengthening the function of the intellectual in secular society, a function which would be fully realized in subsequent ages. Because both authors were rationalists, their ethics tended to establish inequalities in people's abilities to discover the rules governing morality.

DESCARTES'S CAUTIOUS ETHICS

Descartes sees ethics as the product of a rational search for truth. Morality is founded on truth, as is the science from which it proceeds. In his Preface to *Les Principes de philosophie* (1644), Descartes compares philosophy to a tree: the roots are metaphysics, the foundations; the trunk, physics; *the* science par excellence; and the branches, all the other "sciences," regrouped under three headings, medicine, mechanics, and morality. Descartes seeks to establish a universal science, of which morality is part, in that it represented the last step in the systematic search for perfect knowledge. Morality stands at the apex of wisdom, which presupposes, he says, a complete understanding of the other sciences. Knowledge of morality, the sovereign good, is reached through the natural light of scientific reason, the import of faith notwithstanding.

According to Descartes, since we do not initially possess certain moral knowledge, we require provisional rules of conduct. In the third part of the *Discours de la méthode*, Descartes prescribes conformity and moderation as a transitory stage. Writing later in life, Descartes lays down the guidelines one should follow in the triumphant rational pursuit of the moral life: first, one should use reason systematically in order to discover what one ought to do; second, one should follow resolutely the conclusions at which reason arrives; third, and in conformity with stoicism, one should attempt not to desire goods which are out of one's reach (To Elizabeth, 4 August 1645).

Wisdom, in Descartes's terms, is derived from the concurrence of will and reason. More specifically, the wise are those whose wills are at the service of their reason: "That understanding perceive all that is good and that the will be always disposed to follow it" (Dedication to Princess Elizabeth in *Les Principes*, 1967). Or, in other words, one should "to try to know very clearly and to consider with attention the goodness of that which is to be desired" (*Les Passions de l'âme*, 1967, art. 144).

Free will is essential to this process, being the ability to judge, that is, to discriminate truth from falsehood, which for Descartes is assimilated with *bon sens*, good sense (To Elizabeth, June 1645), an aptitude which is not equally distributed among human beings (Laporte 1959, 428). Morality is, therefore, dependent upon knowledge, and should be subjected to the same rules that govern knowledge, starting with methodical doubt.

It is symptomatic that Descartes never wrote a real treatise on ethics. His works on ethics serve as epistemological prolegomena to a work which was never written. His treatise on *Les Passions de l'âme* is not the product of a moral philosopher, but that of a physicist who is absorbed in uncovering the interdependent mechanisms of physiology and psychology in the emergence of passions. Thomas Aquinas too had studied the development of passions from a moral perspective; according to him, passions reflected how an individual was affected by good or bad tendencies (Mesnard 1936, 119). Descartes, however, puts moral considerations aside in order to analyse the passions of the soul, though the two types of passion, passions *for* the soul (the effect of physiology on the soul), and passions *by* the soul (the effect of psychology on the body), always imply both body and soul (ibid., 226). These phenomena are thought to be identifiable and perceivable by scientific methods of observation; they are facts that have a physical bearing of one sort or another. Descartes considered that his treatise would lay the groundwork for a later discussion on morality itself.

For many reasons, he did not further elaborate on his ethics, thus avoiding any deeper involvement. He blamed lack of time (Preface, *Les Principes*), claimed that the undertaking was inadvisable (To Chanut, 1 November 1646), and invoked the exclusive rights of monarchs, or their representatives, to inquire into such matters (To Chanut, 20 November 1647)

As is the case with many philosophers, Descartes' works as a whole converge toward the elaboration of an ethical system. As Gabaude (1970, 214–5) notes, Descartes's famous method is a "purification of the mind" from an *ethical* as well as an epistemological perspective: it is morality applied to the exercise of reason. For Descartes, the search for absolute truth necessarily leads to the search for the sovereign good, which completes the achievement of knowledge. The role of reason is to "examine the true (*juste*) value of goods" in the conduct of life (To Elizabeth, 1 September 1645). We may infer that Descartes' rationalist approach to metaphysics would have also applied to his ethics since the former is the foundation of the latter. In mathematical and scientific matters, Descartes names God as the author of all essences, eternal truths which arise from his will as the Supreme Legislator. Descartes identifies eternal truths as necessary relationships between things that are dependent upon Him (To Mersenne, 15 April 1630 and *Reply* to *sixth objections*, No. 8). For instance, it is God who determined that the sum of the three angles of a triangle are equal to two right angles (To Mesland, 2 May 1644). The same rules apply to morality as well, so human reason is likewise utilized in discovering it.

Descartes is interesting both because his works exemplify an ultimate form of rationalism, which is nevertheless compatible with

Catholic ethics, and because he established a pattern of reasoning that has stood the test of time in France. His rationalism confirmed the usefulness of a deductive approach to the inquiry into the true nature of morals. We can deduce that there exists for Descartes only one true, universal, and eternal morality that is willed by God and ascertained by human reason whenever reason is systematically applied to this effect. Despite Descartes's denials, the influence of his Jesuit education at La Flèche is obvious in his *moral* philosophy. Human beings are considered in the abstract, outside the contingencies of time and space. There is here no contradiction with natural law, and such an approach is bound to require an elite that is able to elaborate this morality. Having been raised to a status that is comparable or superior to science, morality is not left to the consideration of the vulgar. Moreover, it remains to be discovered. All the components necessary for the emergence of the intellectual are well preserved here, if not significantly strengthened. Descartes' confidence in the natural light of reason (though it is itself illuminated by God) thus made feasible the elaboration of an exclusively lay morality, but one that was expounded by rational speculation rather than by naturalistic observation.

MALEBRANCHE'S ETHICS OF THE FEW

The rationalism of Descartes was pursued by Nicolas Malebranche (1638–1715) who was also inspired by Saint Augustine, and who merged the theological and philosophical considerations of ethics. He was a priest belonging to the Oratory of Jesus and he envisioned religion as true philosophy (1939, I, 2, XI). The distance that Descartes established between philosophy and theology is, here, rejected in favour of an all-embracing perspective reminiscent of medieval thought.

In a very Platonic fashion, Malebranche posits the absolute reality of ideas (essences), spiritual beings (1879, III, 2, III) whose existence is objective, immutable, eternal and necessary. They amount to the true nature of things. These truths transcend human beings, as well as God, and lead to the concept of order (an idea from Augustine, but elaborated more fully here), which determines hierarchical relationships independent from God: "This order ... has force of law in regard to God" (ibid., 10e Éclaircissement). Truth and justice are abstract but nevertheless real entities; they establish a definite hierarchy of the values of beings, whatever their nature. A fly is more valuable than a stone, for instance, because the fly is situated at a higher level of being; it is more complexly organized

(1939, I, 1, XIII). Contrary to Descartes, truth and justice are not, for Malebranche, derived from God. For him, God cannot but absolutely agree with and conform to the order of nature, and His role consists in transmitting the understanding of this order to us through Reason.

The term "reason," as Malebranche employs it, signifies more than its common usage. For him, the Word of God (Jesus Christ), which is the wisdom itself of God, constitutes the reason that enlightens the minds of human beings (1939, I, 1, I). Reason, in Malebranche's terms, must be universal, since its purpose is to capture the universal nature of truth. God knows perfectly, and reason is consubstantial with Him; it is infallible (ibid., x). We can say, then, that human beings are rational in so far as they conform to the light of the word. "Man is not for himself his own Reason nor his own Light" (ibid., 2, XI). In other words, reason for human beings depends upon their participation in the word. For Malebranche, intelligence is more important than faith, since faith is bound to pass away whereas intelligence exists eternally (ibid.). Faith is simply conducive to intelligence (*Conversations chrétiennes*, 4e Entretien). It is, therefore, not surprising that Malebranche elaborates his ethics in a strictly rationalist manner.

For Malebranche, morality is derived from Truth and is attributed the status of science: "One must clearly understand the principles of this science, and even be a scientist (*savant*) in the knowledge of man" (1939, I, 2, I). The true nature of morality is not readily accessible to most of us. On the contrary, it seems obscure and even confusing to us, probably because of our fallen condition. Access to the immutable order is rendered difficult by our propensity to be distracted by our senses and imagination (ibid., x). Everybody, says Malebranche, takes pride in his or her rationality, but ultimately everybody renounces reason. If we all claim to be rational, he adds, it is because our deep nature as human beings calls on us to be so. But being rational requires a "distressing exercise" ("une espèce de travail fort désolant" (ibid., XIII)) since it demands the denial of the senses. Now, because of the Fall, people are more inclined to listen to their senses than to reason. Our attraction to objects of the senses and the imagination (Malebranche often groups them together) translate into the search for glory and worldly recognition. Scholars are pointedly identified as easily seduced by the chimera of reputation (1879, Preface). Ordinary people live either by "opinion" – in its pejorative sense – or by mere imagination (1939, I, 2, XIII), when what really matters is the "internal Truth" which one can achieve by looking inward. *But,* Malebranche adds, we must be very careful not to let loose our own corrupt imagination; it is better that we obey the passions of those entitled to rule than be free but susceptible to our own passions (*Traité* I, 2, XIII).

Malebranche's conception of ethics, like that of Descartes, implies the existence of a very precise intellectual elite It amounts to *la crème de l'élite*, since very few people are admitted into it. It is limited to those people who are capable of distancing themselves from their worldly condition in order to reach the exclusive realm of reason. But, he adds, experience shows that those most concerned with reading books and searching for truth are the same ones who have diffused the greatest number of errors (1879, II, 2, III). In a part of *De la Recherche de la vérité*, significantly entitled "De l'imagination," Malebranche devotes many chapters to a discussion of scholars, whom he calls "*personnes d'étude.*" He is far from impressed by well-read people, for they are likely to be distracted from thinking for themselves. He himself was not overly fond of intensive reading, instead preferring to meditate on abstract truths, an exercise that, he claims, very few either enjoy or are able to practice.

According to Malebranche, all human beings have at least an intuition of natural law, but very few are able to reach the highest sphere of real contemplation of the immutable order of nature. For him, the goal is not so much a matter of knowledge acquired through education but rather access to the reason of God gained through self-discipline. His approach is, therefore, bound to rest on intuitions which are subsequently subjected to abstract deduction. The conditions that will allow for the consecration of the intellectual are here strongly reinforced. Malebranche's concept of the moral thinker foreshadows the intellectual who will have to rely more on his or her intuitive and speculative abilities than on systematic sources of knowledge. Malebranche did not share the Jesuits' predilection for Baroque rhetoric in which style is paramount. Nonetheless, the rationalism that he inherited from Descartes and that he further develops, recognizes the existence of an objective justice and the use of personal reason to discover it; at the same time, however, those who possess adequate intellectual faculties to engage in this kind of moral reasoning form a very select group.

Neither Descartes nor Malebranche questions the existence of an objective justice that is to be defined by an elite; on the contrary, their respective rationalisms reinforce this view, which is essential to the emergence of the intellectual in subsequent generations.

7 The *Philosophe*: The Prefiguration of the Intellectual

Calling eighteenth-century French authors either *philosophes* or moralists is a misnomer in both cases, for they were usually neither. They identified themselves as *philosophes*, but they had little in common with philosophers like Hume or Kant. There was no intention to deceive on their part. By posing as *philosophes* they intended to stand in the name of reason, outside any considerations of religion or even of metaphysics. Unlike most of their predecessors, who usually stopped short of tackling revelation, the *philosophes* openly crossed this threshold and claimed total intellectual freedom. Abstract metaphysics was also put aside in favour of a more accessible mode of thinking, for most of the *philosophes* were basically *littéraires* animated by a strong urge to transform their intellectual landscape.

By its avoidance of the world of ideas, the French aristocracy left the door open for the emergence of a *noblesse de plume*, as I call it. Social mobility was generally difficult, but some found it possible to elevate themselves by creating a new class of sorts side by side with the *noblesse d'épée* (the military elite) and the *noblesse de robe* (the magistracy). Even under Louis XIV, most writers were commoners. With the slow but progressive ascendancy of the bourgeoisie, especially the petty bourgeoisie educated by the *collèges*, there appeared an ambitious and turbulent group which could claim a social position of its own.

The *philosophes* recognized each other without sharing the same points of view. The definition they gave of themselves was seldom satisfactory and lent itself to different interpretations (Lough 1975;

1982, 1–3; Dieckmann 1948). It is therefore advisable to use the term "*philosophes*" with caution. My purpose is not to designate a specific group by this label but simply to indicate how eighteenth-century French writers involved in intellectual discussions saw themselves. Despite major differences, especially over the existence of God, a series of writers shared a preoccupation with the status to be ascribed to morality and the means of discovering it.

The *philosophes* were not, on the whole, full-fledged moralists as those within the British tradition would understand the term. They were not too concerned with morality itself; they either circumvented it or merely alluded to it. It seldom crossed their minds to become involved in epistemological inquiries over the fundamental aspects of ethics and the ways of discovering them. Throughout their writings, justice is taken as a given which is sometimes imputed to God, sometimes to nature in general; there is little further development of the concept.

Natural law remained largely unscathed throughout the eighteenth century in France. According to the Catholic tradition, justice amounts to laws made for human beings by God. Universal and immutable, justice is grasped by reason, which acts as a guide or a discoverer, but not as a creator (Crocker 1963, 5). Nevertheless, reason is considered to be central to the recognition of justice. This point may have been disputed at times, but nobody denied the existence of a law of nature in the abstract. While the *philosophes* were not in total agreement with the Scholastic conception of natural law, they did carry on a discussion about it, emphasizing its different aspects and, at times, simply paying it lip service. Even in the latter case, natural law remained a referent for which no substitute was proposed.

The transition from Descartes and Malebranche to the authors of the Enlightenment did not challenge the role of reason in ethical matters, but extended it, while putting aside any references to or respect for a supernatural order. Descartes's epistemology served, in the hands of his eighteenth-century successors, to emancipate ethical discourse from Church control and place it in the hands of those who were deemed sufficiently rational and knowledgeable. French Enlightenment secularized the agency responsible for elaborating ethics without, in all cases, secularizing morality itself.

Pierre Bayle (1647–1706) is usually considered either the precursor or the initiator of the Enlightenment in eighteenth-century France. Indeed, he was an important influence. But because he was a Protestant, we have to consider him as somewhat of an outsider; this is also true of Jean-Jacques Rousseau. We can find in both authors the influence of the Reformation. The role of conscience as a feeling conducive to moral integrity is obvious in their writings, in Bayle's *Système de philosophie* (1968, IV: 260–2), and in Rousseau's *Le Contrat social* (1762). This understanding of conscience, which, as we have seen was common currency, especially among Calvinists, was alien to the Catholic tradition in which reason rather than conscience, was the ultimate judge.

MONTESQUIEU: THE KNOWLEDGEABLE JURIST

Montesquieu, who opens this era, is representative of a position on natural law that many commentators find ambiguous and confusing. Waddicor (1970, 16–21) has neatly summarized the primary positions of the commentators: some argue that Montesquieu gave up on the natural law, in which case, they either lament this renunciation, if they are traditionalists, or celebrate it if they are progressives; others of humanist inclination argue that Montesquieu did not surrender the notion of natural law; and, finally, certain logicians conclude that he never made up his own mind.

Without becoming drawn into such arguments, it is possible to detect that, on numerous occasions, Montesquieu readily adheres to the idea of natural law. In *Mes Pensées* (1949, I: 1458) he plainly states that something is not to be considered just because it is legal, but rather it is considered legal because it is just. He is also explicit in the *Lettres persanes* (Letter LXXXIII) when he identifies justice as a relationship of appropriateness that exists between two entities, and always remains so. Justice, he writes, is eternal and never depends on human conventions. The opening chapters of *L'Esprit des lois* [The spirit of the laws] (1748) follow in the same vein; here he establishes the indubitable existence of invariable rules of equity that are prior to any positive law. As many observers have noted, Montesquieu puts forth this principle at the beginning of the book but pays little attention to it subsequently, preferring to elaborate on the social determinants of state law, or, in other words, on the general laws of social nature. One could add that even Montesquieu's references to natural law illustrate empirical preoccupations; he focuses on particular aspects of human behaviour such as feeding oneself, sexual attraction, or life in society (Shackleton 1961, 250–1), which have little to do with the normative aspect generally attributed to natural law. Though this is true, one cannot ignore the fact that for Montesquieu, natural law in its traditional sense is prior to any other laws on earth (bk 1, ch. 1). By positing its existence, he also makes a direct appeal to reason as the ultimate guide in social life.

Montesquieu's *Esprit des lois* proceeds from two approaches involving reason, but reason as used in different senses. The work opens with an appeal to reason as the means of understanding the nature of the world; there is also a deistic reference to God as the being who establishes order in the universe. Then the discussion takes an empirical tack, in which reason functions mainly as a means of observation, but rarely as a guide or judge.

The most famous section of the work, Book XI, deals with laws that relate to political liberty and the constitution. Chapter VI of this book entitled *De la Constitution d'Angleterre,* sets out how political freedom can be secured through the appropriate organization of power. The exercise amounts to a rational contrivance which is not so much concerned with the separation of powers as a juridical device, but rather with a judicious equilibrium among social powers or classes. Montesquieu focuses on how the Crown, the House of Lords, and the House of Commons, each representing specific interests, can work together in such a way that no one entity will hold an overwhelming authority. For Montesquieu, the device procures a well-tempered exercise of power, and it therefore prevents despotism. This is the crucial issue. Montesquieu is haunted by the arbitrariness of despotism as exemplified by Asian countries. By despotism he means the state in which each person fears others. By freedom he means the peace of mind that emanates from each person's sense of security regarding others, a security Montesquieu applies to a person's own life and property (1949, I: 1152, 1431; *Esprit*, bk XI, ch. IV). His liberalism is decidedly aristocratic since freedom, which is merely the absence of non-legal constraints, is well entrenched within a system sensitive to distinctions of birth, wealth, and honours, to use Montesquieu's own terms (*Esprit,* bk XI, ch. IV).

Throughout his works, Montesquieu considers law to be a product of reason, even though law can be affected by social factors. Early in *L'Esprit des lois,* he identifies law in general with human reason, which leads all people of the world, while each nation's body of laws is specific only to it (bk I, ch. III). With this conception in mind, it is quite natural for him to adhere to the Platonic view that "Laws are made to declare the orders of Reason to those who cannot receive them directly from it" (1951, II: 1042). This is the *raison d'être* of legislation. Laws should not be subtle, because they are made for people of mediocre understanding (bk XXIX, ch. XVI). Montesquieu sums up this conception of law in the preface to *L'Esprit des lois*: "Could I but succeed so as to persuade those who command to increase their knowledge in what they ought to prescribe, and those who obey to find a new pleasure resulting from obedience – I should think myself the most happy of mortals" (1900, xxxii).

If Montesquieu exemplifies the role of the enlightened legist, Voltaire supplies the prototype of the intellectual.

VOLTAIRE: THE FIRST OF A LINE TO COME

To a large extent, Voltaire exemplifies the *philosophe* as the figure was understood in eighteenth-century France. The *philosophe*, as we have seen, was not expected to be a metaphysician. On the contrary, he was not to indulge too frequently in metaphysical speculations. Metaphysics was considered appropriate only to the extent that it led to ethics, for the purpose of human beings on earth was to act, not to speculate. The *philosophe*'s role was, therefore, that of the moralist. Voltaire confided to Frederick the Great, that as much as possible, he reduced his metaphysics to ethics (15 October 1737), conceding in another letter his suspicion of metaphysical ideas as carriers of uncertainty[1] (8 March 1738). But even here, the moralist is not conceived of as one versed in the problems of ethics, or one who is concerned with the epistemological status of morality. He is seen as one who spontaneously addresses the miseries of this world and offers possible remedies. Voltaire is the first intellectual, as I have defined the term, who involved himself on specific issues, such as the Calas affair (1765), for example, which was an obvious case of miscarriage of justice. But in addition to acting as an intellectual, Voltaire set the frameworks for intellectual action. Much of his work is devoted to the rise of the *philosophe* and the demise of the clergy, the former taking over the latter's privileged position.

Voltaire never intended to elaborate any sort of system. Being primarily a *littéraire* and having few claims to exhaustiveness, he preferred to make short comments on a variety of topics that, when brought together, form a kind of a whole. Voltaire was well aware of his limits, comparing himself to little streams "which are very clear because they are very shallow" (Brumfitt 1972, 9). He hoped that his message would eventually sink in, that people would be convinced that religion leads to misery if not to disorder, and that the wise should take over and impose the rule of reason in place of the rule of superstitious passions. Voltaire conducted his crusades primarily

---

1 "The great, the interesting object, as it appears to me, is not to argue metaphysically, but to consider whether, for the common good of us miserable and thinking animals, we should admit a rewarding and avenging God, at once our restraint and consolation, or should reject this idea, and so abandon ourselves to calamity without hope, and crime without remorse" (Voltaire, IX, *Philosophical Dictionary*, "God, Gods," sec. v).

by means of harassment tempered with irony, allusions, and occasional elaborations. He wrote for a large audience and seldom confined his work to a select group of thinkers or philosophers. He had little in common with academics.

Voltaire and the Encyclopedists sought to destroy Church authority by undermining its doctrine and dogma, as well as the influence of the clergy. For them, the Christian faith, like all faiths, depends upon superstition and leads inexorably to fanaticism and, therefore, to chaos. But Voltaire was a man of order. His purpose was to topple clerical authority while keeping morality intact, since he deemed it eternal, immutable, and universal.

It is most likely that Voltaire, who claimed to be a deist, actually believed in God. Many of his writings, public as well private, support this claim, even though his faith seems to have been dictated more by expediency than by any deep conviction. In a letter to the Count and Countess of Argental, he wrote, "Yes, I serve God, I believe in God and I wish it to be known" (30 January 1761). But his basic concerns lay elsewhere.

If Voltaire was opposed to established religions, he was also opposed to atheism, for it too could have a dangerous effect. He considered arguing against fanaticism and superstition laudable, because it is useful to humanity, whereas atheism is conducive to abuses. He apprehended the arbitrariness that would ensue on the parts of both rulers and ruled (To Sr. de Vilevieille, 26 August 1768; 1901, VI: "Atheism," 104–28). A profound belief in a rewarding and vengeful God is, for him, indispensable. Society, in order to work properly, cannot function without this "opinion" (To Duke of Richelieu, 1 November 1770). And if God did not exist, he adds, we would have had to invent Him (10 November 1770). God serves as the guarantor of moral truth against any form of nihilism. This is the real point. Like rationalist ethicists, Voltaire equates morality with truth, but he simultaneously sees God as the Supreme Legislator. God, who is also the "Eternal Mathematician" (To Mme du Deffand, 20 June 1766), ensures the rationality as well as the legality of justice. Voltaire's strategy is to reconcile reason with nature, and, at the same time, the natural with the transcendental (Crocker 1963, 36). For him, there is only one morality, just as there is only one geometry (1901, XII: "Morality," 18–20). And after discussing the universality, immutability, and divinity of morality, Voltaire considers its social usefulness. Pomeau's reading of Voltaire's *Traité de métaphysique* traces the sinuous course Voltaire at times follows (1956, 223). For Voltaire, justice is defined by its own usefulness to society, so much so that virtue and vice amount to what is useful or noxious to society (1785, XXXII: 69). God, having determined that human beings should live in society, could not but provide humanity with the idea of justice, which is indispensable to social life (To Frederick the Great, 15 October 1737).

Natural law is for Voltaire an obvious reality, and thus it needs little proof. He claims that there are rights in all societies, rights that are necessary for human happiness and that must be respected (1785, XXXII: 68–9, n.2). While Voltaire recognizes the impressive diversity of laws in different countries, he also argues that human beings abide by the same basic rules; this enables him to determine that laws, if they are in fact laws, must be just (ibid.).

The interesting feature of Voltaire's discussion is not so much his belief in natural law, which is hardly original, but rather the way in which he manages to grant individuals just enough autonomy and intelligence to grasp the rudiments of justice, but not enough for them to be entitled to enter public debate. Voltaire's strategy was to free the people from clerical influence by attributing to them the ability to develop a natural religion, while simultaneously refusing them the civic ability to rule the state.

As his first step, Voltaire secularizes natural law by rendering its basic tenets instinctively accessible to all. Religion is necessary, but priests are not. For him, God has provided human beings with the capacities both to *feel* and then to *reason* about the basic rules of social life. Initially, morality arises from our disposition to act with pity and kindness rather than with cruelty; we all possess an "instinct by which we feel justice"; afterward it becomes a matter of comprehension, and reason exercises its power of discrimination between right and wrong. (1901, VII: 235; XI: 60). Here for Voltaire, are the foundations of civil society, but they are rudimentary forms or conditions of social life.

As his second step, Voltaire legitimizes the role of superior minds, which are expected to perfect the rather primitive state described in the first instance. Morality "is the same among all men who make use of their reason"; it proceeds, he adds, "from God, like light" (1901, XII: 20). Thus an objective justice can be discovered by human beings, but only if they make use of reason. Similarly, he contends elsewhere that arbitrariness comes from ignorance, not from the nature of things (1785, XXXII: 69, n.2). Justice does not appear spontaneously, but requires the intellectual elucidation of the wise.

Voltaire's conception of society is basically elitist. He argues in two directions and tries to reconcile a purportedly egalitarian view of human beings with the unequal organization of society. On the one hand, he holds that human beings as such are equal, in the sense that all people are equally human, submit to identical passions, and are able, to some extent, to use reason. (1785, XXIX: 25; 1901, VIII: "Equality," 260–6). On the other hand, people, by the very fact that they live together, are unequal. Voltaire sees society as naturally unequal; and, from this "fact," argues that this situation is desirable.

From utilitarian arguments of his own, he advocates the maintenance of the severe divisions that were typical of the time. Voltaire makes no secret of his convictions that, in order to work, society needs an "infinite number of useful individuals possessed of no property at all" (1901, VIII: "Equality," 264). With his distinctive irony, he triumphantly claims that equality is simultaneously the most natural and the most fanciful thing. Every person has the right to think in his or her own heart that he or she is equal to others, but no more. Inequality is inherent to social organization; without it, human society would be corrupted.

As one might expect, the next step consists in disqualifying the mass of people from the domain of thinking in order to justify the status of the *philosophe*. This move is quite easy for Voltaire. The "populace" has to earn a living and is, therefore, condemned to ignorance; it simply does not have the time to think (1955, 19). Voltaire goes even further in his correspondence with Damilaville; not only is it indispensable to society that there be ignorant "boors," but one should note the problems that arise when the "populace" starts to reason (1 April 1766).

This reasoning places those few who know, especially the *philosophes*, in a privileged role. They are granted a virtual monopoly over moral and rational discourse.

But who are these *philosophes*? Their names are readily found in Voltaire's *Dictionnaire philosophique*. The *philosophe* is defined, so to speak, as a "lover of wisdom, that is, of truth" (1901, XII: 169). But it is also apparent that Voltaire's reference to wisdom and truth pertains exclusively to morality. *Philosophes* are to be moralists, but only in so far as they exemplify virtue and dispense moral truths. They are not expected to speculate on the nature of ethics. This allows Voltaire to state that Cicero, by himself, is probably worth all the philosophers of ancient Greece. Voltaire thinks that morality is not difficult to understand, but it requires, nonetheless, wise people to discover and practise it.

Voltaire celebrates the *philosophes*' freedom from any specific social class or power; they can, therefore, claim to be disinterested representatives of the people's as well as the monarchs' interests. He insists that the *philosophes* share no interests of their own and can, thus, speak in the names of reason and public interest (1785, XXIX:

15). The sovereign can congratulate himself when he is surrounded by them, for they are guardians against superstition and fanaticism, both of which are conducive to troubles in the realm.

Voltaire identifies the function of the *philosophes* as one that is basically social, this being consistent with his understanding of morality in general. The progress of reason is largely conditioned by moral imperatives. The *philosophe*'s role is to guide both king and subjects down the right path: "Opinion governs the world, and in the end the *philosophes* govern men's opinions" (27 January 1766).

Epitomized here is the function of the intellectual as the perfect representative of the people's real interests. Justice is an objective entity which is to be elaborated and illustrated by the few.

Voltaire was not much of a liberal. He argues in favour of certain freedoms, but does not provide either a demonstration of their legitimacy or a discussion of the conditions of their implementation. Claims for the security of property and for freedom of speech and conscience are frequent in Voltaire's writings, but he offers no logical demonstrations. He spontaneously envies the English system of government without considering how such a system might be established on the continent. John Lough (1982, 17) argues that prior to the Revolution, there was, in France, a consensus that, because of its size and population, France could not conceivably become a republic. Voltaire's contemporaries usually refrained from disputing the legitimacy of the monarchist regime then operating in France.

Voltaire promoted absolutism for reasons of efficiency. But as in many other cases, he offers no theoretical justification for his position (Besterman 1976, 315). The absolute monarchy he advocates is alien to the absolutism of divine right. Instead, it is based on the appropriateness of a concentration of power against the elements of anarchy. Hence Voltaire opposed the *Parlement* (which had nothing in common with its British counterpart) and unswervingly supported the king, Louis xv, against the robed nobility, the magistrates, whom Voltaire considered reactionary and divisive; this, even though their challenge to the king was popular. Voltaire wished to guarantee the rule of law, derived from justice and reason, through the unified authority of the monarch. His preoccupation with unity is fundamental here and comes from his reading of history. Voltaire detested the internecine conflicts that afflicted France during the wars of religion and the *Fronde* when Louis xiv was still a minor. Furthermore, he thought that the great eras in the history of thought and the arts were dominated by grand characters who had imposed their ambitious projects onto their surroundings. Voltaire admired Philip of Macedonia, Alexander the Great, Julius Caesar and Augustus, the

Medici, and ultimately Louis XIV, who for Voltaire came closest to the ideal (1901, XXII: 5–12)

Voltaire believed in an absolute but enlightened monarchy. Ideally, the king would be a *philosophe*. However, there was an immense political role to be played by the *philosophes* who constituted an elite group of opinion-makers. In sum, Voltaire supported a new type of aristocracy, one of thought, whose members would have the ears of the king and who would act as representatives of the public interest.

In Voltaire, we find assembled the components that would constitute the requisites for the emergence and maintenance of the intellectual. These amount to a consistent set of beliefs: first, that an objective justice of a transcendental nature exists, an ethics whose rules and principles are external to humanity; second, that these rules and principles, as laws, can be discovered by reason; third, that because the ability to reason is unevenly distributed among individuals, certain people are better equipped than others to discuss ethics; and fourth, that this elite should be officially recognized by being granted an appropriate social status.

The distance that separates Voltaire from Thomas Aquinas is, of course, great. But it is interesting to note that the elements indispensable to the constitution of an intellectual elite can be found in both authors. Both authors point to the objective nature of justice and to the necessity of keeping intact the privileged status and role of the knowledgeable. With Voltaire, all references to revelation disappear; revelation is even combated, which leads to a process of secularization, the demise of the clergy and the ascendancy of the intellectuals. Contrary to the Protestant process of secularization, where individuals are invested with full moral responsibility, the Catholic course ends with a simple transference of moral authority from one elite to another, from the clergy to the intellectuals.

Voltaire not only provided a framework which legitimized the role of the intellectual, but also acted as one. Here is a man who, thanks to his high reputation as a writer of histories, essays, poems, plays, stories or novels, was able to attempt to redress what he considered public abuses. As a prominent *littéraire*, he could become involved in public matters and receive recognition for such involvement. Voltaire is known for the role he played in a number of judicial cases, including the Calas case previously mentioned, and the Sirven (1764) and La Barre (1765) cases. In his own individualistic way, his actions prefigure the more collective action undertaken by those whom I label intellectuals who, over a century later, intervened in the Dreyfus Affair. The famous "apotheosis" that was conferred on Voltaire at the Comédie française shortly before his death was due largely to his reputation as an intellectual. He was celebrated as "l'homme aux Calas," as he was called, the defender of Calas against the judicial apparatus. In the spirit of a second apotheosis, his remains were transferred to the Pantheon in 1791; in a sarcophagus, they were placed on a coach drawn by twelve white horses, on the front of which was inscribed: "Il vengea Calas, La Barre, Sirven et Montbailli. Poète, philosophe, historien, il a fait prendre un grand essor à l'esprit humain, et nous a préparés à être libres" (Pomeau 1994, 360).

Besterman (1976, 466) argues that Voltaire's involvement in the Calas case "created public opinion as a new and increasingly weighty factor" in France. This may be a bit far-fetched; nevertheless, he rightly indicates the importance to be attributed to subsequent intellectuals who took similar action. Voltaire foreshadows the intellectuals who would follow him. He paved the way for them by establishing a legitimate sphere in which intellectuals could act, and by being the first intellectual to place himself and act within this newly created realm.

Lanfrey (1857, 55) aptly sums up Voltaire's character: "(Voltaire) is a moralist, but one who attests to an offended morality." In this way, Voltaire foreshadows the intellectual to come.

DIDEROT: ETHICS AS A SOURCE OF INCONSISTENCY

The notion of an objective justice, whether openly called natural law, or more surreptitiously located within nature itself, appears to have been the stumbling block of most eighteenth-century *philosophes*. This problem is apparent in the case of Denis Diderot, for instance, who was torn between two philosophical tendencies: naturalistic determinism and abstract moral theory. He himself was conscious of his propensity to moralize and of the inconsistency it might have introduced into his professed naturalism.

Diderot begins his study of human nature by examining its basic unit, the individual, in whom he recognizes an impulse toward happiness. From this perspective, Diderot makes no distinction between the moral and the physical world, since both are moved by the same laws drawn from the necessary relations between things. There is thus at this stage no merit or demerit to be attributed to them. He considers human beings to be identical in their respective constitutions (*"organisations"*) and, thus subject to the same search for pleasure and avoidance of pain. Because he sees human beings as responding to the same determinants, he makes no value judgment.

His views are in keeping with a naturalist interpretation of human behaviour. However, his argument becomes twisted when he gives his account of human beings as social creatures. He sees them as motivated by similar needs; all people feel the same necessity to be together. From this Diderot infers that they constitute an entity in its own right; they constitute a species.

It is from his notion of the social human species that Diderot develops his conception of morality. Like Voltaire, Diderot asserts that morality is essentially a social reality but is also identified with its utility for the public, the latter being a distinct whole. One pursues one's own real interests by conforming to the general interest. This conception of the individual vis-à-vis society is not that distinct from those of the Aristotelian and Scholastic schools, even though the approach is entirely different. For Diderot, there is an equation to be established between one's happiness and one's conduct that is to be adapted to one's own "nature and condition" (1773, v II: 309). Justice determines what we owe to ourselves and what we owe to others (From Tourneux 1970, 315).

The whole argument rests on the conviction that society, being itself a product of nature, abides by its own laws. Moral law is part of the nature of things and must be discussed as a science dealing with truths. Diderot argues that the principles of justice are ingrained in nature, and that they are, therefore, necessarily eternal, immutable, and universal. They exist prior to any rules established by legislators and should be discussed in scientific terms. There exists a law of nature, or, in other words, a natural law, which has nothing to do with mere conventions, and which can only be grasped by reason.

Everybody must be able to act morally, but only the *philosophe* is able to possess a profound understanding of morality itself: "The magistrate administers justice; the *philosophe* teaches the magistrate what the just and the unjust are. The soldier defends the homeland; the *philosophe* teaches the soldier what the homeland is... The sovereign commands all; the *philosophe* teaches the sovereign about the origin and limit of authority. A particular man has duties to fulfill in his family and in society; the *philosophe* teaches everyone what his duties are" (1986, *OC*, XXV, *Règnes de Claude et de Néron*, II: 25).

Whenever Diderot speaks of reason he refers to an abstract entity that transcends the individuals' personal conceptions. Only the enlightened mind can reach the heights of a reason that is "the reason of the human species."

The *Encyclopédie* was meant to instruct future generations in order to allow them to be simultaneously virtuous and happy. Happiness is achieved through virtue which in turn is achieved through knowledge.

Conversely, ignorance and stupidity are the frequent companions of injustice (To Sophie Volland 22 September 1761).

It is now obvious that the *philosophes* are an elite few. For Diderot, there is nothing as rare as a logical mind. It is lacking among an "infinity" of men, and is totally absent in almost all women (1961, 593). Governance becomes a matter to be discussed by the enlightened.

With Diderot, natural law is totally secularized, whereas nature becomes somewhat sacred. And from Diderot onward, nature replaces God as the repository of law, and becomes an abstract reference point for intelligibility and stability. The rationale that supports the emergence and importance of the intellectual is evident here as it is in Voltaire. While Diderot's approach is more naturalistic, at least in appearance, than is Voltaire's, it is equally rationalistic when it comes to ethical matters. This situation is not uncommon among the openly avowed naturalists of the period.

THE MATERIALISTS AND THEIR IDEALISM

Self-proclaimed naturalists and materialists are even more interesting to analyse since one would expect that they would oppose the notion of an objective justice and that they would be less inclined to recognize the importance of an enlightened elite. For our purpose, three authors of the period stand out: Helvétius, D'Holbach, and De La Mettrie. We could look at Condillac who attempted to combine a "sensationalist" approach with a form of rationalism; he thought that, through the interplay of pleasure and pain, the individual could grasp the nature of God-given moral law (Knight 1968, 36). Condillac was quite bold, but desired to remain within the boundaries of Christian orthodoxy. Hence, it is more satisfactory to address ourselves immediately to those less likely to indulge themselves in compromises of this sort.

Both Claude-Adrien Helvétius (1715–71) and Baron d'Holbach (1723–89) initially adopt a naturalist framework. They see human beings as being motivated only by self-interest in the adjustment of their sensations to the environment. Because they believe that utility is both the primary motivating force of human action and the sole measuring rod of action's worth, they also believe that moral laws can only be discovered empirically. They each look for a science of ethics that is parallel to the science of physics. But from these naturalist premises, both authors develop arguments that seem to be inspired by considerations which are foreign to materialism.

In their accounts of society, both Helvétius and d'Holbach move from an individualistic approach based on human nature to a rather holistic account of human interests. Morality, as the Baron d'Holbach sees it, emerges from the recognition by human beings that they have to live together in society. Hence, a new natural reality emerges from the necessity for reciprocity and cooperation. The problem, as Helvétius perceives it, is how to organize society in such a way that individuals can pursue their own self-interests while, at the same time, helping to realize the general interest (1969, II: 249).

For both authors, the sole purpose of ethics remains throughout the happiness of people, which is the *raison d'être* of morals. Yet, neither author seems overly concerned with establishing means of evaluating happiness. Instead, both claim, at the outset, that there is a situation to redress.

Helvétius boldly assigns to law and education the full responsibility for the people's vice and virtue. But the quality of law and education presupposes, as he says, the knowledge of human nature. Expressing similar sentiments, d'Holbach maintains that people are unhappy, antisocial and wicked because they are not told about their true interests (1971, II: 125). According to Helvétius, when human beings initially gathered together and formed society, they did not possess knowledge of the true principles of morality (1967, III: 99). The initial remedy to this situation is law and, subsequently, education, which is itself established by law (ibid., VI: 181). Law is a type of constraint, whereas education is a form of inducement. For Helvétius, the science of morality is the science of legislation (1969, II: 276): "The masses of a nation are never moved except by the force of laws" (ibid., 245). Similarly, d'Holbach states, "Legislation must set public opinion straight, and should be guided by the latter only when it is in conformity with reason and the good of society" (1971, II, 126). Morality, here the means by which the original flaws of society are to be redressed, is imposed from above.

Both authors consider morality to be founded upon invariable principles that should lead to "public felicity" (Helvétius 1967, XI: 173). D'Holbach, who is more inclined to attribute an absolute character to it, associates justice with truth (1967, 7): it is unchanging because it is ingrained in the nature of society (1971, II: 271). Both authors make explicit references to a natural law which entails the rights of security and property (Helvétius 1967, XIV: 196; d'Holbach 1969, II: 8). Like their predecessors, Helvétius and d'Holbach point to reason as a means of determining how human beings should behave in society. The aim, this time, is to maximize utility; but the approaches taken are rationalistic and have little in common with the authors' original naturalist premises (Crocker 1963, 126). Helvétius and d'Holbach begin their accounts of morality by considering individual psychology, but very quickly, both authors grant society the status of a distinct entity, from whose nature moral laws are derived, but only by those who, because of their superior knowledge, are best suited to the task: the *philosophes*.

Again the *philosophe* enjoys a privileged status. He functions as the "architect of the moral edifice" (Helvétius 1967, XII: 138). Helvétius argues that it is up to the *philosophe* to use his foresight to detect the true opinion that, though individual and little known, shall become the general and accepted opinion (ibid., 152). Again, ethics becomes a matter of *reason* and *knowledge* to be defined and explicated by the few. Helvétius uses the traditional argument of disinterestedness to legitimize the role of the *philosophes*. They are those who, because of their education, knowledge and detachment from "personal interests," are able to pass judgment on the appropriateness of laws and conventions (1969, II: 255). Both Helvétius and d'Holbach give the specific responsibility of enlightening the legislator's actions to the *philosophes*, or moralists, as they are sometimes called. For these authors, the role of legislator is often reduced almost to that of a rubber-stamp. Helvétius is explicit: "It is up to the moralist to articulate the laws, for which the legislator secures the execution by affixing the seal of his power" (ibid., 250).

This is almost the definition of the intellectual. Similarly, d'Holbach maintains that the politician's function is to use his power to sanction the lessons of the moralists, or, in other words, to be the "faithful interpreter of the moral oracles" (1967, 2, 190).

The public in general is reduced to a role of passive receiver. According to Helvétius, few individuals have the leisure to educate themselves, so the people at large shall be content with a catechism of simple maxims (1969, II: 47, 263). D'Holbach is somewhat more adamant in his elitism. He claims that few people, in any case, have clear ideas about the moral (social) order; it is difficult to understand, and one needs a sophisticated mind to grasp "the true relationship between things" (1969, I: 100–2). In fact, the true principles of morality are unknown to most people (1970, I: 44):

"By a fatal and natural inclination, people and those who rule them are subject to passions ... which make them deaf to the voice of duty, to the eternal laws of nature" (1971, II: 187).

Baron d'Holbach's conception of society verges on the totalitarian. He sees society as a generic entity – a notion alien to Helvétius – which is prior to the individuals that compose it. He bluntly asserts that citizens are obligated to serve their country, by offering it the use of their talents and ideas. The country can, therefore, decide how it will use these talents and ideas (1969, III: 156). D'Holbach seems satisfied to give the people the minimal amount of education necessary to secure satisfactory support for the state (1971, II: 127). Here, we are very far from liberalism. Though utilitarian in his approach, d'Holbach is more concerned with the "general utility," as he points out that "Society must provide for the welfare of those who are useful to it" (ibid., 276).

Thus, the two most prominent materialist utilitarians in France arrive at a reinforced conception of the *philosophe*, which articulates the exact nature of the intellectual: one who serves as a self-appointed representative of the general interest to the legislator.

Julien Offroy de La Mettrie (1709–51) differs from Helvétius and d'Holbach to the extent that his materialism remains unscathed by rationalist considerations. Having been educated in the medical profession, he retains throughout his works a physician's outlook on society. In the *Discours préliminaire* (1750), he brushes aside any references to justice, equity, vice, or virtue as such, though previously, in *L'Homme machine* (1748), he had entertained the notion of a natural law located in sentiment (1970, I: 324).[2] Morality and justice are merely the products of politics, religion being an instrument of the state used to keep the people under its control. La Mettrie views these phenomena as the simple expression of interests. Nature is the only thing to be understood, and nature is what it is: facts. Philosophy is defined for what it has to be: "the science from their effects" (1981, 241).

In the quest for knowledge, individuals are not equally equipped; some are better "organized" to think than others, and they happen to be a small minority. This situation is understood to be a simple fact of nature. The vast majority of people are dominated by passions, obeying blind interests and responding to prejudices. Again, only the *philosophes* are able to find the "just" and "equitable" actions, that is, actions that benefit society (1981, 238). La Mettrie advocates a kind of utilitarianism when he declares that the interest of society provides the sole criterion with which to evaluate actions as just or moral. One may wonder what the nature of this interest is, but La Mettrie does not elaborate. It is worth while to note here that the more these authors adhere to materialism the more communitarian they become. Without reference to the Church or the notion of God's people, they create a community whose interests transcend those of individuals and establish a new clergy in the *philosophes*.

Quite cynically, La Mettrie argues that the more knowledgeable

---

2 As long as one excepts *L'Homme plus que machine* as La Mettrie's; it was published anonymously, and was never absolutely recognized to have come from his pen.

and enlightened the elite becomes, the easier it will be to control the people (1981, 241) So, he concludes, the legislators have a great interest in being informed by philosophers.

RAYNAL: THE COMMON DENOMINATOR

The Abbé de Raynal epitomizes the spirit of the time, its convictions and contradictions, and he was very popular among his contemporaries. The *Histoire philosophique et politique des établissements et du commerce des Européens dans les deux Indes* (1770) in seven volumes made his reputation, even though today we cannot tell which sections are actually his, since some of them were written by contemporaries such as Diderot. The work appears to be a synthesis of the writings of a number of authors: Montesquieu, Rousseau, the Encyclopedists, and the Physiocrats. At the outset, Raynal posits that human beings possess a social instinct that makes human associations necessary; and, from this condition, arise the indispensable laws of society. As he proceeds, morality becomes a question of reason and philosophy, a science whose object is the conservation and happiness of the human species (1777, VII: 302). Like some of the other *philosophes* such as Diderot, Helvétius, and d'Holbach, he identifies both needs proper to society and needs proper to the individual. The "common interest" (ibid., 304) determines what is good. Society is deemed to have interests of its own, called the "common profit" or the "common utility," which is completely dissimilar from Bentham's sum of individual interests. Morality, which is universal and which should determine all government laws, arises from the nature of society itself (ibid., 305). These premises allow the author to explicate the intellectual's role: "(Governments) should allow ... for the superior minds to attend in some way to the public good. Any writer of genius is a born magistrate of his country ... Being always noble, his spirit takes its qualifications from its own rights. His arbiter is the nation at large, and his judge is his audience, not the despot who does not hear him nor the minister who does not want to listen to him" (1777, VII: 187–8).

The role of the representative of the public interest is here very well expressed. For Raynal, the ideal situation could certainly be classified as that in which rulers listened to the advice of "superior minds."

THE LEFT

To the left of Raynal stood Morelly and the Abbé de Mably (1709–85) whose respective collectivisms helped pave the way for the intellectuals. We know very little about Morelly's life, but he left a *Code de la nature* (1755) which did not pass unnoticed. The book proposes no less than the complete suppression of private property and a return to a God-given natural order of benevolence. Nature, he argues, had its own laws, which were distorted by the introduction of private property. Morelly's goal is to return to the original condition, but in order to do so, people have to become acquainted with the former values. At the present, he claims, individuals are blind to the true interests of humanity (1950, 153). Against "vulgar morality" (ibid., 157) which is false and alien to nature, he recommends the one universal morality, which can be discovered through the use of reason. According to him, morality can be logically demonstrated; just as in mathematics one can use equations to determine the value of the unknown, so too in the analysis of morality one can, by discarding falsehood, arrive at the truth (ibid., 161). Here again we find rationalism coming to the rescue of naturalism. And again the enlightened are invited to carry out the operation and to bring the people to utopia.

The Abbé de Mably, for his part, strives for the equality of fortunes in society; he does not, however, advocate any form of democracy. Like Morelly, he sees reason as having been thwarted because it has been corrupted by the passions, which are the lot of the majority. Human beings have followed their passions rather than reason, thus transgressing the laws of nature; they are punished by nature itself. Each individual's search for satisfaction through splendour, luxury, and voluptuous pleasures has contributed to the decay of life in society (1789, IX: 20). In the present state of society, people have to endure oppression because they have progressively removed themselves from *truth*. Like Morelly, Mably says that people must recapture their original condition and submit themselves to the laws of nature, which lead to the happiness of all (ibid., 202); for nature provides the rules of justice as secured by providence (1821, XIII: 140–1).

Mably's judgment is harsher than that of Morelly: "(The) multitude is unable to think by itself and is therefore condemned to be, at all times, ignorant, stupid and fickle" (1821, XV: 166). For him, the great majority will always be in need of direction to control and harness its passions. Direction is to be provided by governments which rule in conjunction with the wise (ibid., XIII: 351). The wise comprise a small group which nature produced for the purpose of enlightening nations: they are those who can discover truth through reason untampered by passions (ibid., XV: 179). If all people were capable of disinterested reasoning, there would be no need for politics or laws; but nature has provided a different arrangement.

Whether the *philosophes* approached the question of ethics from the right or the left, they maintained the need for an enlightened minority, even though their rationales differed.

THE PHYSIOCRATIC CONSTRUCTION

In a category of their own, the Physiocrats (led by François Quesnay (1694–1774)) developed an entire theory of society to justify their conception of economics. Taken as a group, they have almost as much to say about society as they do about economics, which is considered to be their primary concern.

The starting point of the Physiocrats is the physical and moral exaltation of nature. Following a line of thought, which has become familiar, they ascribe to nature the full capacity to furnish laws that govern both the physical and moral worlds. Nature, which is created by God, obeys rules that make its functioning harmonious; it is up to the human mind to discover these rules and apply them to the organization of society. The whole argument depends on the immutable character of natural laws and the interrelationship of the physical and moral orders.

Society is considered to be some sort of extension of the physical order. Nature provides human beings with needs, or interests that can be fully satisfied only by society. The Physiocrats' primary project was to reconcile the individual's natural propensity to maximize his or her happiness (which stems from the law of self-preservation and from other natural needs) with the human species' propensity to multiply its numbers, its need for growth. Not surprisingly for an informed reader, the Physiocrats conclude that individuals, when left to pursue their own interests, will unknowingly promote the interests of the social whole. These considerations are set out in a discourse that pretends to be exclusively scientific. The Physiocrats claim that the language they use is the language of reason and that they simply uncover and enunciate the laws of nature. This ethics is derived from naturalist and utilitarian premises but remains nonetheless rational in tone. Quesnay readily equates justice, which is objective and immutable, with natural rules and rights that can be found by enlightened reason (1958, 731). And any defiance of the laws of nature is punishable by the misery that results. As Le Trosne mentions, there is a necessary connection between the just and the useful, but justice does not have anything to do with moral feelings (1980, 180, 82).

Justice is absolute. It is part of the nature of things (Le Mercier de la Rivière 1910, 8), since human beings possess a social nature that is prior to society itself, and that implies abstract rights and duties.

Society is said to arise from two natural needs: the multiplication of the human species and the promotion of individual happiness. From these considerations, the Physiocrats argue that the primary right and duty of an individual is self-preservation. From this, they conclude that the individual has an inalienable right over his or her own body and property. The interesting aspect here is not the type of rights that are established, but their epistemological status. Nature is governed by rules that apply equally to the physical and the moral order, and these rules have exactly the same status and can be discovered by the same process of reasoning.

In the Physiocrats' terms, knowledge is absolute because of its self-evident nature. It is worthwhile to note the emphasis a physiocrat like Le Mercier de la Rivière places on truth. Any belief that is neither true nor evident is an opinion, and therefore an error; there is no middle ground (1910, 39–40). Evidence, in the sense that a proposition's truth is evident, is the first attribute of knowledge. Consequently, public education is necessary for the proper functioning of society. The purpose is obviously to secure the diffusion of unambiguous arguments which, in turn, ensure the full understanding of order as an essential characteristic of the world (ibid., 53). In order to achieve this goal, "doctrinal books" are to be used to make the conclusions of the learned accessible to all.

The Physiocrats favour the unimpeded workings of the market, which, they claim, will maximize the public good. They consistently apply their notion of "laissez-faire, laissez-passer" to the discussion of ideas. Le Mercier de la Rivière insists upon the full freedom of discussion since, through the contradiction and clash of opinions, truth will emerge as evident (1910, 40, 42). But since very few people are actually able to think or elaborate judgments on their own, leadership is left to the most able.

The universe, according to the Physiocrats, is comprehensively ordered. Every part of the world is so well integrated with the whole, that the need for politics is almost nullified. The Physiocrats first use the term "legal despotism," to refer to legal authority, but they subsequently replace this with "tutelar authority," which is probably more consistent with the reality the Physiocrats wish to describe. For the Physiocrats, law is not made but merely "declared" or applied (Du Pont de Nemours 1910, 17). The essence of law exists prior to the existence of society, and there is only *one, universal, immutable,* and *objective* order. The only actions the legislator may take are to make the law known and to impose it. Law, in order to be law, must conform to natural law. If a government is enlightened by reason, all elements noxious to society and its sovereign shall disappear

(Quesnay 1958, 741). Authority is labelled "tutelar" to illustrate its role as transmitter of the law, the state's function being to reaffirm the right of individuals to security and property.

The law secures the right of property but does not address natural inequalities. Justice is intended for all, but since the faculty to acquire differs from one individual to another, some will unmistakably gain more than others. The Physiocratic law is one which defends the right to hold property and the total liberty of exchange, including the right of property of anyone over his or her own body.

In order to insure the most efficient and expedient mode of government, the Physiocrats favoured the concentration of power in one person, thus joining the defenders of enlightened despotism. Their economic liberalism does not entail any form of political liberalism. The latter has little meaning for these authors, who are convinced that government influenced by truth and moral evidence is the only acceptable form. People, generally speaking, should obediently submit themselves to the laws insofar as they are the products of an enlightened ruler: "All men are born to be subjected to order" (Le Mercier 1910, 42). But this type of regime is not simply autocratic, its laws conform to the "despotic authority of evidence" (Sée 1925, 210). It is a question of knowing how to lead public opinion in order to control and transform mentalities (Le Trosne 1980, 294–6).

But this coherent system also requires a special category of enlightened individuals whose role is to oversee the legislator's actions; these people are called the magistrates. Their primary function is to measure the degrees of accordance between the laws of government and the laws of justice as such (Dupont de Nemours 1910, 18). Well versed in matters of justice, they are in a position to inform the legislator when his laws do not conform to natural justice. Because of their superior knowledge and privileged status, the magistrates act as "depositories and guardians of evidence itself" (Le Mercier 1910, 87) for both the legislator and the people in general. They are the enlightened, the morally knowledgeable, who, because they possess truth and evidence rather than opinion, are able to discern the correct course of action that a society should follow. Their purpose is to check ("vérifier") the legislator's actions (Einaudi 1938, 31, 55–6). This is not entirely different from the French Parliamentary tradition of registration and remonstrance (Laval-Reviglio 1987, 199–201). But, with the Physiocrats, a class is instituted to serve as privileged experts.

The Physiocratic thought depends on a unified view of nature and society. It expects total social harmony from the proper functioning of moral laws, just as the working of mechanical laws leads to equilibrium. Although Physiocracy's premises and conclusions differ from those of Thomism, both philosophies share certain concerns, particularly the near-magic power of nature. For the Physiocrats, the power of nature stems not so much from its divine origins but from nature's own inherent rationality and harmony. People's actions, when they conform to nature's rules, lead to the felicity of all. Dr Pangloss's claims that everything unfolds in the best possible world were, from Voltaire's point of view, gibes at traditional philosophers, but they could equally apply to the Physiocrats (Voltaire's *L'Homme aux quarante écus* was intended as an ironical work explicitly about the Physiocrats).

CONDORCET: THE ULTIMATE PHILOSOPHE

The French Enlightenment comes to a close with the figure of the Marquis de Condorcet (1743–94), who espoused both the naturalism and rationalism of his age while opening the way for historical progress.

As is typical of the *philosophes*, Condorcet posits the priority of sensations over ideas in the acquisition of knowledge, but then proceeds rapidly into a rather rationalist discourse. He characterizes man as a "sensitive being, capable of reasoning and of acquiring moral ideas" (1933, 149). From this premise, he elaborates a theory that advocates the rational search for justice.

In his reception speech at the *Académie française* (1782), Condorcet states that the moral sciences are homologous to the physical sciences: both are governed by the observation of facts, by a strict methodology and by the use of a specific language (1968, I: 392). His entire address rests on the assumption that truth is to be ascertained through science, through the rigorous use of reason. The history of humanity unfolds as the progressive perfection of humans' intellectual and moral faculties. It rapidly becomes obvious that Condorcet's moral discourse avoids empirical considerations, even though he makes incidental references to morality's utilitarian consequences.

Like his fellow *philosophes*, Condorcet identifies justice as an objective and eternal product of nature, though he does not discuss its actual origins. Justice is understood as given by nature, as is the desire for happiness. Again knowledge, this time scientific knowledge, enables societies to realize justice, and this realization is conducive to the happiness of society. In Condorcet's writings, justice is defined in terms of natural rights: the right to liberty and security, the right to property, the right to be subject only to general laws (in opposition to the arbitrariness of specific laws), and the right to participate in collective decision making. These rights and others should arise when a society reaches maturity. Condorcet views such rights as inalienable and imprescriptible. They are there to be discovered and be put to work for a happier and more harmonious world.

Condorcet calls for a thorough knowledge of our "moral constitution" (1933, 227) to be achieved by means identical to those of science. The "voice of reason" is to be found, as expected, among the enlightened people, those who are naturally inclined to love of the general good and who dedicate themselves to it (1968, 1: 393, 395). Being profoundly involved in education in general, he suggested a formal institutionalization of the *philosophes*' role whereby the state would establish a hierarchy among the men of knowledge.

Condorcet's basic commitment is to truth, of which the identification of justice is part. According to him, the science of morality was formerly made impossible because the priests were the only authorized voice (1933, 133). But since Descartes's confirmation of reason, humanity has developed an appropriate method by which to search for truth. It is now up to the learned to diffuse knowledge and, in so doing, to facilitate the progress of justice in the human species. Because truth is eternal, it is bound to triumph in the long run; error, on the other hand, is naturally transitory (Schapiro 1934, 139).

Condorcet's conception of politics is consistent with his belief that justice is to be discovered by rational means. The legislator is expected to have two primary qualities: rationality and justice (1968, 1: 364). In fact, we could suppose that rationality alone should suffice, since justice is derived through reason. However, Condorcet is concerned with establishing the rule of reason, or, as he says, establishing "a method for the collective discovery of truth" (Baker 1975, 228). Hence, he desires the establishment of a calculus of consent, which would provide a means of arriving at a rational process of decision making. This calculus would allow the emergence of the "common reason" rather than the "general will," reason that is based on individuals motivated solely by rational considerations (1968, x: 590). Whereas Rousseau, with his notion of the general will, is concerned with what is right, and Montesquieu, with moderation through the separation of powers, Condorcet is preoccupied with truth. He wants to ensure that majority decisions conform with it.

Since justice is tantamount to natural rights, the legislator's role is to articulate them in society. In 1790, Condorcet wrote, referring to the National Assembly, that since it was elected by the people, its function was to restore the people's natural rights (1968, x: 25).

People have different degrees of rationality which should determine their political rights. Most people should merely have a say in the selection of their representatives, just as certain representatives should act only at local levels and should select the representatives for upper or national levels of government. The whole theory is constructed around the establishment of reason as the ultimate judge. Baker observes that if Condorcet was a democrat, he was surely a very reluctant one (1975, 256).

It is interesting to note the privileged status Condorcet provides for the enlightened, the *philosophes*. In one instance, he suggests that there should be a tribunal of the wise at the very top of the power structure; this tribunal's role would be to determine the amount of "truth" in the decisions made by a given assembly (Baker 1975, 237).[3] In the name of reason and its ability to discover justice as truth, the enlightened have the final say, they are the ultimate judges.

According to Condorcet, truth, happiness and virtue resemble a chain linked by nature (1933, 228). But we must recognize that truth dominates happiness and virtue. Condorcet's thought represents Catholic (so to speak) secularization *par excellence*, in which morality is understood only by reason.

CONCLUSION

Most of the *philosophes* claimed to be following the tenets of Lockean empiricism; they agreed with Locke that sensations were prior to any knowledge. This was a common point of view, endorsed extensively by Voltaire, whose purpose was to dissociate the *philosophe* from any idealism. By declaring their faith in Locke's epistemology, the *philosophes* hoped to conform to the scientific mode of understanding.

Locke's *Essay Concerning Human Understanding* was the work of reference for the French Enlightenment. In it, Locke claimed to have elaborated an exact science of ethics, though, as we have seen, he remained faithful to a rationalist optimism. Locke's view is theocentric (if we accept Dunn's interpretation of Locke); and the notion of a divinely created world was well suited to the purposes of the *philosophes* who desired the rational organization of the universe. Those *philosophes* who were atheist merely substituted nature for God and argued that a natural order exists. While the British moralists moved progressively toward the dissolution of natural law, the *philosophes* strengthened it. It is not surprising that Samuel Clarke was also well known to the *philosophes*; his rationalist ethics assumes an "eternal rule of equity" in conformity with an eternal reason for things. But, whereas the British moralists made knowledge of morality accessible

---

3 The Physiocrats had envisioned a controlling apparatus of the same sort (Einaudi 1938).

to the people, in keeping with Protestant ethics, the *philosophes* always claimed a monopoly over the interpretation and diffusion of moral truths.

French authors of the period made a habit of professing their commitment to naturalism. One of Diderot's first works, for example, was a translation of Shaftesbury's *Inquiry Concerning Virtue or Merit*. But if the French authors' works begin from naturalist premises, they quickly evolve into rationalist accounts of morality. And although there are a few exceptions, such authors almost never give inner feelings primacy over reason; quite the reverse, since reason is always victorious, even when Gassendi's epicurism is invoked as a guarantee of naturalism.

Indeed, few French authors subscribed to the naturalism of the British. Jean-Baptiste Robinet in *De la Nature* (1766) espoused the theory of a moral sense as expounded by Francis Hutcheson. In "De l'Instinct moral" (1: 227–33), he identifies the existence of a sixth sense through which we can feel the natural moral impulse without recourse to reason. From these premises, Robinet posits that there is no need for interpreters of morality, since morals are naturally apprehended. We are told that he renounced his naturalism toward the end of his life (he died in 1820), but this adds little to the discussion.

Delisle de Sales, who followed in Robinet's footsteps, claims, in *De la Philosophie de la nature* (1770), to be a follower of Hutcheson and Hume. He believed that the moral instinct, not reason, expressed the laws of nature (1770, 75). But this did not stop him from asserting the existence of natural laws construed in very idealistic terms: "Prior to any system, there are things whose essence is in the obligation that they be done, just as there are other things whose essence is in the obligation that they be believed in" (ibid., 15).

This represents quite a concession in a discourse which, on the whole, tries to be respectful of the naturalist school. It shows the strong attraction of objective justice as the ideal measuring rod of moral action.

All types of English authors were translated and quite widely read. But this did not mean there was a wider acceptance of the naturalist trend that developed through Hume and Bentham. The case of the Baron d'Holbach is a good example. Cosmopolitan because of his education outside France, familiar with the critical deist writings of Toland, Collins and Woolston, and acquainted with the works of David Hume, d'Holbach developed, as we have seen, a secular ethics that remained faithful to a form of rationalism.

The rationalists of the French Enlightenment agreed on the need for an intellectual elite which was thought to be legitimized because it held no interests of its own and could therefore act in the general interest of society. Seventeenth-century authors such as Descartes and Malebranche advocated a metaphysical rationalism, but they did not explicitly formulate the need for an elite, although their writings implied it. The eighteenth-century *philosophes* did explicitly propose a *raison d'être* for a class of intellectuals. They did not extensively discuss the foundations of ethics; instead they demonstrated how and why only the enlightened few could discover the true nature of objective justice.

In passing, it is interesting to note that many of the *philosophes* would agree with Diderot that laws are necessary for the people but not necessarily for the enlightened. This form of elitist anarchism reappears from time to time. "The truth of the matter," writes Diderot," is that strictly speaking there are no laws for the wise man" (1963, 443). Intellectuals in the future will have a propensity to profess a form of anarchism for themselves while demanding strict rules for the people at large.

The profile of the ideal *philosophe* is well drawn by Condorcet who, without naming them, refers to a certain class of people. Such people, through reason, destroy prejudices and superstitions, criticize their own societies and governments, and publicly denounce abuses perpetrated in the name of war, justice, or punishment (1933, 9e période). This portrait generally outlines the intellectual, whose features become better defined as we progress in time.

Now, whatever the soundness of their arguments, and despite their differences, the eighteenth-century French largely agreed on the necessity to do away with the power of the clergy, and replace the clergy with an intellectual elite. Moreover, most of the *philosophes* claimed that their ethics were based on science and needed no further elaboration.

Natural law remains as indispensable point of reference. But by the eighteenth century it is invoked to support a supposedly naturalized conception of justice. During this period a great number of French authors defended and promoted individual rights. All of them agreed that these rights were natural, that they were either willed by God or part of a natural order, and that they were, therefore, binding on all societies, in all times and all places. Voltaire, Diderot, Helvétius, d'Holbach, the Physiocrats, and many others made explicit claims to this effect. What is startling is that few of them ever extended these reflections to the political domain.

The *philosophes* contributed to the reversal of the perspective on natural law, from the traditional conception of natural law, which focuses on society as a whole, to the modern conception which is concerned with the individual. At least this was their claim. It was not the particularly original, since it merely followed what was happening abroad. The *philosophes*' approach seems individualistic, but their individualism was very limited. They readily adopted the universal principles of individual liberties over one's own life, preservation, property and speech. But, more often than not, their ethics was formulated from the perspective of society as an entity in itself that had a nature of its own. Typically, most *philosophes* argued that the public good was distinct from, and prior to, individual interests. It was thus logical to limit discussions of the public good to those most suited for this purpose. So, from Voltaire onward, the trend was in favour of assigning *philosophes* the role of guides to an enlightened form of authority. This has little in common with liberal democracy, and is in sharp contrast with the British and American tendencies of the time.

8 The Revolutionary Reading of Justice

The different opinions expressed during the French Revolution crystallize conceptions of the individual and society that the *philosophes* had entertained but never completely developed. On the whole, the revolutionary ideologies expressed values that were far from liberal; thus they provided fertile ground for the emergence of the intellectuals. The *Déclaration des droits de l'homme et du citoyen* (1789) together with the writings of Sieyès, who is quite representative of his time, and the discourse of the Jacobins, show a convergence of ideas that share a perception of reason and its function in the workings of society.

The preamble of the *Déclaration* has a pedagogical tone. Written chiefly by Jean-Joseph Mounier and the Marquis de Mirabeau, it purports to remind the "members of the social body" – the organic reference is not fortuitous – of their rights and duties, taking into account that the causes of "public misfortunes and the corruption of government" are "ignorance, neglect, or contempt of human rights."

As has been often noted, the *Déclaration* remains an abstract proclamation of principles, unlike its American counterpart, which was pragmatic and was aimed at redressing specific unjust practices. The 1789 *Déclaration* is an eloquent discourse setting out philosophical and political principles (Boutmy 1907, 139; Godechot 1985), even though it was also meant to counteract specific abuses. Inspired in some respects by the American Declaration of Independence and subsequent state declarations, such as that of the state of Virginia, the French document is fundamentally different. Its abstract nature creates a distance that embues the whole exercise with a sense of the sacred. We are no longer dealing with a specific collectivity, such as the American colonies, but with humanity and its social fate. The *Déclaration* adopts a tone that leads one to believe that it emanates directly from the grand book of justice.

In conformity with the contemporary conception of natural law, the first rights that are declared are basic rights: the rights to liberty, property, security, and the right to resist oppression (art. 2); these are followed by others such as due process before the law, freedom of conscience, and freedom of expression. But, as a counterpoint to these individual rights (a counterpoint that seems to contradict article 2), article 3 establishes the principle of sovereignty as residing "essentially" (in the original sense of belonging to the essence of a thing) in the nation. The nation here refers to an indivisible entity that "supplants" the former realm that was unified by the monarch. Whereas the Virginia Declaration, for instance, vests "all power" in the "people," who are understood to be a free association of individuals (art. 2), the French document endows the nation itself with a mystical aura. Sovereignty is no longer expressed by the king but by the nation as a whole, and from the nation, the general will emerges.

The *Déclaration* combines two juridical principles that are hardly compatible: natural law and absolute sovereignty vested in the nation as a sacrosanct entity. As they are stated, both principles betray a Catholic reading of politics. On the one hand, the belief in natural rights here assumes the existence of an objective justice. But the notion of rights being somewhat alien to the Catholic tradition, it is understandable that rights can be readily disposed of. On the other hand, the nation, as a consensual community, suggests a sacred conception of unity and authority. The nation here is construed in the same way as the Church. It is built on a type of coherence that cannot bear the divisiveness of Protestant individualism. We are dealing with a community, not a collectivity.

The writings of the Abbé Sieyès (1748–1836), which immediately preceded the *Déclaration*, help us to understand how, at the time, it was possible to reconcile the notion of natural law with absolute sovereignty. Sieyès wrote elaborate and "reasoned" pieces that unite the concepts. *Qu'est ce que le Tiers État?* [*What is the Third Estate?*] published in the early days of 1789 together with *Préliminaire de la Constitution* explores the notions of natural law and absolute sovereignty beyond the terse phrases found in the *Déclaration* (some of which were, in fact, influenced by Sieyès).[1]

For him, the solution to the problem seems simple: nature and logic together provide the answer. His starting point is natural law. Next comes the nation, which is itself a product of natural law. At the same time, it is considered to be a natural and moral entity: "A nation is always in a state of nature" (1963, 128). A nation is not merely the product of social convention; it is a real entity in itself. It is not only a natural entity, but also an absolute moral being. For Sieyès, politics is exclusively a question of morality, as it was for the Jacobins who followed him.

Even though Sieyès uses individualistic terms to establish the nation as an "aggregate of individuals," just as the "national will" is the combination of individual wills, he is concerned only with the nation itself, not with its components (1963, 156). He writes:"Every attribute of the nation springs from the simple fact that it exists" (ibid., 126). This enables him to argue that only the common interest is important and ought to be considered. Like the *philosophes* who directly preceded him, Sieyès sees morality solely as a social, albeit real, phenomenon, not as the result of conventions. And in order to resolve the conflict between individual and common interests, he says that "the law, by protecting the common rights of every citizen, protects each citizen in all that he can become..." (ibid., 163). Natural law comes to the rescue of both: natural rights and the national interest are reconciled through a process of integration in which the former becomes an aspect of the latter. Society is said to derive from natural law and can be only advantageous to humanity (1789, 94–5). Reason alone, he claims, would lead human beings to form society, if feelings were not already conducive to it. For society "ennobles and perfects" human beings (ibid., 95) and provides them with greater freedom. Sieyès then goes on to describe the nature of society as a distinct entity. He quickly identifies it as a type of political body, which, like the human body, has the ability to will and to act.

The national interest is assimilated with "virtue," civic indeed. For Sieyès, only corporate interests can be divisive, for individuals are

---

[1] Sieyès's own epigraph to *Qu'est ce que le Tiers État?* is not without interest for its recognition of the *philosophe*'s role. "As long as the Philosopher does not go beyond the boundary of truth, do not accuse him of going too far. His function is to show us the goal and first, therefore, he must get there ... The duty of the Administrator is the reverse. He has to set his pace according to the nature of the difficulties ... If the Administrator does not see the goal, he does not know where he goes" (1963, 51).

isolated and their particular interests are not dangerous so long as the individuals do not act in concert. When individuals form what we would call special interest groups, their interests then become deleterious to the community (1963, 159). The subsequent Le Chapelier Law, which abolished the corporations of medieval origins and forbade any associations of a professional nature is consistent with Sieyès's fear of special interests. As Sieyès writes, "*One* society can have only *one* general interest" (1789, 101). Such being the case, the nation possesses the same attribute as its components, i.e., a "natural (but) common will" (1963, 128). In unequivocal terms, Sieyès affirms the nation's overwhelming authority that it expresses through its will: "The manner in which a nation exercises its will does not matter; the point is that it does exercise it; any procedure is adequate, and its will is always the supreme law" (ibid., 128). Absolute sovereignty is here invoked, though it is not named; the spirit of Rousseau haunts the entire discussion.

This sovereignty resides in the nation, *not* in its representatives; as Sieyès makes clear, without specifying the actual relations of power between the nation and its representatives, the power of the delegates is not unlimited. It is up to the constitution to establish the limits of their power. But since it is necessary for the nation to determine the rules, and since the nation, due to its sheer size, is unable to meet as a whole, Sieyès suggests that certain extraordinary representatives be given constituent powers (1963, 130). In brief, it is the Third Estate that assumes this function, for the nation resides in neither the aristocracy nor in the clergy.[2]

Prominent jurists of twentieth-century France such as Maurice Hauriou, Emmanuel Esmein, and Carré de Malberg still argued that sovereignty lay in the nation as a whole (Bastid 1970, 572–85). The electorate is considered to be only a means by which sovereignty is expressed; it is not the source of sovereignty. The unity of the nation is prior to the equality of its members as citizens (Bastid 1966, 580).

The Constitution of 1791 was just as explicit; it claimed that sovereignty was singular, indivisible, and inalienable, and that it rested in the nation.

With these considerations in mind, we can make another reading of the *Déclaration* that puts the emphasis upon the sovereignty of the nation. The *Déclaration* can be seen as consisting of two basic considerations. The first is the defence against absolute monarchy. In this

---

2 Sieyès developed more liberal views at the time of and after the Jacobins' *grande terreur* but that was a long time after the *Declaration* was written. See Forsyth (1987, 119–27).

case, natural rights provide limits to monarchical power. The second consideration functions as a second step and establishes a new régime based upon the nation. The first provision then vanishes, for there is no need to protect the nation from itself. Instead, the *Déclaration* establishes a new legitimacy, that of the people as a nation.

Sieyès is very explicit about this. He maintains that the French *Déclaration* has an entirely different nature than the American (1988). He situates the latter in a line of political arrangements extracted from rulers who made concessions to the people. The Americans, he claims, wished to protect themselves from the expression of an arbitrary authority. For him, this notion of contract or convention is obsolete. There is no need for the people (here identified with the nation) to take preventive measures against themselves, since they form the only power, the only authority.

The transition from the mere affirmation of rights to the assertion of the new legitimacy is made all the more obvious by the terms that are used to sanction the new mode of authority. In the *Déclaration*, two terms, and the concepts they denote, stand out: *nation*, which denotes an abstract whole, and *law*, which signifies a neutral, rational, and impersonal product. The law, not the laws, permeates articles 4 through 11, and its authority is recognized as absolute. Because it emerges from an impartial general will, it is attributed the same impartiality, "anonymous impartiality" (Gauchet 1989, 118). Furthermore, the law determines the limits placed on natural rights (art. 4). The law judges itself.

At this stage of the discussion, two authors naturally come to mind: Locke and Rousseau. The *Déclaration*, at first glance, looks more or less like a convenient fusion of their respective ideas. One can easily identify the influence of Locke in the claim to basic rights and in particular the right of people to be governed by consent. The inviolable right to property, ultimately granted in article 17, partakes of the same Lockean spirit that pervades the whole of the eighteenth century. The departure from Locke is noticeable in the conception of the nature of society. In the case of French eighteenth-century political thought, the tendency, as we have seen, was to confer on society a nature of its own. The *Déclaration* confirms and even reinforces this tendency which would reach its apex in the Jacobin conception of the people. Locke's conception of society is definitely more individualistic, even though he does not equate society merely with the sum of individuals.

By stating at the outset that the chief end of the political society is the preservation of property, Locke limits the scope of his discourse (1948, *Second Treatise*, ch. IX). He indeed provides a notion of the common good, but this good remains confined by natural law. Furthermore, the legislator's action is bound by a trusteeship, which ensures that individual rights are strictly respected. Nowhere in Locke is there the idea of positive law determining the understanding of natural law. The majority assumes the supreme political power but it is not an unlimited power (Pangle 1988, 254–5). True, Locke is not explicit about this matter, but we may presume that he supported a monarchy that was limited by parliament (Gough 1973, 51; Dunn 1969b, 149; 1984, 51–4).

Locke's persistent popularity among French authors prior to the Revolution was probably due to ambiguities within his works. For these authors, Locke's writings provided a rationalist discourse with utilitarian and empiricist considerations. They had all the trappings of scientific discourse, but could be read as containing an essentialist conception of nature. In political terms, Locke could be invoked to defend natural rights and sovereignty at the same time.

As for its relationship to Rousseau, the *Déclaration* uses terms that seem to refer to the *Contrat social*. The authority of the law as the expression of the general will appears to be taken directly from Rousseau. But it does not refer exactly to the same reality. Rousseau's general will rests on the psychological drive of the people whose decisions belong solely to the category of goodness[3]; whereas the *Déclaration* depends on the rational quest to find the true nature of society. The law, in this case, is an expression of reason, and can, therefore, make universal claims, as the *Déclaration* itself did. Moreover, the *Déclaration* sanctions representation in two respects; first, it declares the formation of a National Assembly, and second, it lays down the legislative rights of its successors. These notions of representation are alien to the *Contrat social*. But they were directly conducive to the absolute supremacy of Parliament which was made official under the Third Republic.

By contrast, the American Declaration of Independence, the other state declarations that followed, and the first ten amendments to the American Constitution are juridical documents whose purpose is to delimit the legislator's actions. They are meant to guarantee individual rights whatever may subsequently happen. They offer a means of influencing, or even controlling, the future. French constitutional thought did not address these issues.

---

3 The general will is considered to be a regulative power, a moral faculty (Shklar 1969, 184), an affective imperative (De Jouvenel 1947, 115), a rule of justice that corresponds to conscience for the individual (Derathé 1950, 236, 343).

The *Déclaration* soon lost much of its judicial significance; it was superseded in 1793 by other texts of a declaratory nature. The constitutional laws of the Third Republic (1875) make no reference to it at all, leaving later jurists like Léon Duguit, Maurice Hauriou, and Carré de Malberg to ponder its judicial relevancy. Under the Fourth Republic (1946), the *Déclaration* was incorporated into the preamble but not into the body of the Constitution itself. It is, finally, with the Constitution of the Fifth Republic (1958), which provides for a Constitutional Council, that the legal impact of the *Déclaration* was recognized. But in practice the *Déclaration* was legally recognized only two decades ago. (One might also want to note that the Constitutional Council is consulted only at a specific stage of law making and cannot be addressed by private individuals, although there are ongoing political discussions about the future possibility of this as well as of granting the Constitutional Council certain powers over existing laws).

On the whole, former constitutions in France were procedural texts that were intended to determine the manner in which decisions were to be made but not which decisions could be made. Because sovereignty was unlimited, the people or its representatives were to act according to a specific procedure (Godechot 1985, 37–8).

With the Jacobin movement, the search for unity was exacerbated and virtue – "public virtue," the fundamental principle of democratic government – was brought to the fore. Jacobins' tone was moralistic and the exercise of authority became a sacred vocation. The search for unity, which reached its apex with the Comité de Salut public, led to the notion of the people as a "collective individual" (Jaume 1989, 153). Any reference to politics was likely to be frowned upon because of its divisive character. Billaud-Varenne, a member of the Comité de Salut public, distinguished between citizens who were duty-minded and wholly committed to the public good, and those who were totally preoccupied with their own interests (ibid., 190).

Despite its "heart-to-heart politics" (Hunt 1984, 45) and despite its recognition of the people's moral instinct (Robespierre 1967, 461), the Jacobin movement depended on a deeply rationalist discourse. Its main spokesman, Maximilien de Robespierre (1764–94), could be particularly rationalistic. His two speeches in 1794 on the subject of political morals are direct calls for the sound establishment of the democratic state based on reason.

His argument is all too familiar but, as such, it is revealing. Robespierre contrasts the high level of artistic and scientific knowledge attained by the people of Europe with their apparent ignorance of public morals: "They know everything, except their rights and duties" (1967, 444). To correct this state of affairs, he delegates to what he calls the political and legislative science the responsibility of realizing "in the laws and in government, the moral truths that have been relegated [*reléguées*] to the *philosophes*' books" as well as the responsibility of ensuring that justice prevails (ibid., 446). He desires the ascendancy of reason in the quest for eternal justice (ibid., 352). Truth will overcome fiction, just as reason will overcome foolishness (ibid., 457). A year before, 27 April 1793, in his own *Déclaration*, he had asserted that laws that were not derived from the "eternal laws of justice and reason" should be considered to be "attacks by ignorance or despotism against humanity."

All this talk of reason does not forbid Robespierre from finally proposing an ideal situation where the latent intellectual elitism of his position would be made manifest: "The masterpiece for society would be to create in (man), on moral matters, a quick instinct that, without the belated help of reasoning, would bring him to do good and avoid evil, because the individual reason of each man who is carried away by his passions, is merely a sophist who pleads its cause" (1967, 452).

For want of this utopia Robespierre, as we know, fell back on civil religion. It is worth noting here that human beings as individuals are not to be trusted and therefore have to be correctly manipulated (or managed if "manipulated" is too strong), by those who actually represent the interests of society.

Jaume draws an insightful parallel between the Jacobins' defence of state unity and that offered over a century earlier by Bossuet (1989, 368–82). In both cases society is absorbed by the state in order to counter the threat of division, or "schism," among the consciences of the people (ibid., 370). Bossuet feared the Protestants, whereas the Jacobins distrusted their political rivals, the "enemies of the people." In *Politique tirée des propres paroles de l'écriture sainte*, Bossuet elaborates a conception of absolute monarchy that, because of its Gallican premises, could later be replicated in secular terms, though this was definitely not his intention. Bossuet was acquainted with Hobbes's works and some aspects of his discussion are reminiscent of *The Leviathan*. But whatever the influence, he asserts that the unity of the nation is achieved "when each (person) renounces his will and hands it over and joins it to (the will of) the prince" (1818, bk I, art. III, 3rd prop.). The operation is performed in the name of reason, as Book V makes clear. There, Bossuet states that "the government is a work of reason and intelligence," and then he conjoins this reason to the unity of the state: "Look at a people united in one person ... look at the secret reason that governs the entire state body, this reason enclosed in one head" (ibid., bk V, art. IV, 1st prop.).

The Jacobins' rationale for the necessity of unity and the means to achieve it is not very far from that of Bossuet. The individualist claims against royal authority at the start of the Revolution are progressively attenuated and are ultimately superseded by collective necessities.

It may not be accurate to sum up the nature of the Jacobin Republic by citing Robespierre, but his views illustrate the impressive continuity of French rationalism through a series of severe breaks in political ideologies.

9 An Anti-Individualist Liberalism

The decades that followed the Revolution were, in France, a period during which authors from all political horizons drew conclusions about the *philosophes* and the consequences of their writings. Whether the *philosophes* did or did not have the influence frequently imputed to them matters little in the context of the present discussion. What does matter is rather the status they were assigned by their successors. In other words, how was the role of the intellectual appreciated in nineteenth-century France? As weakened, obliterated, or as strengthened?

Traditional conservatives such as Joseph de Maistre (1753–1821) and the Vicomte de Bonald (1754–1840) made no bones about their absolute opposition to eighteenth-century rationalism as well as to any abstract claims for humanity. But, as we shall see, they agreed on the need to secure an absolute status for the Church, a status founded on the eternal value of its presence.

More liberally inclined authors of the period showed a wide variety of opinions ranging from those who supported liberalism, such as Benjamin Constant (1767–1830) to those who advocated the republicanism of a later period.

Because he was a Protestant, Benjamin Constant's liberalism is not representative. (The same applies to Madame de Staël.) Constant stands in complete opposition to Jacobinism; he claims that the value of individual liberty is prior to any other considerations. From this principle, he derives freedom of conscience and opinion, and other freedoms. He opposes, therefore, state education and any form of press censorship. As examples of the freedom of the press, he readily points to England, Sweden, Denmark, Prussia, and other Protestant German states (1957, 1275). Because "society" is merely a word used to convey the idea of an abstract entity, an aggregate of individuals, no state nor any other authority can claim to express the "common good" which simply does not exist. It is interesting to look at Constant's thought, if only because it did not receive any subsequent following.

More representative of the period are the supporters of the French Restoration who proposed a new type of constitutional monarchy. They formed a group inaccurately referred to as the *doctrinaires*. They were involved in politics but were often associated with the university. Though neither very articulate nor particularly original, they nonetheless represent a mode of thinking which was widespread at the time, a mode Victor Cousin would further support when, as minister of public instruction during the July Monarchy (1830–48), he tried to impose it on university teaching.

Pierre-Paul Royer-Collard (1763–1845) was a typical *doctrinaire*. He tried, through his speeches both inside and outside Parliament, to elaborate a middle course between the despotism of absolute monarchy and the despotism of Jacobin democracy. He associated this with a middle course, the golden mean, which would be realized by the middle-class. Victor Cousin (1792–1867) took over this project. His goal was to extract truths from previous philosophical systems and to fuse them in one true philosophy or science, he called this venture eclecticism.

Royer-Collard and his contemporaries strongly reacted against the sensualism they perceived in the preceding century. The trend moved away from the political passions that the Revolution was thought to have unleashed, and toward a return to reason. Using oratorical terms, Royer-Collard advocated the "divine sovereignty of reason and justice" (in Rémond 1933, 36) as opposed to popular sovereignty.

It was left to Victor Cousin to elaborate more extensively the role of reason, truth and philosophy as a whole. Acquainted with the works of the Scottish philosopher Thomas Reid through the writings of Royer-Collard, Cousin attempted to make a strictly rationalist reading of Reid's vague notion of common sense, in order to expand the distinction between common sense, which all human beings share (it is a property of the species, not of the individual as such) and science or philosophy, which is the prerogative of the few. According to Cousin, there exists a general and universal way of reasoning that gives rise to language, general beliefs and fundamental social institutions; he traces these notions to Bossuet and Malebranche (1895, 56). At the same time, however, there is a type of knowledge accessible only to an aristocracy that then works in the people's interests. This aristocracy forms an "elite, avant-garde of humanity" (1866a, xxxi, lxxii) and it is devoted to philosophy. Because reason is considered to be both a universal phenomenon and a source of certainty in the search for the true, the good, the beautiful, and the great, it cannot be left to the individual to establish these on his or her own (ibid., lxx). Cousin criticizes the Protestants, and particularly the Methodists, for their individualist conception of reason, which, he claims, ultimately works against reason itself (ibid., lxix). His goal is to establish an organon of truths, as opposed to opinions, from which one can derive universal moral rules. Théodore Jouffroy, a follower of Cousin, called these rules the "social natural law", and defined them in terms of the *ends* of society (1886, 179–80; 1876, 17).

Because it is eternal and universal, justice constitutes "absolute truths"; the difference between the just and the unjust is a matter of necessity (Cousin 1836, 309). For Cousin, morality is the ultimate goal of philosophy, and it is thus judge of all the other aspects of philosophy (1866b, ii). Ethics becomes the fulcrum of philosophy.

From a global perspective, politics is expected to provide a framework for the administration of justice, so that freedom is equated with what one ought to do (Cousin 1895, 171). Cousin argues that society does not repress what he calls natural freedom; it merely represses passions. Therefore, politics must be managed by those who, in the *doctrinaires*' words, have the capacity to rule. With a very limited electorate and an even more limited number of people entitled to be candidates, government is confined to the "true, intelligent and enlightened nation, and not the ignorant mass, which is now carefree, now restless" (1851, xxix). This echoes Royer-Collard's reference to the "antisocial passions of the multitude" (Barante 1878, II: 36). The rationale behind this scheme is that the select nation represents the "legitimate interests" of society more accurately than the "multitude" does by itself (Barante 1878, II: 36). Cousin hopes to install what he calls the pure and disinterested sovereignty of eternal justice (1836, 312). The whole operation, as we can see, calls for the aseptic work of reason.

With this aim in mind, Victor Cousin considered the university a useful tool to secure national consensus on his own ideas of governance. He wished to create a body of professors that would be analogous to the clergy and the magistracy; it would be hierarchically arranged and would enjoy an existence of its own (1850, IX: 81, 47).

The intention was to create what Bénichou calls an intellectual corporate body, a social guide that would play the same role that the Church had done (1973, 470, 250–1). Cousin wanted to establish a new supreme power which would take over from the Church and enjoy the same sphere of influence. The purpose of Royer-Collard and the *doctrinaires* was to create a political elite; Cousin subsequently added an intellectual element of leadership. His notion of politics comes close to that of Auguste Comte.

Despite the pervasiveness of romanticism in the first half of the nineteenth century, those ideas which gained "official" status remained within the rationalist tradition, just as most of the eighteenth-century *philosophes*, despite their naturalist pretensions, were preoccupied with the notions of objective justice and reason, and with the need for an elite to bring the two together.

François Guizot (1787–1874) was a prominent *doctrinaire*; he became a key minister under Louis-Philippe and held the post for years under the July Monarchy. Of Protestant extraction, he shared the *doctrinaires*' points of view on the sovereignty of reason, justice and law (Rosanvallon 1985, 87–8), but his treatment of these concepts was somewhat more sophisticated.

Because of his profound Calvinist convictions, Guizot was very sensitive to the religious character of the human condition. He was indeed very proud of the progress accomplished by the Reformation in the emancipation of reason; the Reformation, which had acted as an "insurrection" of the human mind, had led to "the abolition of absolute power on spiritual matters" (1985, 261–5). Henceforth, people were entitled to think for themselves. But one should never forget, Guizot claims, that justice emanates from the absolute *legislative* power of God, the only sovereign (this is a canon of Calvinism). Contrary to Victor Cousin who treated ethics as an independent and autonomous reality, Guizot emphasizes its subordinate position. As he clearly states, moral law does not belong to the general working of nature, it is distinct from nature and must therefore be an aspect of religion (1864–68, III: 61, 77.). The law is not of this world, but superior to it; thus it cannot be left solely to science.

Guizot also stressed the fallibility of our reason, hence no one can aspire to sovereignty or absolute authority. This is in keeping with the position of Royer-Collard, but Guizot is more articulate and more concerned with religion. Conscience, the "instinct of justice and reason" in all of us, is an independent rule that governs human will, that dictates to us that tyranny is morally unacceptable and, therefore, that sovereignty cannot be claimed by any particular group or individual.

Guizot shared the *doctrinaires'* desire to set limits to the exercise of power. He also agreed with the notion of reason as a collective guide. The belief that only certain people possess a political capacity is a direct consequence of this conception of reason.

But Guizot stood somewhere between the *doctrinaires* and Protestantism. His concern was often religious; he tried to reconcile Catholic and Protestant values. He frequently refers to Christianity as *the* religion which because *it* possesses a body of values, provides a frame of moral reference. Guizot saw in Protestantism a dynamic of progress which Catholicism lacked. He claimed that Catholics were afraid of too much freedom whereas Protestants were afraid of too much authority (1864, I: xiii). Despite his attempts to achieve a better understanding of morality, reason, and politics within the Christian faith, Guizot was always considered as somewhat of an outsider in France.

TOCQUEVILLE: THE FEAR OF INDIVIDUALISM

As does Montesquieu, Alexis de Tocqueville (1805–59) stands out as one of the very few liberals in French political thought. As he noted himself, he was a liberal of a peculiar breed. He agreed with his predecessors, the *doctrinaires*, that justice and reason are sovereign. Although he never discussed it in detail, Tocqueville argues that there is a general unwritten law which is prior to all those passed by legislators (*OC*, II: II, 371; I: I, 261). Like Montesquieu, he was a magistrate, and, again like Montesquieu, he tends to attribute to law an overriding power, but only so long as it conforms to justice and reason. Law is opposed to arbitrariness and injustice.

Tocqueville is indeed a liberal when it comes to his intense opposition to absolute power. He is opposed to this power, whatever form it takes, whether it comes from majority rule in legislative assemblies[1] or from the insidious weight of public opinion, which is, for him, the most severe expression of the tyranny from the majority. But contrary to Benjamin Constant, Madame de Staël, and even to Guizot, all of whom were Protestants, Tocqueville is not satisfied with identifying freedom with the freedom which individuals might enjoy in their private lives. He would not have agreed either with later thinkers who claimed that "the only freedom that deserves the name, is that of pursuing our own good in our own way (without of

---

1 Tocqueville is ironic about the situation in some European parliaments where, as he says, it is not the people who decide, but rather those who best know what is good for the people.

course depriving others of theirs)" (Mill, *On Liberty*, CW, XVIII: 226). For Tocqueville, there is more to liberty than this individualism that may, in fact, be conducive to despotism.

Tocqueville submits the following paradox: though logically opposed to despotism, individualism, in its extreme forms, may lead to a new form of despotism. Individualism, Tocqueville notes, is a new term in the French language that refers to a new concept, and it must be distinguished from egotism. According to him, it is not a passion but a considered choice that inclines one to withdraw from society and to confine oneself to a limited circle of friends and relatives (*OC*, I: II, 105–6).

Being completely absorbed by their private interests, individuals are too ready to leave their collective governance to politicians; this enables "private" individuals to devote themselves to what are considered more serious matters, their own business. For Tocqueville, this tendency is typical of democratic societies whose egalitarian cultures deny the use of political intermediaries who are associated with aristocratic, or, non-egalitarian elements in such societies. In this case, people are isolated from one another and are therefore more vulnerable to being influenced or manipulated, if not controlled by an authority of one sort or another. "A despot," he writes, "readily forgives his subjects for not liking him so long as they do not like each other" (*OC*, I: II, 109). Tocqueville feels that in egalitarian societies, people are induced to live together without social bonds, and that in such circumstances, equality can ultimately lead to the surrendering of freedom.

Tocqueville's argument foreshadows a model proposed by William Kornhauser in *The Politics of Mass Society* (1959) where the vulnerability of isolated people is conducive to their alienation within mass society, a situation deemed most propitious for the eventual disappearance of democratic institutions.

A large part of Tocqueville's *De la démocratie en Amerique* (1835) is devoted to showing how Americans used their freedom to thwart the individualism created by equality (*OC*, I: II, 110). By setting up different levels of decision making, especially at the local level, and by multiplying the number of intermediaries through parties and associations of all sorts, the Americans provided a substitute for the long chain of collective units which aristocratic societies had introduced between the king and his subjects, guilds, trade corporations, and parishes. The idea in so doing is that every individual should be furnished with a sense of belonging and that nobody should consider him- or herself isolated.

Tocqueville challenges a form of individualism that, he thinks, could ultimately lead to the destruction of individualism itself. He is a liberal to the extent that he sees freedom as a value that must not only be protected but promoted through rational means. In other words, he sees freedom as the product of a well thought-out conception of society as a whole. Tocqueville is not a liberal *tout court*, he is an aristocrat as well as a sociologist. To what extent these two characteristics are consistent with liberalism is for us to determine.

Tocqueville wished that freedom be secured through the appropriate organization of the political arena; he was, in this sense, a liberal. He considers that the interplay of voluntary associations and parties, together with community political life, which operates as a kind of civic school, are all considerations typical of liberalism. Although he admits that free elections and a free press may create social division in the short run, Tocqueville praises their long-term effects (*OC*, I: II, 110; I: I, 185–91). In his eyes, freedom of the press is not a good in itself; it is more valuable because of the evil that it prevents than the good it may produce (ibid., I, 185). In fact, as a liberal, he maintains that it is the competitive character of the American press that guarantees the expression of diverse and even contradictory opinions. He applies the same rule to education, when he writes to Louis Bouchitté that," in order to improve it, it needs, as in all matters, the spur of competition" (4 February 1844, ibid., 1864–6, VII: 219).

Tocqueville's emphasis on participation as an absolute condition for the functioning of democracy is also typical of liberalism. To the extent that he is concerned with the maintenance of the system, his thought remains within the boundaries of liberal orthodoxy. He explains the incentive to participate in public affairs in rational terms; participation proceeds from enlightened self-interest which in the long-run becomes civic instinct (*OC*, I: II, 127–30, 112). People naturally come to understand the advantage of working in common for their common improvement. They are, of course, sacrificing certain interests but, as Tocqueville point out, in order to realize others (*OC*, I: II, 129). This leads him to consider further societal systems of mutual support about which he provides a comprehensive analysis of human beings living together in society.

Tocqueville's sociology, particularly what we might call his aristocratic sociology, signals his departures from orthodox liberalism. His treatment of religion is hardly compatible with liberalism. In his analysis of religion, he proceeds from Machiavelli-like conception of society, which, though not necessarily cynical, is very realistic. His approach is basically functional and focuses on the stability of the entire system. Religion is considered solely in terms of its positive effects on society, and more precisely, on politics. Borrowing the terminology David Easton employs to analyse the political system, one could read Tocqueville's writings on religion as follows: religion is necessary as a culture inhibitor which regulates the inflow of wants which are translated into demands upon the system; it reduces the volume of demands, and helps to avoid a demand input overload (Easton 1965, 101, 112, 58–62). In other words, for Tocqueville, religious beliefs have a regulatory function in the sense that they tend to reduce people's expectations while encouraging them to respect their fellow human beings. Religious beliefs contribute to defining culture as a barrier against the whims of what would otherwise be unbridled public opinion. The aim of religion in Tocqueville's mind is to set boundaries for the political arena.

The strength of Tocqueville's analysis is that it shows the importance of culture in the maintenance of political patterns of behaviour. *De la démocratie* is, in large part, a demonstration of this social phenomenon, though Tocqueville also discusses politics' influence on society. This is in keeping with Montesquieu. Tocqueville is quite explicit in a lesser-known text, *Voyages en Sicile et aux Etats-Unis*, where he concisely expresses his view of religion and society: "I do not think that a republic can exist without mores and I do not think that a people can have mores without having a religion. Therefore I consider the maintenance of religious spirit as one of our greatest political interests" (*OC*, v: 1, 231).

In a system of political checks and balances, religion could function as a counterbalance to individualism and its by-product, the tyranny of the majority. Though not a believer himself, Tocqueville easily detected that religion was socially useful. In this respect he was not entirely liberal. But he saw religion and liberty as interdependent, and he considered religion more as a cultural asset than a supernatural phenomenon. This led him to say that only despotism could do away with faith (*OC*, 1: 1, 308), whereas religion, as the guardian of social customs, could be the safeguard of liberty (ibid., 43). From this perspective, Tocqueville's vision was of a liberal culture that is sustained by compatible religious values. Only in this respect does Tocqueville rejoin the liberal camp.

Throughout his work, Tocqueville always considers politics as inseparable from society, so much so, in fact, that both politics and society form a single reality. Freedom has to be both political and social if it is to have any meaning.

One should never forget that implicit in Tocqueville's discourse is the idea of one justice that is accessible to reason, a justice in which religion participates. This is the meaning we can attribute to his intention to reconcile liberalism and religion.

Tocqueville's implicit notion of justice, together with his aristocratic origins, contributes to his definition of society in terms that are foreign to liberalism. He definitely does not consider society to be an aggregate of individuals, but rather a whole that is based on the sense of community. At times, he reveals an aristocratic bias toward the glory and pride that can be achieved by national collectivities; these are values he considers more noble than the mere pursuit of economic prosperity (Boesche 1987, 63–4). Tocqueville often complains about the mediocrity of the industrial age. The threat of war in the early 1840s gave him a "certain satisfaction," tired as he was of the "little democratic and bourgeois pot of soup" (To Beaumont 1840, ibid., 63). In a letter to J.S. Mill, Tocqueville refers to the *grandeur* of France, a theme that bridges the era between Louis XIV and Charles de Gaulle (ibid., 64).

Tocqueville is probably the most moving author among political thinkers. His works reveal an inner tension between a rational disposition toward the political environment and a deep feeling of nostalgia for a régime that he knows will never return. There is for him no clear break from his social background. Thus he could write: "I love liberty, law (légalité), and the respect of rights with passion, but not democracy. This is from the bottom of my heart" (*OC*, III: II, 87).

As a liberal, Tocqueville criticized social attitudes or behaviour that did not fit into the liberal picture. And the emergence of intellectuals was an illiberal trend. In *L'Ancien Régime et la Révolution* (1856) (*OC*, II: 1, 193–201), Tocqueville places the *philosophes* in the context of a new social reality in the making.

He suggests that in the eighteenth century, men of letters became the most important spokesmen, due to the prestige of their social position. They were not politicians themselves, nor did they claim to be. But while others were busy governing the nation, these people enjoyed exclusive authority, at least in a symbolic sense. The political arena was moved into literary circles, and writers became leaders of public opinion, holding a position that in "free countries" is usually reserved for leaders of political parties (*OC*, II: 1, 196). So much for their status. As for their message, Tocqueville describes the *philosophes* in unambiguous terms; they revelled in abstract and sweeping views, hoping to reconstruct society by the sole operation of reason. In so doing, they constructed fictitious entities that bore little relation to the real workings of society. For the complexity of reality, Tocqueville contends, they substituted simple rules drawn from reason and natural law (ibid., 194). The *philosophes'* lofty attitudes led them to mistrust the "mob," and to hold no respect for the wishes of the majority, whereas, he adds, the situation was much different in England and America (ibid., 306).

Tocqueville's observations on the intellectual in the making are interesting for they describe quite well the prototype of the intellectual, which evolved through time. In Tocqueville's age, as we shall see, the trend was toward a more direct involvement in politics – so much so, that a great number of French writers became active politicians. Tocqueville, for instance, spent much of his energy in becoming known as a proficient political seer so that he would subsequently be recognized in the political arena. He was a deputy in the Lower Chamber (1848), and, for a short while, minister of foreign affairs (1849).

Despite his deep-rooted opposition to despotism of any kind, Tocqueville remains sensitive to and suspicious of what he considers the logical evolution of individualism. He admired Bossuet's *Histoire des variations des Églises protestantes*, in which Bossuet describes the divisive propensities of Protestant individualism (Boesche 1987, 139).

His belief in reason and objective justice, and his fear of individualism bear the marks of his Catholic environment, and these features of his thought place Tocqueville's liberalism in a category of its own. He had very few followers and was forgotten under the Third Republic. In fact, the expression "as Monsieur de Tocqueville would say" was used in farces, since nobody knew anything about this author who had fallen in oblivion. Antoine Redier's book entitled *Comme disait Monsieur de Tocqueville* (1925) was meant precisely to counter this state of forgetfulness (the last edition of *De la démocratie en Amérique* to be published in France before 1951 was that of 1888 (17th edition)).

Édouard Laboulaye (1811–83) pushed the French liberalism to its logical conclusions. In *Le Parti libéral, son programme et son avenir* (1863), he set the rules for a truly individualistic conception of politics. For him, democracy could mean only the sovereignty of the individual, which translated into natural rights: freedom of conscience, of speech, of education, of association, of voting, and so on. A great admirer of the United States, he was the initiator of the idea of presenting the Statue of Liberty to the Americans. He was against any form of monopoly, be it the monopoly of the press, of public utilities (gas, water, public transportation), or of education. Laboulaye was among the very few French authors who extensively subscribed to the sort of liberalism that was standard currency in many Protestant countries.

On the whole, in France, few of those frequently called liberals, whether they are politicians or writers, are what we might call true liberals, that is, they rarely subscribe thoroughly to liberal tenets. As we have seen, the call for individual rights was widely heard in the eighteenth century, though this did not lead to the establishment of a true liberal discourse. The same can be said of the nineteenth century, even though the claims of liberalism were then considered more acceptable. Étienne Vacherot (1809–97) provides an interesting case that illustrates the contradictions that were introduced into French political thought.

In 1860, Vacherot wrote a book entitled *La Démocratie*. This was during the Second Empire of Napoléon III, and the work earned him the honour of a condemnation by the French judicial system. Vacherot tried to define both the absolute character of individual rights and the sovereignty of the state. On the one hand, society is said to exist for the individual, not the reverse. Human dignity is sacrosanct; therefore individual rights are not only inviolable but are prior to positive law; their entrenchment forms the ultimate goal of any constitution, the rest being of a purely instrumental importance (1860, 34, 231, 240). On the other hand, social law, as he calls it, is expected to prevail over individual rights. We find intact in Vacherot the rationalist conception of ethics, which is ranked as a science. Politics and justice are matters of truth; they are apprehended by reason and subject to demonstration. As for freedom, it can be defined only in terms of justice, which is the absolute point of reference. Vacherot admits that the equilibrium to be established between social law and individual rights is not easy to determine. Nonetheless, he believes that social law is derived directly from justice itself. He concludes, therefore, that the "subordination of individual rights to social law is absolute, and must be accepted in all its consequences" (ibid., 236). Social law knows no boundaries since it is just.

Vacherot exemplifies the type of reasoning that republicans and radicals would subsequently develop during the beginnings of the Third Republic.

FROM THE MAGI TO THE PROPHETS: THE RECOGNITION OF THE INTELLECTUAL

Although liberals such as Tocqueville were very rare in France, many authors who, at one time or another in their lives claimed to be liberals, acted as inspired spokespersons for the nation. They were romantics whose liberalism, when they had any, barely concealed their other ideas. They embued politics with a sense of history and "grandeur." Paul Bénichou (1988) refers to them as the romantic magi. Victor Hugo conceived of the poet as a source of inspiration for the nation, since he, the poet, was able to reveal its hidden essence (ibid., 493).

Jules Michelet, a historian at the Collège de France, called for a man of genius to express the people's true voice, a voice the people could not, apparently, find all by themselves: "The people, in its highest expression, can hardly be found in the people ... It is, in its full truth ... solely in the man of genius ... This voice, is the people's; silent in itself, it speaks through this man, and God with him" (1965, 213).

This man of genius is indeed exceptional, particularly in his intuitive understanding of the people. Michelet exalts him while simultaneously exalting the true popular instincts, those which should ultimately define the leading role of France in the world. We are here in the wake of romantic populism, but it is a populism that is tempered by the political and moral mediation of the exceptional few.

Almost all of the authors of the time were involved in politics. They argued for or against monarchy, and, later on, for or against Napoleon the Third. At the beginning of the period, Chateaubriand, Lamartine, Vigny, and Hugo supported the restored monarchy. Later on, Chateaubriand, Lamartine, Lamennais, Michelet and others opposed the July Monarchy. It was common, if not perfunctory, for authors to be appointed or elected to a national political body of the nation. Hugo was appointed to the upper house in 1845, elected in 1848, 1849, and 1871, and became a senator in 1876. Lamartine played a significant political role, especially during the Second Republic (1848–51). He was trounced by Louis Napoléon in the presidential elections of 1848 (5,400,000 votes to 8,000; there were, of course, other candidates in the race) (Agulhon 1973, 85).

It is worth noting here that authors of all hues became actively involved in politics at a time when political parties were not well organized. This enabled them to avoid the prosaic aspects of political life and placed them beyond the control of any particular political party. The notion of allegiance to one specific party is alien to the intellectual tradition at this formative stage. When full-fledged parties did finally emerge, intellectuals withdrew from the immediate political arena and aspired to the disinterested and the more distinguished spheres of representation outside the houses of Parliament.

As the nineteenth century progressed, many philosophers made scientific claims in opposition to the spiritualism imposed by Victor Cousin upon the official channels of education. When positivism emerged, it brought a new method for establishing an official status for the philosopher, a status that was outside the commonplace discussions of politics.

10 Positivism: The Path Leading to the Intellectual

Even though French positivism is correctly identified with Auguste Comte (1798–1857), the formative influence of Henri de Saint-Simon (1760–1825), Comte's predecessor, should not be neglected. Comte borrowed much from Saint-Simon, and both authors celebrate the social role of the scientist. Comte did indeed depart from Saint-Simon; Comte was more organically inclined and less organizationally oriented than his predecessor.

Auguste Comte is best known for his theory of the law of three stages in the development of history: the theological, the metaphysical, and the positive stages. Saint-Simon more than prepared the way for this theory. Both authors agreed on the necessity of a unified body of knowledge, a wholly scientific discourse that is formed and diffused by a scholarly elite.

Because they were eager to trace the development of a scientific theory of society, Saint-Simon and Comte were ready to recognize, in the theological stage, features that fitted into their framework. It is obvious that the theory of the three stages is primarily aimed at legitimizing the third and last stage, the positive stage. This stage is brought about only after stage one, the theological stage, has been negated by stage two, the metaphysical stage. The metaphysical stage is then negated by the positive stage. The dialectical process serves to rehabilitate forms of thought that were considered obsolete at the time.

Whatever their criticisms of the theological stage, Saint-Simon and Comte always praise the unifying action of the Catholic Church in the Middle Ages. First, it unified the religious systems of its time by imposing monotheism onto the Western world, as opposed to the polytheism of the Ancients. Second, it introduced a separation of authority between the spiritual and the temporal powers, a separation that did not previously exist. Through these two operations, the Church, they argue, ensured the autonomous development of a body of ethics external to politics. Their purpose becomes transparent; Saint-Simon and Comte wish to reinstate this former ethical model but to replace its contents with positive science.

Comte does not hesitate to affirm that dogmatism is the normal state of human intelligence (1854b, 202), just as Saint-Simon wished to put an end to the "parlage" and the "parleurs" [talking and talkers]. Thus, it is logical and in the order of things that an elite should establish its moral authority over the masses.

Saint-Simon and Comte recognize that Catholicism established the social supremacy of ethics over the use of force (Comte 1908, VI: 334). Comte is struck by the immense authority that the Church gained over a vast territory. It is this sort of influence that he and Saint-Simon envisioned for the philosophers of the positive era to come. The Church enjoyed a strictly moral power, independent of politics, and this situation should be recaptured.

According to Comte, his own age was metaphysical. This metaphysical stage is understood as a transitory period whereby the human mind departs from the belief in supernatural agents and adopts new but illusory abstractions before proceeding to true scientific knowledge.

Comte sees this second stage as negative but necessary. It is negative to the extent that it destroys the existing consensus and, therefore, entails profound confusion. Unlimited freedom of thought was necessary, he feels, to destroy the theological power of the Church. The destruction of established authority occurred first in the spiritual realm and subsequently reached the temporal one; its apex was the Revolution.

Comte identifies Protestantism as the trigger of the metaphysical stage. It introduced freedom of conscience, which led to freedom of thought and the other freedoms this entailed: freedom of speech, freedom of the press, and freedom of education. This translated into the dissolution of public morality, which was, for Comte, all the more evident in the further breakdown of Protestantism into sects in the United States (1908, I: 64). For him, Protestantism amounts to moral chaos, to sterile and perpetual discussions that no society can accept in the long run (ibid., v: 174). The unlimited competition among philosophers can lead only to the intellectual anarchy which Comte ascribes to his own age.

This moral freedom, indiscriminately granted to all, necessarily implies the recognition of equality, that is, the moral sovereignty of each and every individual, and ultimately the political sovereignty of the multitude, which amounts to the rule of the ignorant majority.

Among the "moral aberrations" of Protestantism, Comte singles out as fundamental the severe alteration made to the principle of "universal justice" (1908, v: 361). Here we find the still resilient notion of an objective justice that, in Comte's case, amounts to the social laws of human nature.

In order to counter this situation of decomposition and anarchy, Comte calls for a "reorganization of the minds" (1854b, 187). For him, the difficult task is to reintroduce organicism into the thinking about society. Critical doctrines have fragmented society, and the difficult job is to reconstruct it when all minds accept an individualist conception of society.

Comte considers Protestantism and liberalism as temporary evils. They are considered evil because, as the reader might expect, they work against the re-establishment of an exclusive moral elite. At this stage of the discussion the stakes become more obvious. The major differences between Catholic and Protestant conceptions of ethics are brought into the open. Comte combats both the relativism that the Reformation introduced into the interpretation of morality (he posits an eternal objective justice) and the concomitant dismissal of the need for an elite who are best equipped to explicate morality. The two tenets of traditional Catholic ethics, objective justice and a clerical hierarchy, are, as we know, the two conditions for the recognition of an intellectual elite. Comte sees how Protestantism and liberalism, which follows it, can hamper the emergence of this same elite.

In describing the attributes of the positive stage, Comte integrates the Catholic model of morality and society with his purportedly scientific conception of society. He envisions a society in which scientific philosophers would discover the eternal laws of justice and would then propose the laws to the political authority for legislative application. There is, Comte believes, only one set of universal and eternal laws; and just as there is no independence of mind in mathematics, so too would there be no reason for independence of mind in a full-fledged social science that would possess true knowledge about the laws governing humanity. Stage one, theological society, and stage three, positive society, both depend on absolute moral certainty.

Now, in order to achieve the positive era, a new spiritual order must be introduced. And just as the former theological order was undermined by critical philosophy, by ideas, so too shall the metaphysical stage be undermined by a new set of ideas, scientific ideas. The pattern proposed by Comte follows the same process: ideas bring about social change. But in order to trigger the process, a moral authority is required to achieve a consensus about the changes that shall occur.

Comte's immediate purpose is to recover a communion of ideas, such as existed in medieval monotheist theology. Comte longs for a social consensus, a convergence of minds that, he says, implies the voluntary renunciation of freedom of thought. "True freedom" comes only from the "rational submission" to the fundamental laws of nature (1908, I: 103). It is not to be found in popular assemblies. Comte claims that "unanimous consent" can be achieved through proper education provided by a spiritual authority (ibid., VI: 326).

The role of the spiritual power, as Comte describes it, is to influence opinion, that is, to establish and maintain those principles that govern social relations. Scientists take the priests' place as the social group that ensures the intellectual and moral foundations of society.

Saint-Simon had also been preoccupied by the intellectual confusion of the age, and he too underlined the necessity for scientists to redress the situation (1966, III: 19): "Scientists, artists, look with the eyes of the genius at the present situation ... you will see that the spectre of public opinion has fallen into your hands; grab it vigorously" (1925, 25).

But, as in the theological stage, intellectuals do not take control of the state. They are attributed a power, or if we prefer, an influence of their own. For despite the references to a spiritual power, Saint-Simon and Comte speak only of the intellectuals' influence, influence over the masses through education and other means, and influence over the temporal power from their (the intellectuals') status as privileged representatives. It is a role of persuasion that they are granted, but there are no competing views from the outside.

Distinct from the temporal power, as theory is from practice, the spiritual power is expected to direct opinions and mores (Comte 1908, VI: 304–5). It is a moral power that rests on the people's confidence in the intellectual superiority of scholars, a confidence that should lead the masses to accept their authority (ibid., 325). Comte ascribes three features to this spiritual power: rationality, elevation and impartiality (ibid.,V: 336), elements that intellectuals claim naturally to have. Intellectuals form a "sacerdotal" or "speculative" class that has the responsibility of ensuring the prevalence of universal positive ethics (ibid., V: 160; VI: 354). At the same time, though independent from the temporal power, the spiritual power is given a consultative role, and it establishes the moral boundaries of political action (VI: 262–3).

Comte foresees two types of members of this speculative class: those devoted to science and philosophy (the difference between the two disciplines is negligible), and those devoted to aesthetic and poetic considerations.[1] The first category is considered superior because it is more abstract than the second. Those in the former are charged with the responsibility of reshaping society from the inside, that is, from the positive values provided by science.

According to Saint-Simon and Comte, if the best minds are to fulfil their specific functions, they must keep away from politics; because moral solutions are prior to political solutions, they are more important. As Saint-Simon writes: "The temporal power shall naturally be second in consideration once the spiritual power is in the hands of the learned" (1925, 66 n.1).

Comte agreed; he believed that the learned had a perspective that encompassed the whole, as opposed to politicians, who had only a partial view (To J.S. Mill, 17 January 1842). He holds that the reorganization of society is primarily spiritual and only incidentally temporal (1908, VI: 262–3), since the ultimate purpose is to achieve a consensus of minds, which will then serve as a foundation for the exercise of temporal power.

It is easy to understand the many hesitations that John Stuart Mill had in relation to Comte's theories; these ultimately led to the break in their relationship. Mill had originally been sensitive to the Saint-Simonist idea of spiritual power, at least so long as it remained the "insensible influence of mind over mind" (To Gustave d'Eichtal, 7 November 1829, *CW*, XII: 41). But from the start he objected to any sort of institutionalization of this power, which he identified with spiritual despotism (*CW*, X: 314). Mill also disagreed with Comte's downgrading of Protestantism. He believed that far from being regressive, Protestantism, and particularly Calvinism, was conducive to a scholarly tradition, as was evident in the case of Scotland. Giving direct moral responsibility to the individual could lead only to an increase in intellectual activity rather than the reverse (ibid., 321). The contrast between the two religious traditions is obvious here: in one, intellectual dynamism is vested in the learned few; in the other, it is vested in the laity, the common people.

---

1 Emile Littré, a disciple of Comte, maintains that there will be no distinction between philosophy and science in the future, to the extent that philosophy becoming positive will be the science of humanity or social science, the ultimate end of the scientific process. The science of humanity will naturally continue the "regulating function" philosophy had over society in the past (Littré 1876, 60–63).

Comte's works had little influence in the United States (Hawkins 1936), probably for the same reasons that Mill rejected them, though they were influential in Latin America.

It is worth noting that Auguste Comte continued his quest for the re-clericalization of society. His famous meeting with Clotilde de Vaux in 1844 and her death a short while later (1846) had a deep effect on him; so much so, that some of his disciples, such as Emile Littré, had to leave him. After her death he developed a mystic love whereby she became a saint who partook of the religion he considered establishing. One can get the gist of Comte's thought without having to dig through the excesses in which he indulged in at the end of his life.

Comte's model serves as an almost ideal defense of the intellectual. All the ingredients are present and are well integrated: a learned *elite*, which, though *independent* of politics, commands the attention of both rulers and ruled, and reveals the laws of an immutable and *objective justice* through the *rational* interpretation of social reality.

Even though Ernest Renan (1823–92) found Comte's positivism too abstract and felt that Comte had not left sufficient room for aesthetics, he, like Comte, continued a tradition of scientific elitism. Like Comte, he could assert that his religion amounted to the progress of reason, that is of science (1947, III: 719) He too called for the scientific reorganization of society (ibid., I: 231). Philosophy is equated with science; Renan believes that one day humanity will have as sound a knowledge of metaphysics and ethics as it presently has of science (ibid., III: 800). This enables him to claim that science should lead, as the positivists had argued, to the "triumph of ethics over politics (ibid., I: 231). Politics, having been up to now the mere product of passion and instinct, shall in the future follow the path of reason (ibid.; III: 755). Here again is the proclamation of the "sovereignty of reason"; the "general reason" (in contrast to Rousseau's general will) of the nation must prevail, and this has nothing to do with any numerical majority (ibid., 1001; I: 379). It is the right of reason to reform society through science (ibid., 756); and like Comte, Renan says that it is up to the learned to fulfil the task of rehabilitating the people.

Renan also discusses society in organic and hierarchical terms. He considers society prior to the individual; one is born into a society and is not, therefore, born free (1947, III: 995). The needs of society and the interests of civilization take precedence over individual needs and interests (ibid., 1031). Furthermore, the good of individuals must be sacrificed for the good of the collectivity (ibid., I: 402–3).

It is easy to understand from these considerations that Renan thought that freedom of speech should be reserved for the few who can use it properly: the learned. They are the true aristocrats (1947, I: 470). The masses are too unrefined and superficial to discover or know their own interests (ibid., 344). Freedom left to insane (*insensé*) people can be only detrimental to society and conducive to anarchy (ibid., III: 1012). Renan considers fallacious the argument that claims that freedom is necessarily favourable to the development of new ideas (ibid., 1014). The present liberal conditions benefit only agitators and do not foster the emergence of progressive ideas. France has become, he states, a nation "without a prophet to tell it what it feels" (ibid., I: 355). "The consciousness of a nation resides in its enlightened part, which leads and rules the rest" (ibid., 375).

From a pessimistic reading of human society as it was in his time, Renan proposes a rather optimistic program of rehabilitation, but only through the true source of moral energy: the intellectuals.

11 The Emergence of the Intellectual

The last three decades of the nineteenth century in France witnessed a significant interest in ethics.[1] This trend coincided with the onset of the Third Republic. The Third Republic was proclaimed in 1870 but was more officially established through a series of laws which culminated in 1875. Thinkers of the time envisioned the republican era as providing a solid ground on which to build a secularized state. The debate over secularization, which progressively materialized from the early 1880s to the famous Combes legislation of 1904 testifies to the importance of the issue on the political agenda of the time.

---

1 At the turn of century a number of philosophers made noticeable attempts to circumscribe ethics, to establish its sources, its nature, and its consequences. Eminent sociologists such as Durkheim and Levy-Bruhl broached the question from their own perspectives, summing it up in a science of norms that one can observe in societies throughout history. But a more philosophical concern in the tradition of Renouvier can be discerned among authors like Gustave Belot (1921), Frédéric Rauh (1903), and others. For the former, there exists a positive ethics that is demonstrable, a rational one, whose ends (the general interest) do not have to be proven; they are immanent in society, and they subordinate the individual to society (1921, II: 106–9, 247–57, 263–6); morality is objective and universal (Benrubi 1926, 73). On the other hand, Rauh opts for individual consciousness since it can be rational and impartial in the establishment of its own rules; he recognizes, at the same time, the importance of collective moral experiences, thus the relevancy of sociology (1903).

A NEW ETHICS LEADING TO "SOLIDARISM"

The call for scientific rigour was taken seriously in the 1860s. Though they were not necessarily followers of Comte, many writers showed an interest in the scientific character of ethics. Etienne Vacherot used the terms "moral science" and "scientific ethics" interchangeably; for him, moral laws are *a priori* principles, necessary truths as opposed to questions of personal conscience (Vacherot 1864, 254, 283–4, 289). Charles Renouvier (1815–1903) entitled his major work *Science de la morale* (1867) which again shows a major concern to distinguish ethics from metaphysics and religion.

Nonetheless, Renouvier strove to preserve a rationalist approach to ethics and his works are consistent with the emerging neo-Kantian movement of the time. Kant's works had been recognized in France by Victor Cousin, but were widely read only somewhat later. They permeated French moral philosophy well into the twentieth century. Renouvier can be considered the most influential initiator of Kant's philosophy in France. As we shall see, this philosophy was readily adapted to the scientistic leanings of the era. Renouvier's goal was to construct a purely rational ethics, which was derived from pure concepts expressed by an "abstract moral agent"(1867, I: 16).

His neo-Kantian leanings lead him to rely on the notion of duty, but not without, at times, stressing the existence of a natural law to which positive law ought to conform (1867, I: 231). The term "natural law" is not explicated; all we are told is that it is also the rational law of any rational agent,[2] and that it is compulsory, since it is derived from justice.

One should note that Renouvier also made concessions to philosophies derived from Protestant ethics. He acknowledged the role played by natural benevolence and sympathy, feelings or a moral sense that provide instinctual support for moral laws (1867, I: 183). Renouvier made no secret of his leanings toward Protestantism which, at the time, was attractive to a number of authors, such as Hippolyte Taine. In fact, the reforms in education at the end of the century in France were largely influenced by Protestants, including Félix Pécaut, Ferdinand Buisson, and others.

Though he favoured universal suffrage, Renouvier considers that because of the natural inequalities of talents and intelligence, the task of legislating should be entrusted to an aristocracy. This aristocracy is to be composed of men of "right reason," and we should entrust ourselves to them (Scott 1951, 66).

---

2 In this he likely meant to follow Kant's *Metaphysics of Morals*.

Renouvier developed a contractual conception of society that would find its full expression in the movement called solidarism. If there is one ideology representative of the Third Republic at the turn of the century, it is solidarism. At the Paris World Exhibition of 1900, both Emile Loubet, president of the Republic, and Alexandre Millerand, who later became president, expressed the official commitment of the political class to the "higher law" of solidarity (Hayward 1961, 22). Solidarism was considered to be the official social philosophy of the régime. It had the great advantage of situating itself between liberalism and socialism, in that it avoided both excessive individualism and excessive collectivism. This was French radicalism at its best.

Alfred Fouillée (1838–1912) can be considered the originator of the solidarist movement. Coming after Renouvier, he elaborated a moral philosophy whose goal was the reconciliation of idealist and positivist ethics. He argued that philosophers should consider not only the universal character of conscience, but also biological, psychological, and, above all, social data (1896b, 297). Fouillée looked for a "metaphysics of morals" that took naturalism into account, a metaphysics that considers the natural or causal action of ideas; those ideas that have causal power over man or nature and that he calls "*idées-forces*" or "power ideas" (1899, 408). These, he avers, belong to both the ideal and the natural worlds; thus, Fouillée achieves a tentative reconciliation between Plato and Comte. Ideas are seen as forces in themselves that work to achieve their own realization (Gunn 1922, 80). After Saint-Simon and Comte, any discussion of ethics had to claim a scientific legitimacy, otherwise it was likely to be dismissed as utterly metaphysical (one-stage *dépassé*) or worse still, religious (two-stages *dépassé*). By claiming to ground their speculations on scientific foundations, ethicists could consider that their accounts of morality were true. In this respect, Fouillée follows the rule.

The notion of "power ideas" has the advantage of accounting for both thought and action. When considered from the social level, power ideas become collective ideas and therefore collective forces. Fouillée's conception of society is revealing. Like others at that time, when noticeable progress was being made in biology, he defines society as an organism, but an organism born from an idea: a contractual organism working for the mutual dependence of its members. Here solidarity, or society, is understood as a living being (1880, 115, 128, 250). On the one hand, Fouillée's account is idealistic; he considers society to be an idea that realizes itself in the state. And on the other, he makes scientific claims; he identifies society with a physiological organism (ibid., 145, 245). Fouillée concludes with a synthesis of *a priori* justice and naturalistic solidarity (Hayward 1961, 27): "The search for the true and scientific principle of human fraternity ... has led us to know its fundamental identity with justice itself" (1880, 409).

Like Comte, Fouillée was pessimistic about the condition of society at the time, particularly in France. In *La France au point de vue moral* (1900), he diagnoses this country as being in a state of moral crisis and degeneracy. People, he complains, are left on their own without any political or moral guidance (1900, iv). The masses, being always the same throughout history, are described as tainted by a chronic disposition to barbarism, which became all too obvious in this age of democratic affirmation. In his search for solidarity, Fouillée asserts the need for the fusion of the individual with society (ibid., 236). He considers that education at the turn of the century suffers from an excess of individualism (ibid., 341). From this consideration, he concludes that the people should be morally instructed and led by elites; if left to themselves, they would pursue their own degeneration (ibid., 409).

Léon Bourgeois (1851–1925), a former prime minister, followed Fouillée and became, at the turn of the century, a champion of the solidarist cause. Since then, history has identified the movement with his name, even though the idea was, by that time, widely accepted in France. He may well have been more of a propagandist than a profound thinker, but he remains nonetheless representative of the movement.

As I have already mentioned, solidarism's great virtue was its position between liberal individualism and communist collectivism. Both liberalism and communism were considered extremes that had to be reconciled one way or another. French philosophers, at the time, were inclined to manage opposites through dialectical syntheses. There was no question of falling into the trap of Victor Cousin's former eclecticism, but the propensity was great to find a course of speculative action that would reconcile those views that were rendered incompatible by their mutually exclusive reductionism. The times were indeed propitious for this mode of thinking; writers and politicians felt the imperative need for France to finally put an end to its internal divisions and to agree upon one major collective project.

Léon Bourgeois illustrates well this search for a unifying ethics founded on purely secular grounds. His goal was to elaborate a moral doctrine for society that would be dependent on scientific premises. With this in mind, Bourgeois identifies solidarity as the "resultant" of two "forces" that had been separated for too long: science and ethics (1906, 16). Bourgeois wanted both of them to work in unison. He believed that laws of the moral and social world exist, which, when discovered, should transform society and make it realize its own true nature. The argument is simple: society obeys natural laws, and it is up to reason to discover and ultimately impose them. Bourgeois was heavily influenced by the progress that was occurring in biology, and which was exemplified in France by the work of Claude Bernard, Louis Pasteur and others. This influence certainly induced Bourgeois to put forward the notion of solidarity as being grounded in nature itself. Since they are detectable in living bodies as well as in species, the laws of solidarity should equally be found in social life (ibid., 61). It is up to reason to discover these true laws, and it is left to the state to impose subsequently the "rule of justice" (ibid., 36, 23).

We find again the idea of a true and objective morality (Boutroux 1927, 158–9). Rights and duties shall be derived from the truths discovered by scientific inquiry (Bourgeois 1906, 79–80). For Bourgeois, objective or natural laws exist which reason has to uncover in order to comprehend justice (ibid., 173). Without explicitly calling for an intellectual elite, the argument follows the same rules as those found among Bourgeois's predecessors.

These were the views shared by both ethicists and politicians at the time of the Dreyfus Affair. That event projected intellectuals to the fore and served as the catalyst that subsequently consecrated their collective existence.

The model inherited from Catholic ethics has remained relatively unscathed until the turn of the century, that is, until full secularization was achieved and intellectuals took over. As we have seen, the idea of natural law was recognized well into the nineteenth century. The notion of an objective justice remained relatively stable, even though it became identified with scientific laws that held nearly the same status. Reason continued to be considered the only acceptable judge in ethical matters, so it was thought best to leave its exercise to the more enlightened.

As time passed, the cause of democracy advanced, but not without concessions being made to the collective responsibilities that were left in the hands of the privileged. Representative political figures such as Jules Ferry could refer to "eternal morality" and to the importance of a "moral power to govern individual wills" (Barral 1968, 192, 248).

Reason was seen as fundamental, but only so long as it was understood as a collective phenomenon. Claude Nicolet, a student of the republican movement in France, underlines the role the republicans assigned to reason, a role which is exercised collectively: "From

Reason to politics and from politics to Reason, there is, for the republicans, a reciprocal relationship that extends inevitably beyond the individual stage (of reasoning)" (1982, 483).

Léon Gambetta (1838–1882), spearhead of the republican radicals, maintained that the sovereignty of the people strengthened the sovereignty of the individual (Nicolet 1982, 481). In this case, the sovereignty of the people is expressed by politicians. Nonetheless, the idea of a rationality to be elaborated by representatives remains untouched. This perspective allows room for the intellectuals who, in the radical tradition, were given full credibility.

THE DREYFUS AFFAIR

It was not fortuitous that the Dreyfus Affair became the reference point of the intellectuals' actions. It occurred at the exact moment when French society achieved its final stage of secularization. In the 1880s, a first set of measures had already been adopted to severely reduce the part played by clerics in education; this was followed by the Combes laws, which were almost simultaneous with the Affair. These laws were to lead in 1905 to the total separation of the state from the Church, implying the complete exclusion of religious orders from schools and also from certain monasteries. Beyond the judicial aspect, the Affair signalled a deep social conflict between the established values and those of the republican ideology; this translated into the fight for complete secularization. New rules were set which would determine the way public discussions would unfold in the future. A place within the political arena was provided for the intellectuals. The Dreyfus Affair opened the era of the intellectuals who, as independent spokespersons, now had a vital part to play. Since the time of the Affair, intellectuals have tended to form a distinct group. Voltaire fought as an individual, whereas Zola was one of many who fought for or against the review of Dreyfus's trial.

Interestingly enough, the action to review Dreyfus's conviction was initiated by Protestants such as Auguste Scheurer-Kestner, Edmond de Pressensé, a parson, and the historian Gabriel Monod. Ferdinand Buisson was also active. But as Encrevé notes, though a Protestant minority played a role in the Dreyfus Affair, as they had in the secularization of education, their role, in both cases, can be considered only supplementary (1985, 223–4). The great majority of those favourable to Dreyfus (the *"Dreyfusards"*) were from Catholic backgrounds. This did not prevent Jewish scholars, including, among others, Emile Durkheim and Lucien Lévy-Bruhl, from taking part in the debate. By the time the Affair occurred, the Catholic notions of a moral elite had been entirely integrated with the secular culture and were, therefore, common currency for all those brought up in the French system of education.

Theoretically, we could stop here. We have seen how secularization was secured and the status of the intellectual recognized. It is less important to trace the details of the evolution that followed, as long as we remember that intellectuals retained their status in one way or another. The purpose of the present discussion has been merely to show the connection between a religious conception of morality and its ultimate impact on secular society. The history of the intellectuals therefore becomes secondary, even though it is not devoid of interest. I will, therefore, content myself with focusing on certain patterns in the evolution of the intellectuals.

Scholars generally agree that the Dreyfus victory was one of the university, and more specifically of the *École normale supérieure* (*"rue d'Ulm"*) over the academy, the academy being those recognized writers who sat under the dome of the *Académie française* (Rémond, 1959, 869; Bredin 1983; Ory and Sirinelli 1986). To fight for Dreyfus was to fight against the traditional institutions: the hierarchy, the military, and the Church.

This event gave the *École normale supérieure* an impetus that ultimately led to a number of its former students being elected to Parliament. It also led Alfred Thibaudet to write a book on the "republic of professors" (1927) that compared their role to those played by Guizot and Cousin in constituting what had been called the monarchy of professors.

Created during the Revolution, the *École normale supérieure,* under the reign of Napoléon, resembled a secular version of the earlier Jesuit colleges. Its purpose was to educate teachers for the *lycées* (schools corresponding to upper secondary and lower college levels in English-speaking countries). It reached its zenith during the Third Republic. The *École* maintained a literary tradition, offering classes in criticism, rationalism, idealism and classicism; it was aimed at providing the "culture générale" (Smith 1982, 78, 2). The preparatory stage for entrance to the *École* was conducted, as it still is today, at prominent *lycées*, and this stage amounted to one or two years known in the jargon as *"khâgne"* and *"hypokhâgne."* It is at this specific level of French education that the Jesuit tradition was most influential. If one reads Bourdieu (1989, 112–18), one can see that, even now, the French system of education still resembles the pedagogical framework of the Jesuits. Education in the *lycées* is designed with the *École's* selection contest in mind. For two years students are imbued with a spirit of competition, and they are trained to have brilliant answers to any type of question that may turn up on the exam. They are mentally isolated from the rest of the world and submitted to the rules of intellectual virtuosity. These generalizations are most true of the literary disciplines in which many intellectuals in the making were educated during the Third Republic. We shall see, when we get to Jean-Paul Sartre, the extent to which literary values were well internalized.

The Dreyfus Affair strengthened the connection made between intellectuals and rational progress, or, in other words, between intellectuals and the political left. At least this is the way it would be understood by Jean-Paul Sartre, who tried to finalize the connection between intellectuals and the left in his extensive "Plea for the Intellectuals." Of course, not all intellectuals were left-wing. The right could also make claims to the systematic use of reason, even though it first had to identify itself with an irrational conception of politics.

FROM RIGHT-WING ANTI-INTELLECTUALISM TO RIGHT-WING INTELLECTUALS

French anti-intellectualism developed when secularized forms of authority began to appear. Initially, the anti-intellectual position was shared by people like Louis de Bonald and Joseph de Maistre who, from their own experience of the French Revolution, favoured tradition over reason. During the eighteenth century it had usually been clerics who had opposed the *philosophes*, but with the advent of secular institutions, laymen took over this critical role. Their arguments were at odds with the traditional teachings of the Church. Like Edmund Burke, their contemporary, these arch-conservatives ridiculed eighteenth-century rationalism from a very secular perspective. De Maistre, for instance, considered human beings to be historical products of their respective nationalities, a position that excludes any universal rules of conduct. At the same time, however, he severely qualified this relativism with his notion of a providential unfolding of history. Being also an ultramontane, he defended the position of the Pope at the top of the social hierarchy, Such aspects of his thought severely weaken his relativist posture. For de Maistre, there existed one true *eternal* form of religion that, he held, was perfectly realized by Catholicism (1821, II: 59). As for de Bonald, he believed in a wholly, not to say holy, theocratic world that obeyed the absolute laws of society as designed by God. So in both cases justice was secured through divine authority. If there was any relativism, particularly in the case of de Maistre, it was qualified by the absolute character of divine justice. So until the beginning of the twentieth century, anti-intellectualism was the almost exclusive domain of traditional monarchists for whom the Church served as guarantor of order. Intellectuals had no part to play, since the clergy was called upon to fulfil its customary function.

At the time of the Affair, secularization in France was all but complete; therefore, arguments against rationalism or scientism had to be established on proper secular grounds. Religion, wherever it is relied upon, becomes merely a functional adjunct to the harmonious working of society.

It is interesting to note, however, that the most committed opponents of intellectual activism were themselves active intellectuals. Their anti-intellectualism merely voiced their stringent opposition to rationalism; they were not opposed to the role of intellectuals as such.

The fiercest opposition to the intellectuals' claims of universal reason came from Maurice Barrès (1862–1923), who at the time of the Affair was already a well-known author. He derided, as did some others, the term *"intellectual,"* which was first used in France to identify those authors, professors and scientists who supported Dreyfus. Being an *antiDreyfusard* and a nationalist who was concerned with the moral unity of France, Barrès took up a relativist stance reminiscent of de Maistre's; he held that temporal and cultural conditions determine truth within a specific social context. A national reason existed which articulated national interests, as did a French truth and a French justice (1902, 13). Barrès brought together the notions of truth and justice, as is typical of intellectuals, although he set them within national boundaries. Despite his severe criticisms of intellectuals who revel in universal abstractions, Barrès rallied around him a *Ligue de la "patrie française,"* twenty-five members of the *Académie française* (made up of a maximum of forty members), if only to prove that "intelligence and intellectuals are not only on one side" (ibid., 65). The *Ligue* was designed to work outside the direct networks of politics. It was set up to analyse the anarchic situation in France and to shed light on public opinion about the true interests of the country. The purpose, to use Barrès's terms, was to remedy the paucity of French political thought, and to transform public opinion by providing principles and discipline; it was the search for common consciousness (ibid., 94, 101, 104).

Though he was critical of the *Dreyfusards*'s arguments about a true and universal justice, Barrès shared their conception of an elite which would represent, in some sense, the national interest. Later on during the First World War, he extolled the virtues of the sacred union of the diverse spiritual families of France, families which were comprised of Catholics, Protestants, Jews, socialists, and traditionalists. In these circumstances, Barrès proclaimed that the mission of France was to aid humanity as a whole through her national genius whose scope is universal. Though he states it in a different fashion, Barrès legitimizes the role of intellectuals by appealing to their universal understanding of the world.

Although they were few in number, there were authors who challenged the legitimation of the intellectual, usually by an appeal to intuition as opposed to reason. Edouard Berth's *Les Méfaits des intellectuels* (1914) offers an example of a certain type of anti-intellectualism, one which opposes the very tenets of intellectualism. The work, whose title refers to the damaging effects of intellectuals, brings together articles written between 1905 and 1908. It is inspired by Nietzsche, Henri Bergson, and also Georges Sorel, to whom the book is dedicated. In it, Berth combats the "government of intellectuals" (1914, 36). The first intellectuals that he identifies are to be found within the Church which, he claims, should content itself with mysticism, since this is where its real strength lies. Berth also opposes Cartesian rationalism, the Jesuits' formalism, and the tradition of both the Encyclopedists' and the Auguste Comte, all of which are manifestations of unbridled intellect (ibid., 36–7, 43, 56). In his eyes, these various forms of intellectualism can act only against the silent trends of history which are committed to the warring nature of human beings in society. Intellectuals, because they soften the minds of the people, encourage the ruin of the motherland. In other words, they destroy the beneficial myths by which society lives.

Similar views against the intellectual were voiced by various right-wing thinkers and militant activists, especially during the 1930s. However, this minority became extinct at the end of the Second World War.

Instead of pursuing the exclusively intuitionist approach of Edouard Berth, most right-wingers, particularly nationalists, rallied around the *Action française* and its leader, Charles Maurras, who had led the movement almost since its inception. The *Action française* was the extreme right-wing movement *par excellence*, and it commanded public attention for decades, although it never managed to become a widespread, powerful, or even politically successful movement (Wilson 1969, 328). It performed poorly when it tried to field candidates for the House of Deputies. Nevertheless, it attracted a broad range of political opinion and it influenced generations of intellectuals. If the *École normale supérieure* served as the matrix for progressive intellectuals, the *Action française* fulfilled a similar function for the right, though on a much greater scale. Its influence on the right can be compared to the influence that the French Communist party had upon numerous left-wing intellectuals after the Second World War.

The *Action française* had its own daily newspaper, and its influence spread to many journals, both literary and historical, as well as to other right-wing movements at its periphery. Even though its authors both used and abused invective, they still had a certain style. The *Action française* was run, not by scholars (for it attracted almost none) but by writers who caught the public's attention by their high literary qualities. Some were even widely recognized for their historical productions; some, like Jacques Bainville and Pierre Gaxotte after him, wrote best-sellers that remained works of reference for many people. Between the two world wars, the *Académie française* was filled with authors under the direct or indirect ascendancy of the movement. Indeed, almost all of its primary activists and sympathizers became academicians, starting with Maurras.

Among this group of rather literary-minded people, Charles Maurras (1868–1952) emerged as the principal thinker of the group, even though he also had strong literary inclinations. He set up a framework that gave the *Action française* its ideological legitimacy. Because of Maurras's contribution, the movement could pride itself on having established its discourse on rational grounds. One commentator has cogently noted that Maurras was more concerned with having reason on his side than with being on the side of reason (Barko 1961, 152).

Not only did Maurras claim that his discourse was rational, but he claimed it was scientific. His writings were meant to express no ideological preferences, but merely scientific propositions that would establish the true nature of politics. Maurras wanted to counter the sentimental and romantic irrationalism that nationalists such as Barrès were supporting. Moreover, he wished to establish the solid grounds for a convincing demonstration that favoured an "integral nationalism," a vision of society in which full-fledged monarchy topped the social order. Since our interest lies not in the detail of his thought but in its relevancy to intellectuals' action, we shall focus only on those aspects most relevant to our discussion.

Claiming to follow the same procedure as Comte, Maurras attempts to base his main arguments on scientific premises. Thus, he sees society as subject to laws of nature that are inflexible over time. He proposes no less than a "social physics of natural politics" that justifies the hierarchical organization of society (1937, lxxxix). Politics, in other words, corresponds to the natural and essential order of things. Reason's role is not to invent rules, but merely to discover them as facts of truth. The principles by which society operates are considered to be given, but they are accessible only to the knowledgeable. In this framework, justice is set aside, for it has a bearing only on voluntary relationships between individuals. It occurs at the level of individual conscience, whereas politics is social and obeys laws that have nothing to do with morality. Society is prior to any ethical considerations since it is imposed by nature itself.

Though his argument is not totally alien to that of Comte, Maurras's is probably more secularized. Maurras posits that the laws of nature, as he had characterized them, were in complete agreement with Aquinas's conception of natural law. While there is little use here in showing the profound incompatibility between the two, it is important to note that, like Aquinas, Maurras's conception of the laws of nature serves to legitimize political interventions by the knowledgeable. Morality is virtually discarded; *nature* fulfils the same function of legitimizing the actions of those intellectuals who possess the appropriate knowledge. In Maurras, we find the same conception of an enlightened reason that searches for an objective truth with which it can properly organize society.

Maurras identified the nation as the natural state of society. The nation, since it exists prior to the individuals who comprise it, has a life of its own and a right to perpetuate itself, independent of any ethical considerations. If de Bonald and de Maistre had attributed to society a status superior to that of the individual, it was in the name of transcendency, whereas for Maurras it is in the name of nature and its essential laws (Capitan Peter 1972, 17).[3]

In a statement reminiscent of Renan, Maurras alleges that French society is in dire need of reform; it needs to be reorganized by an inspired elite (1905, 15). The people should rely on "intelligence," whose function is "to *see* and *show*" which regime is best (ibid., 97). What he proposes is no less than a "Counter-Revolution," a kind of intellectual movement: "[The goal is] to bring [public] opinion to feel the profound insignificance of its power and to abdicate its fictitious sovereignty" (ibid., 98). Of course, Maurras is in favour of monarchy, and in the name of *reason* and nature, for the salvation of social order (ibid., 99). The goal was to "monarchize" public opinion before actually reinstating the king; the "*coup de force*" would come afterward (Capitan Peter 1972, 135–7). Being fond of wars, and particularly of religious wars, which, to him, were the most human form of war, Maurras felt that the *Action française* had to turn people's minds against the folly of the religion of democracy. In

---

3 In this regard Maurras, in agreement with Barrès, argued that individuals form society because of an instinctual feeling; this feeling was taken as given. Thus, Maurras opposed any voluntaristic or contractual models of the formation of society.

order to achieve this effect, the movement adopted a strategy of excesses of language in its writings and speeches as well as of physical violence on the streets and in the university. Maurras could write that Léon Blum was a monster of the democratic republic who as a Jew had usurped the French nationality and had tried to dismantle it, he should be shot "but in the back" (*Action française*, 9 April 1935, from Bodin and Touchard, 1961, 33–4).

It is usually felt that the *Action française* never seriously considered taking power – taking power, for the movement, would have meant taking power by force– since it never rallied even a significant minority to its cause. When it could have attempted to seize power during the demonstrations of 6 February 1934, for instance, it refrained from doing so. Violent actions that were undertaken by the movement were intended to be symbolic and were initiated by intellectuals who revelled in such exchanges. Because it had an impressive following of writers, the movement extended its influence through numerous networks that enabled it to reach competing groups and publications of the same political hue.

Having begun in direct opposition to the rationalism of the *Dreyfusards*, the nationalist movement led by Maurras moved rapidly toward a position that celebrated a mode of reasoning that enabled right-wing intellectuals to attain recognition and status. From the beginning of the present century to the end of the Second World War, the *Action française* served as *the* rallying point for intellectuals. Ironically, it was disavowed by those whom it claimed to defend: by the Church in 1926, which was quite a blow, and by the pretender to the throne, the Duke of Guise, in 1937. During the war, the Vichy Regime and the German occupation allowed some of the traditional values professed by the movement to be applied. But by 1944, the movement was discredited, and after the war, it was considered totally irrelevant. The Cold War period was rather the opportunity for the left to make itself heard.

Even though, as is commonly admitted, the *Dreyfusards*' victory was a victory of university professors, the decades that followed were to belong to the people of letters. Whether they emerged from the *École normale supérieure*, like Romain Rolland, or went into politics like Léon Blum, they were identified as people with a literary bent. The first four decades of this century were among the richest for French literature. Men of letters readily became involved in politics, particularly during the thirties, which reached their political apex with the *Front populaire*. Newspapers, weeklies, and monthlies of all political hues furnished forums for these authors, whose exchanges and arguments took place largely through these channels.

BENDA'S *GREAT BETRAYAL*

It is in this context that Julien Benda in 1927 published his famous *Great Betrayal*. His purpose was to counter the influence of the Bergsonian intuitionist school. In the book, Benda expresses his opposition to what he calls political passions moved by worldly considerations of class or nation (1928b, 60). He objected to the national mystique which he found pervasive at the time.

Borrowing the language of the Church, Benda extols the detached stance of the cleric who, engrossed in the contemplation of universal truths, abstains from squabbles over temporal issues. Benda has in mind the scholar whose contribution is valuable for society, but only in so far as it remains at a highly abstract level where universal truth and justice can be perceived. Benda consciously refers to a spiritual ministry in which scholars, like the priests before them, participate; and again like priests, devote their energies to universal principles and disregard national particularities. Benda's goal is to perpetuate a special social role for the scholar that will ensure the continued existence of humanism as a way of thinking. His intention was to discredit those who, like Barrès and Maurras, claimed to be scholars but were deeply involved in the political arena. For him, such people were mere polemicists; they were not living up to the status they claimed to have.

Benda accepted that scholars sometimes opposed political authority, as did intellectuals, but he approved of this opposition only when it was carried out in the name of truth and universal values. He considered that such had been the case for Voltaire in the Calas affair or Zola in the Dreyfus Affair (1928b, 61). Consistent with this moral position, Benda is said to have become a "fellow traveller" of the French Communist party, one who stands outside the party's official structures while remaining sympathetic to the cause (Schalk 1979, 41). He agreed, it seems, with the party in so far as it defended universal principles.

Benda accused his contemporaries of discarding the traditional Catholic distinction between the part of the Church that teaches (the priests) and that which is taught (the laity). The betraying scholars were precisely those who abode by the Protestant belief in democratic egalitarianism on matters of truth and justice (1968, 262 n.l, 263).

Benda, who was Jewish, recognizes the influence of his years at the *lycée* where the Jesuit mode of education shaped his mental structure as well as his moral judgment. (1968, 43, 54; 1937, 37–8). The Jesuits, he states, were universalists with respect to the nation, so much so that the Jacobins who followed them wished to spread truths to people all around the world (1937, ll). Benda nicely illustrates the internalization of Catholic values via the secularized education of the *lycée*.

Benda's concern for the cleric's social role was aimed primarily at defining the function of the professional thinker, who was a scholar or philosopher, rather than that of the writer as such. Without denying the latter some room, his references are more immediately directed to higher levels of abstraction where contemplation is necessary.

If French intellectuals were not generally known for their philosophical thought during the period between the two world wars, some social thinkers, such as Emmanuel Mounier, and the periodical *Esprit* foreshadow the era that followed the Second World War. This is the period that extends from the end of the Second World War to the mid-1970s and it sees the rise of a different kind of intellectual. With Jean-Paul Sartre emerges a new and charismatic type of intellectual. Although he became popular through his novels and plays, it was his philosophical preoccupation that supposedly gave these literary works their raison d'être.

12 The Consecration of the Intellectual

Jean-Paul Sartre was the intellectual who most closely approximated the ideal type. He was the intellectual *par excellence* because of both his writings and his frequent participation in political debates. He consciously placed himself in the tradition begun by Voltaire and continued by Zola. In this respect, he was faithful to the examples set by his predecessors. He was innovative in that he asserted that a commitment to politics was compulsory for writers, whereas his predecessors had considered political involvement to be a matter of discretion.

Sartre's itinerary follows a progressive path that leads ultimately to the consecration of the intellectual. His first writings, such as his novel *La Nausée* (1938) and his philosophical work *L'Être et le Néant* (1943) assume a somewhat individualistic approach to the ontology of consciousness in the world. His approach to consciousness had moral implications that he readily recognized; ontology could not be separated from ethics (Jeanson 1980, xxxix). He planned to write a treatise on ethics but, significantly, never completed it, having been "stymied," he said, in the process of developing it (1976, 207; 1983). This certainly did not prevent him from making statements on ethical matters, far from it. But, as we have seen, few authors in the tradition were ever very explicit on this subject.[1]

---

1 It is interesting to note, in passing, that the most influential philosopher in France during the first half of this century, Henri Bergson, came out with his work on ethics (*The Two Sources of Morality and Religion*) very late in his life (1932) when his actual influence was waning.

Like his prominent predecessors Voltaire and Zola, Sartre admits to having been initially "apolitical and impervious to (social) commitments" (1960, 46–7). He became an intellectual, just as he had seen others do, after having gained recognition in a specific field of philosophical, artistic, or scientific endeavour. However, Sartre always had the literary tradition in mind: "And quickly I came by the notion that that was how a man's life should develop – to begin with one was not political, then toward fifty one did become political, like Zola" (Beauvoir 1984, 376).

It was in the process of becoming an intellectual, and a very prominent one indeed, that Sartre felt obliged to explain the nature of his new role. He founded the monthly periodical *Les Temps modernes* in 1945 and then subsequently wrote elaborate texts such as *Qu'est-ce que la littérature?* (1948) and "Plaidoyer pour les intellectuels." He established himself as the intellectual *par excellence* in that he achieved this status to the full while setting forth the responsibilities that went with the role.

Sartre used the term "intellectual" largely in the sense that I have used it: an intellectual is a person who, having gained expertise in a particular field of knowledge, chooses to participate in political and social debates. But for Sartre, a writer does *not* have a choice about whether or not to participate, since participation or commitment is a responsibility that is intimately connected with the function of writing itself. Because of this interpretation of the writer's role, Sartre holds Gustave Flaubert responsible for the repression that followed the Commune of 1871, for the reason that he *abstained* from writing a line against this action (1948, 9–13). Sartre took this same position in *L'Être et le Néant* where he argued that if one declined to take a stand against a war, one could be held responsible for that war. Nizan had already stated in the 1930s that abstention is itself a choice (Nizan 1974, 43).

Sartre addresses himself primarily to writers and secondarily to scholars in general. Their role is to "speak" in the sense of explicating things by "disclosing" them, and in so doing, writers act upon these things (1948, 72–3). This is the gist of his argument which is inspired by Marx and by Heidegger's notion of "unconcealment" (*aletheia*) (Heidegger 1976, 388–91). For Sartre, literature has, in itself, a real function, and any disregard of this function amounts to a social withdrawal and complicity with the bourgeois ideology of social atomism (1948, 16–20). Marcel Proust's psychological "atomism," for instance, is taken to task for precisely this reason.

Sartre's approach implies a dialectical process of grasping reality, and this becomes an imperative for any intellectual wishing to work properly.

Sartre always opposed the idea of values *in se* which had a transcendental existence independent of human subjectivity (1956, 721). In this respect, he seems to deviate from the notion of objective justice as part and parcel of the classic intellectual's lot. He explicitly expresses his disagreement with what he would call an idealistic stance. There is no question of the "abstract universality" believed in by the eighteenth-century *philosophes* (1972, 403); the notion of a human nature is absent. However, Sartre recognizes a dialectical contradiction whereby the intellectual is bound to live an inner tension between, on the one hand, his or her middle-class values, and, on the other, a deep desire to reach universality. In this situation, close to Hegel's unhappy consciousness, the intellectual is charged with the personal mission of discovering from his or her "singular universality" the inner tensions of society as a whole. Being imbued with bourgeois values, society must, so to speak, be exorcised by the intellectuals, who act as its priests.

For Sartre, intellectuals have a responsibility to overcome their own alienation; thereafter they can perform the same operation for society at large. Being products of society and its dominant ideology, intellectuals cannot pretend to transcend its values. They must emancipate themselves from society and its ideology. Their own minds contain the societal contradictions between truth and belief, knowledge and ideology (1974, 265). As Sartre puts it, intellectuals must reveal their own monstrous side and, by so doing, must expose the monstrous aspects that are ingrained in society itself (ibid., 249). Their role is to dissolve ideology; it is a role of consciousness raising which, through the process of "disclosure," establishes the "practical truth" for society, so that people can reach their "organic goals" and ultimately, universality (ibid., 259–60, 265).

From an individualistic ethics which initially revolved around the notions of contingency and ambiguity, Sartre moved to more absolute concerns, as his collective commitments grew stronger. The ultimate goal of intellectuals, who are the "specialist(s) in universality," is to educe the "values of eternity" which can be found in our day-to-day struggle with life (1974, 262, 1948, 15). Thus, for Sartre, there are true social relations based on reciprocity (1974, 251): "He (the intellectual) labours in order that a social universality may one day be possible where all men will be *truly* free, equal and fraternal, certain in his knowledge that on that day ... the intellectual as a species will disappear" (ibid., 254).

The argument unfolds with truth and justice as the ultimate points of reference. With this in mind, Simone de Beauvoir, Sartre's faithful companion, could write: "Truth is one: error is many. It is not by chance that the right-wing professes pluralism" (1955, 93).

Intellectuals cannot be of the right, for in this case, they are merely pseudo-intellectuals or "watchdogs" of the dominant ideology, to use Nizan's words (1974, 252). The idea of an orthodoxy is not surprising here; it conforms to the general pattern. The *philosophes* too claimed that only they perceived the truth.

The intellectuals' audience, which Sartre at times identifies as the masses, requires guidance and representation. Public opinion, he says, is stupid because it is ill-informed, and it is ill-informed because the press is irresponsible (1972, 175). Moreover, politicians always follow the easiest course of action, which is necessarily the least daring. For Sartre, the masses, being deceived by such propaganda, are bound to follow these leaders: "Who, therefore, can *represent* to the government, to the (political) parties, and to the citizens, the value of these actions, if it not the writer?" (Sartre 1948, 309). There is no question of the intellectual joining a political party; this would contradict the self-appointed character of the function.

On the whole, the features that comprise the role of the intellectual and the conditions of its fulfilment remain intact. Universal ethics and an elite to explain its meaning to others remain the essential characteristics of intellectualism, though here they are proposed in a different fashion. This description of the intellectual corresponds to the classical type of intellectual who abides by a tradition with which Sartre was well acquainted. Toward the end of his life, as the "meaning" of the general strike of May 1968 dawned on him, Sartre became sensitive to the French Maoist conception of the intellectual. From being a "left-wing intellectual" he had become, he claimed, a "leftist intellectual" (1971, 118). For him, this meant that he would "suppress himself as an intellectual" and place his skills in the service of the masses (1972, 467). Sartre may have been torn between being a new-born intellectual with a limited Maoist following or being the traditional intellectual of his famous work *Les Mots* [*The Words*], the one who was pursuing his work on Flaubert (Gavi et al. 1974). But he later agreed that he was still a classic intellectual, one who made public denunciations in the name of universality, though he saw a new type of intellectual emerging as an outgrowth of May 1968 (1977, 24, 26).

In a conversation he held with Simone de Beauvoir in the summer of 1974, Sartre still adhered to his commitment to literature as opposed to philosophy, which he places second to literature: "I should like to achieve immortality through literature, and philosophy is a way of reaching literature" (Beauvoir 1984, 150). Here we encounter *fame*, a former Jesuit value, and fame haunted both Sartre and de Beauvoir all their lives (ibid., 162–4). Sartre saw in literature absolute values which he felt philosophy did not have. He knew or at least anticipated that *Les Mots* would be *the* work that would survive for future generations. It was, in his mind, a complete literary work: it was "full of tricks, of clever dodges, of the art of writing" and, as de Beauvoir explains, it was animated by "the desire to charm by words, by the turn of the phrase" (ibid., 214–5). It is quite obvious that the literary values listed here are not totally alien from the Jesuits' insistence upon form and style.

At one time Sartre became aware of the limited impact a writer could have on society: "For a long while I treated my pen as a sword: now I realize how helpless we are" (1964, 172). Nonetheless, he participated intensively in public debates until almost the very end of his life. Although he was at the height of his fame during the 1950s and early 1960s, he was still considered a renowned intellectual when he died in April 1980; thousands of mourners followed him to his last repose. Like Voltaire, Sartre originally became famous because of his literary production, but again like Voltaire, he became even more famous as an intellectual.

Raymond Aron (1905–83) provides a counterpoint to Sartre. Aron was also an intellectual in his own right, and he dared to challenge the conception of the intellectuals held by most leftists. The *L'Opium des intellectuels* [*Opium of the Intellectuals*] (1955) is directed, not against the role or function of the intellectual, but against the clerical and religious attitude many intellectuals assumed, particularly in relation to communism. He criticized their fanaticism, their belief in the infallibility of the party, and their calls for a doctrinaire orthodoxy. As a liberal and a realist, Aron could not brook the discrepancy he noted between certain intellectuals' revolutionary idealism and the crude reality anyone could observe in the Soviet Union. Aron's book is a fierce attack on the misconceived role of the intellectuals. An intellectual himself, he was fully received into the intellectual brotherhood only very late in his life, when events had proven him right. Many considered him to have been more perceptive than Sartre. By that time, people were turning to more liberal views.

Sartre saw the writing of literature as an act that had, in itself, a political meaning. According to this view, writers could not shirk their moral and political responsibilities. Most thinkers who followed took the political implications of writing for granted. While Sartre had introduced the notion of "evil faith" which amounts to the inadequate perception of one's relationship to others, a lie to oneself, the next generation evolved a language that could, following Paul Ricoeur, be called the language of suspicion. Just as formerly Marx, Nietzsche and Freud had previously inaugurated an era of suspicion regarding consciousness, many of the thinkers of the 1960s and 1970s questioned the foundations of both learned discourse and mass culture. *Mythologies,* written by Barthes in 1957, stands as an early example of the "semioclastic" (Barthes 1970, 8) intentions to unmask contemporary myths.

Like Sartre, these authors also abstained from elaborating a political theory of their own. On the whole, they maintained a posture of denunciation by indiscriminately referring to power, domination and class struggle, though they usually shied away from any overly explicit terminology.

This tendency is quite noticeable among sociologists of leftist leanings. Politics, largely ignored by sociologists prior to the 1960s, became an important reference point from then on. Pierre Bourdieu's *La Reproduction* (1970), written with Jean-Claude Passeron, is representative of a way of analysing, usually in deprecating terms, the surreptitious infiltration of politics into society. Politics becomes the hidden social reality which permeates activities that appear politically innocent. In order to illustrate their hypothesis, Bourdieu and Passeron analyse the education system as a case in point. The authors define pedagogical action as the "arbitrary imposition of cultural arbitrariness." For them, education works through the "inculcation" of a "habitus" which, once acquired, manifests itself as the successful internalization of cultural arbitrariness. The pedagogical action is deemed a type of "symbolic violence", since it amounts to the imposition of cultural arbitrariness by an arbitrary *power.*

Power in its most protean form is the point of reference that pervades the trendy sociological and philosophical works of the 1970s. The term remains largely undefined; it thus conveys the sense of an ultimate reality which borders on the inexpressible, while it reinforces the feelings of suspicion that are associated with the word.

Touraine (1974a, 41–2) sees power as a "pathology" of social relations which, nevertheless, can be detected in all societies. So much so that every society contributes to the destruction of its own social reality, due to a process of "desocialization" fed by prejudice, hostility, repression, or exploitation. In view of this reality, the sociologist's *raison d'être* is to question the legitimacy attributed to power by the state or the ideology, and to uncover its alienating effect.

From a similar concern, though from a different perspective, Bourdieu confers on the sociologist the privileged function of disclosing the hidden and sometimes repressed aspects of social life (1980, 20). Bourdieu draws openly from Gaston Bachelard's belief that science's function is to uncover the hidden. Bourdieu considers the sociologist's role to be subversive in nature, since it consists of "uncovering" facts that would otherwise remain hidden, prohibited from sight. Being able to detect the social determinants likely to act as an influence, the sociologist can free him- or herself from them and "offer to others the means of their own liberation" (ibid., 72). This position is not very far from that of Touraine who assigns to the intellectual the responsibility of uncovering the real social relationships which are hidden behind the official discourse of authority and ideology (1974b, 75). The intellectual should be on the side of the oppressed and should support the emergence of science which, he adds, is the opposite of ideology.

Both authors make explicit references to science and both, in discussing the intellectual's role, have the sociologist in mind. The enlightened here are specialists, but the mission remains the same, both in their immediate goals and in their broader social function.

THE NEW INTELLECTUAL

On the philosophical front, Michel Foucault (1926–84) stands out as the most representative of those intellectuals who took over from Sartre while pointing the intellectual in another direction. Foucault was just as involved in public debates as was Sartre but he was more closely connected with the oppression that he identified in the social realities of everyday life.

Foucault's goal was to reveal the existence of relationships of power and domination from which and through which discourses and practices unfold (1973, 11). According to him, practices are strategies of control which shape discourses; discourses in turn, shape new practices. Foucault decries the situation in courts of justice, police stations, hospitals, schools, and armies; he criticizes the mass media, and protests against the social conditions faced by women and homosexuals. Power is never defined, as Foucault himself recognized toward the end of his life, but the theme of power is omnipresent in his works, particularly in the later ones. In fact, he writes that we are ignorant of the nature of power (Foucault and Deleuze 1972,7). After all, he argues, exploitation was identified only in the nineteenth century by Marx. Power remains an unknown which functions through hierarchies, controls, surveillances, and social prohibitions of all sorts. For Foucault, power is "essentially that which represses," whether it represses nature, instincts, classes, or individuals (1980, 89–90).

This search for power partakes of a general proletarian and revolutionary struggle against capitalist exploitation (Foucault and Deleuze 1972, 9–10). It is aimed at disclosing specific mechanisms of power, while at the same time developing a "strategic knowledge" (Foucault 1988, xiv). Foucault believes that there exists a logic or type of rationality that conditions individuals' behaviour, and that it is up to the intellectuals to discover how this logic works (ibid., 105).

Foucault even questions science, since it too depends on the exercise of power; science forces people to think in a certain way, if they do not want to be discredited. Knowledge and power are conducive, he claims, to a certain discourse of truth whose function is to legitimize and reinforce the exercise of power (1980, 93). Following Nietzsche's skepticism, Foucault refers not to truth, but to a "regime of truth," which is part of a "general politics of truth," and which varies from one society to another (ibid., 131).

Foucault contends that politics permeates the private lives of individuals. Thus, he expresses a great deal of interest in the regulation of sex, which is understood as the regulation over the use of the body. This conception of sexuality shares certain features with Gilles Deleuze and Félix Guattari's opposition to psychoanalysis, which, they think, functions as a power that represses desire. Psychoanalysis becomes a political threat to desire which is deemed revolutionary in itself. The latter is thwarted in its action by psychoanalysis which Guattari identifies as a repressive instrument of the bourgeoisie (Deleuze and Guattari 1977).

For Foucault, the function of the intellectual is to reveal the strategies and networks through which power operates. In order to do this, an intellectual must have a degree of expertise. The days of spokespersons for the universal are over (1980, 126–9). Foucault calls for the emergence of the "specific intellectual," who, from the vantage point of his or her own field, can point out specific instances of the working of power, whether in the hospital, the laboratory, or the university. The writer is no longer the prototypical intellectual; he or she is on the way of being replaced by the university professor and the academic. These new intellectuals are to be politically active, as were their predecessors, but only in specific areas where their proficiency ensures maximum efficiency.

Foucault's rejection of the universal intellectual is consistent with his conception of truth, since he does not believe in the existence of a universal truth (*Michel Foucault philosophe* 1989, 193). Truth is not a question of the battle between science and ideology. Truth unfolds, as I previously mentioned, within a régime of truth.[2] But, as he

---

2 "Truth is to be understood as a system of ordered procedures for the production, regulation, distribution, circulation and operation of statements" (1980, 133).

adds: "All this must seem very confused and uncertain" (1980, 132). The goal is to separate "the power of truth from the forms of hegemony, social, economic and cultural, within which it operates at the present time" (ibid., 133). In other words, Foucault intends to expose the present production of truth, and in order to achieve this goal, he proposes a "new politics of truth" (ibid., 133).

The intellectual's role is to shake up the people's mental habits by questioning what is considered self-evidently true or correct in social rules and institutions (1988, xvi). It is a "critical job" of assessment, one which is *suspicious* of accepted systems of values (ibid., 107). But whatever the specific objects of criticism, the struggle takes place within the context of a proletarian revolution (Eribon 1989, 274).

But from Foucault's comments, a question immediately arises: how does one determine the appropriate use of power in establishing truth? After all, Foucault establishes that truth is power. Because both terms are still imprecise, it is likely that Foucault employs certain implicit criteria to evaluate the right strategies. The problem is that he, like other thinkers of the time, claims to be an anti-humanist, in other words, he claims to reject the notion of any intrinsic universal values, yet he frequently refers to global concepts such as "domination" and "repression" (1980, 89–92). The language that he uses to discuss such concepts is ethically loaded, though it is more evocative than specific.

Interestingly, Foucault's attempt to bring together a notion of truth linked with power and an implicit ethical commitment to values is a reiteration of the perennial desire of intellectuals to establish ethics through truth and vice versa. Neither Foucault's insistence on the relative nature of truth, nor his denial of the existence of universal values prevented him from becoming involved in causes that pleaded for specific rights. In these cases, the demand for rights was almost a matter of common sense.

Foucault spoke out on behalf of enough causes to belie his conviction that he embodied the specific intellectual. The discourse he developed to legitimize his own actions differed significantly from that of classic intellectuals who made open references to universality. In practice, he involved himself in too many issues to claim that he was a specific intellectual. In this respect, he did not depart from his predecessors.

And like his predecessors, Foucault, together with contemporaries such as Barthes and Deleuze, not only continued but reinforced, the literary pretensions of the intellectual. This generation cultivated a style of its own; they revelled in paradoxes and literary effects (Ferry and Renaut 1985, 37–8). The weekly *Nouvel Observateur* accepted that prominent intellectuals could be hermetic, but would not grant such a privilege to its own journalists (Pinto 1984a, 91). The intellectual still belonged to a distinct and esoteric elite.

This penchant for obscurity is observable in the discourse of these intellectuals, a discourse in which aesthetic, ethical, and political values are intricately fused. Of the three, politics was undoubtably the unifying thread. Having discarded humanist values and the use of reason to discover them, this generation of thinkers substituted political values, which now had a sacred quality. The new priests preached of the evils of power, and attempted to detect social ills in every layer of society.

Louis Althusser (1971) had already enlarged the scope of politics to include all of the primary groups and institutions of society. His conception of the "ideological state apparatuses" included not only those institutions controlled directly by the state but also institutions such as the trade unions, the churches, the schools, the mass media, the arts, and the family. The authors who followed after him usually shared Foucault's belief in the elusive nature of power, and thus contributed to the "re-enchantment" of the political world. Politics was seen as a realm whose intricacies escaped the uninitiated. The purpose of the intellectuals was to expose its presence in daily social relations. Moreover, the exercise was meant to be as literary as it was philosophical.

Roland Barthes's *Leçon* (1978) illustrates the propensity of authors of that time to extend politics to all aspects of society. In this "lesson," a term that indicates the subordinate position of the readers,[3] Barthes extends the reality of power to language itself. Having already specified that power can be found at all levels of society – in the state, in classes, in groups, in all kinds of activities such as entertainment, sports, and even in certain aspects of individuals' private lives – Barthes here elaborates on the fascist character of language. Whereas Emile Durkheim had considered the constraining aspect of language to be a representative product of society, Barthes sees it as a phenomenon created by alienation, which thwarts the expression of intimate desires. It is thought oppressive because of its legislative and codifying character. Thus a means of escaping the dictatorial power of language must be found. As one might expect, Barthes proposes literature as the means of subverting language from the inside, for literature is the very act of writing language anew. Here again form becomes the significant feature in the art of communication.

In *Leçon* Barthes also confirms that the role of the intellectual is to

---

3 *Leçon* is the written transcript of Barthes' formal *Leçon inaugurale* at the College de France, a standard exercise for the new fellows.

wage war against *all* powers (1978, 11–12). The purpose of the intellectual is to expose the surreptitious workings of power to a previously unaware audience. Intellectuals are called upon to perform this act because of their ability to foil the magic of politics. However, they need this magic to stay in business.

By using suspicion as a method of studying social relations, the intellectuals of this period attempted to demythologize aspects of modern society and culture, that is, they tried to reveal hidden political phenomena to the uninitiated. Yet the discourse was cryptic, even though they intended it to have a dispelling effect. Here one finds the features necessary to keep intellectuals active.

THE DEMISE OF THE INTELLECTUAL

Although most of these intellectuals felt a latent disillusionment with Marxism, they expressed it openly after the publication of Solzhenitsyn's *Gulag Archipelago*. André Glucksmann, a former Maoist, and Bernard-Henri Lévy expressed this disillusion in books that established their authors' reputations (1975, 1977). The young writers of the mid-1970s, or, as they were called, the new philosophers, heralded changes to come. Their message was usually far from new, but they finally had an audience that listened to them.

In the 1980s, the intellectual experienced something of a demise. In 1983, the daily *Le Monde* initiated a discussion on this very issue; the debate occupied the summer months and included articles from a variety of thinkers. Jean-François Lyotard entitled his piece "Tombeau de l'intellecuel." But despite the article's gloomy title, Lyotard does not *de facto* discard the activity of the intellectual. Instead, he envisions more modest forms of political intervention than those which intellectuals had undertaken in the past. The intellectual who advocates universal values and tries to assume the burden of humanity is dead indeed (1984, 12–18, 65). Lyotard feels that the time has come for very circumscribed actions, thus, intellectuals are to be more rigorous and more modest in their approach (ibid., 21–2). Similarly, Glucksmann signs the intellectual's "death certificate" and bids "*adieu* to preaching" (1985, 264, 290). Though Lévy still eulogizes the intellectual, he too prescribes a redefinition of the intellectual's sphere of action. For Lévy, the intellectual remains a precious institution that is as important to democratic culture as is the separation of powers to government. Nevertheless, he calls for a more open, dispassionate, and circumspect type of intellectual.

This demise of the intellectual is as yet uncertain. The intellectual has not entirely disappeared, but the present times do not seem favourable to his or her presence. French magazines still try to sustain the charisma that once emanated from intellectuals (Lamont 1987a, 173), even though they often lament the fading image of a type that was once a natural part of the French social landscape. Whether the withdrawal of intellectuals from the limelight is temporary or permanent is not a question that I shall answer here. But what is striking is the concomitant rise of liberal values. When true liberal values wax, the importance of intellectuals tends to wane, since liberalism is, in the long run, incompatible with the social function ascribed to intellectuals.

Because liberalism is founded on the belief that individuals are the best judges of their own interests, it does not conform well with a social system in which self-appointed intermediaries claim not only to represent the interests of the entire society, but also be able to prescribe the best course for the society to follow. Liberalism is likely to be egalitarian to the extent that it is open to the free expression of opinions. The idea of granting moralists a privileged role in the articulation and representation of the society's interests does not sit well with the brand of individualism that currently pervades France and other nations. Thus in the 1980s we can find complaints about the pervasiveness of individualism, such as those voiced by Gilles Lipovetsky in his book *L'Ère du vide,* whose title reveals its author's opinions of individualism.

The widespread recognition of liberal values in France, which was part of a worldwide trend in the 1980s, contributed to putting an end to the profound ideological divisiveness that had characterized French politics for so long. This situation may be temporary, but for the time being the political game no longer gravitates around the legitimacy of the liberal régime.

Should this liberal and individualistic trend persist, it will probably mean the end of the generalist, the intellectual who could express views on all political issues. People seem to expect specific expertise; they prefer to make up their own minds after hearing the opinions of experts. This tendency is noticeable in academic research in France and it leads to the fragmentation of knowledge (Ross 1987, 52), a fragmentation that is likely to have repercussions on the intellectual arena.

It is interesting to trace the development of the French intellectual in the postwar era. With Sartre we witness the combination of philosophy and literature, and after him, the definite ascendancy of a certain conception of philosophy over literature as the means by which to achieve sufficient recognition to assume the role of intellectual. Academics tended to displace the literati. At the same time, academics depended on modes of recognition that allowed them to circumvent the judgments of their peers and to reach a larger public (Boudon 1981). Their reputations were made in dailies, weeklies, and in the prominent monthlies devoted to the liberal arts. The intellectual structure collapsed at the very time the confusion between the academic and the intellectual functions was at its peak. It does not follow that the intellectual's demise is definitive.

Some events may still serve as opportunities for intellectuals to show that their species is not extinct. The Bosnian civil war mobilized intellectuals who gathered momentarily around Bernard-Henri Lévy, André Glucksmann, and others to run under the banner of the "Sarajevo List," more officially called *"L'Europe commence à Sarajevo"* list in the European elections of June 1994. Its only *raison d'être* was to promote the lifting of the arms embargo, which penalized the Moslem faction in the war. The movement was short-lived since Lévy and most of the other intellectuals left the incumbent Professor Léon Schwartzenberg to fend for himself in his capacity as leader of the list. They felt, if we believe Lévy, that their mission of alerting public opinion had been accomplished. And indeed, the intellectual's function in its ideal form is to remain independent of mundane politics.

The strikes in the late autumn of 1995 also provided intellectuals with an opportunity that they could hardly miss. A number of petition lists circulated at the time. Sociologist Pierre Bourdieu gathered after his name those of Luc Boltanski, Christian Baudelot, and Léon Schwartzenberg; historians Pierre Vidal-Naquet and Michel Vovelle, and actress Marina Vlady also signed, along with about five hundred others, who called for a "radical reflection about the future of our society." This came in response to a previous statement from the periodical *Esprit* and Pierre Rosanvallon. That statement had received the support of three hundred intellectuals, including philosopher Paul Ricoeur and sociologist Alain Touraine, who wished to underline the importance of being responsible in carrying out a reform of the welfare system. On that occasion Touraine summed up the intellectuals' predicament of the day: he saw the necessity of providing a "global model" to avoid a "savage liberalism," while recognizing at the same time the absence of any alternative model in the offing (*Le Monde,* 12 December 1995).

Conclusion

Intellectuals comprise a supposedly enlightened elite who become involved in political matters in order to offer guidance to the masses in the search for their true objective interests. The role of intellectuals is derived from and legitimized by an ethical system that relied on reason to discover and explicate objective justice. While Protestant ethics (particularly Calvinism) is conducive to a subjective understanding of interests in which feelings provide the measuring rod, the Catholic ethical tradition tempers the individual's ability to determine her or his own rules of conduct. Intellectuals claim that because of their ability to reason, they have direct access to the universal. Even when, for one reason or another, they do not claim to have access to universal and objective notions of justice, they may still believe to be acting in the name of their own mission which transcends mere individualism or subjectivism.

Intellectuals usually treat ethics as superior in importance to knowledge, even though knowledge is acquired through the exercise of reason. Their endeavour is primarily a quest for justice in which truth provides a validating element. Intellectuals' activities are usually motivated by moral rather than analytical considerations. Their job is to judge and advise, not merely to observe; their approach is likely to be polemical and prophetical. Following Max Weber's distinction, the discourse corresponds more to an ethic of absolute ends than to an ethic of responsibility. Intellectuals often eschew the contingencies of economics and politics. Thus their language may, at times, resemble the language of messianism.

Whether they are located on the right or the left of the political spectrum, intellectuals usually call for a holistic conception of society (*Gemeinschaft*). They desire to speak to the nation, the people or the proletariat as a whole. They claim to speak to the people, for the people, and on behalf of the people.

Intellectuals usually react against the individualism that accompanies the dual process of industrialization and secularization. Even though they are themselves by-products of this process, they are seldom comfortable with the full moral implications of liberalism. True, intellectuals, as a social group, evolve best within a liberal environment, since they require an arena in which freedom of expression is well secured, and where they may have an influence on the decision-making process. But this does not preclude intellectuals from despising liberalism as a whole. They may even call for individual rights in the abstract without sharing the individualistic values that sustain these claims.

Sartre, for instance, harboured strong feelings against liberal democracy. He maintained that elections, as we know them, amount to a "trap for bloody fools" ("*piège à cons*"), and he identified the secrecy of the polling booth as the "symbol of all the betrayals an individual may commit against the groups he belongs to"(1973, 1100).

The idea itself of a liberal intellectual – an intellectual who proposes classic liberal values – is almost a contradiction in terms. Liberal intellectuals exist, but they are very rare in the mainstream of intellectualism. They are seen in societies which have inherited the Protestant legacy, where they act to remind the society of its basic values, though they are not recognized as privileged spokespersons. In societies of Catholic origin, liberal intellectuals have until very recently had a hard time making any kind of breakthrough, and when they did make such a breakthrough, it signalled the demise of intellectualism in general.

Individualism works against the influence of intellectuals, since it leaves the responsibility to determine one's own interests and preferences to the individual. Such an ideology is readily seen by intellectuals as leading to an undesirable state of atomization, in which society is left rudderless and where people are easy prey to politicians and other carpetbaggers.

It is at this juncture that we can attempt to understand the apparent disaffection that the public shows today toward intellectuals. Secularized countries with a Catholic background such as France may have maintained through their thinkers and their education systems a disposition that favours the enunciation of public concerns by a group of enlightened individuals. Until recently, the political cultures of such nations were likely to be receptive to intellectuals' political involvement. The mass media readily transmitted the messages of intellectuals, which were expressed through a variety of means: public demonstrations, petitions, interviews, press conferences, communiqués, letters to the editors, articles in newspapers, and so on. It is not possible to determine the degree of receptiveness of the audience as such. We can, however, examine the manifestations of such a receptiveness by considering the importance attributed to intellectuals by their own societies, by politicians (such as de Gaulle who refused to have Sartre arrested during the Algerian War, for, as he said, one does not put Voltaire in prison), by the mass media, and by the general public (who frequently show their support for intellectuals by public demonstrations which, in some cases, extend to impressive funeral processions, as was the case at Sartre's funeral).

By contrast, the ethics and theology of Protestantism, which advocated the priesthood of all believers, contributed to the progressive dilution of the clergy's power. When Protestant societies underwent secularization, they developed ideologies that could only be injurious to the intellectuals' claims to an exclusive status.

Individualism is a legacy of Protestantism. The tenets of Protestantism led to specific values of liberal democracy: the free inquiry into religious matters favoured the expression of liberty, and the priesthood of all believers opened the way for the recognition of equality (Gooch 1954, 8). These two features of liberal democracy are usually attributed to the immediate political arena, but they can be transposed to the wider dimensions of political communication and culture in general.

A nation's press is a good indicator of its political culture. The press reflects the types of relationship people expect from the media as a source of information. It is not surprising that the circulation of daily newspapers per capita is higher in countries of Protestant backgrounds than in their Catholic counterparts. In 1992, the circulation of newspapers in three Scandinavian countries ranked among the highest; in Norway, 606 daily newspapers per 1,000 inhabitants, in Finland, 515; and in Sweden, 511. They were followed by the United Kingdom, 383; Denmark, 332; Germany, 331; New Zealand, 304; the Netherlands, 303; Australia, 261; the United States, 240; Canada, 215; *whereas*, for instance, Venezuela had 208; France, 205; Ireland, 187; Italy, 105; Argentina, 144; Italy, 106; Spain, 105; Brazil, 55; and Portugal, 47. Austria, with 400, Belgium with 310 (around 230 in previous years), and Uruguay with 240 did not follow the trend (UNESCO *Statistical Year Book* 1994). It is worth noting that in Canada the pattern is consistent with the cleavage between

English and French communities; circulation per inhabitant is higher among the former. Even if literacy were the reason for the discrepancy among these countries, which is far from being proven, we might remind ourselves that literacy was originally part of the Protestant strategy to enlarge the fold.

Transmission of information by the daily press is a mode of communication that emphasizes the relevancy of facts to the process of making up one's own mind. It is also very egalitarian because newspapers are accessible to large numbers of people. They are relatively cheap and their style of writing is adapted to the abilities of most people. But reading newspapers implies a double isolation of sorts: the reader is usually isolated from other readers, and the facts are isolated from one another. The world tends to be seen in a compartmentalized fashion, and this occurs on a regular, day-to-day basis. One may surmise that when circulation per head is high, people tend to go over more than one newspaper and compare facts as well as opinions; whereas when circulation is low, readers stick to one paper, if they even read one, and content themselves with opinions that are already familiar to them. One would expect the Protestant world-view to encourage a relativistic approach toward newspaper reading, while the Catholic world-view would lead to readers' identification with one newspaper and its opinions. The Anglo-Saxon tradition of distinguishing neatly between the news, its interpretation, and the editorial pages illustrates the preoccupation of allowing the reader to piece together the events and their significance. This does not mean that this press is more objective, it simply shows that it has adapted to a certain type of communication. The French press, on the other hand, is more likely to introduce spontaneous comments and editorial points of view in the treatment of news.

Intellectuals are less likely to influence regular newspaper readers who are used to comparing and weighing different points of view. If the Catholic tradition is favourable to the emergence of the discourse of intellectuals, the Protestant tradition is more sensitive to the opinions of journalists as they are expressed in comments, anonymous editorials or syndicated columns. The difference corresponds to a somewhat distorted distinction made between the two religions, Catholicism being considered a religion of truth and Protestantism, a religion of opinion. Of course, journalism thrives where the rules of the game are the rules of liberalism.

If the Catholic tradition led to intellectuals who have become involved in national and general political debates, the Protestant tradition, by contrast, has tended to confine the political involvement of scholars to their areas of expertise.

Great Britain, for example, has relied for many years on royal commissions as a means of drawing together policy advisers, particularly academics. The Conservative government of Margaret Thatcher accorded a large role to think-tanks such as the Institute of Economic Affairs, the Centre for Policy Studies, and the Adam Smith Institute. This was probably an astute way of securing a sufficient degree of orthodoxy, of which Mrs Thatcher was so fond.

The United States is, even more than Great Britain, a nation of think-tanks, one need only mention the Rand Corporation, the Brookings Institution, the Heritage Foundation, the Hoover Institution, and a host of others. Their typical function is to contribute to debates of policy. Some are more politically oriented than others; the "advocacy tanks" often adopt militant stances. Funded by government contracts, endowments, fees, private grants, and gifts, think-tanks offer a platform of sorts for scholars and researchers, but it is a role which is highly specialized and institutionalized. In all these cases the opinions expressed are those of specialists who work within the bounds of their respective fields of expertise but who may at times extend beyond them. They are far from being intellectuals as we understand them. They can hardly be compared with novelists, playwrights, and artists who, from a well-established status among the public at large, take it upon themselves to expound on public policies.

In the same fashion, the United States makes use of consultants as immediate advisers to the White House but also in government agencies and bureaucracies. These consultants may even become policy-makers, as did Henry Kissinger during the Nixon administration.

Allan Stoekl's comments come apropos: "In Protestant countries, and especially the United States, the tradition of the authority of anyone and everyone to interpret (correctly) the Bible for him- or herself effectively precluded the formation later of a powerful secular intellectual corps. There may be pragmatists, trained experts and technicians, safely ensconced in government facilities – but not a group of independent but authoritative generalists writing and interpreting for ... the larger public sphere" (1992, 2).

Involvement in actual political debates by intellectuals is rather rare in the United States, at least when compared to those of France. One may recall the open letter of the Ad Hoc Committee for Panama to President Bush; it expressed grievances concerning the American invasion of Panama in search of General Noriega. Members of the committee included author E. L. Doctorow and poet Allen Ginsberg (*New York Times*, 10 January 1990). Woody Allen's exceptional condemnation of Israel's treatment of rioting Palestinians (ibid., 28 January 1988) contrasted with the usual discretion of the actor. One may easily find illustrations of the sort, but they remain, on the whole, relatively isolated cases.

When compared to those of the United States and Great Britain, the Canadian situation is particular, since it opposes the two traditions, Catholic and Protestant, which are reinforced by the two languages of this society, French and English (see Brooks and Gagnon 1988). A comparison between the two experiences, those of French (Catholic) and English (Protestant) Canada, confirms our expectations.

With the secularization process that occurred in Quebec in the 1960s – a process which had been preceded by fifteen years of anticipatory movements (Bélanger 1977) – appeared a generation of intellectuals who dominated the period extending from 1960 to the beginning of the 1980s. Their presence was visible at every level of political life. It was a period of intense mobilization, when even singers and actors joined with writers, professors and artists to promote a politically independent Quebec. But, as in most Western societies, the emergence, and subsequent spread, of individualist values, in the form of the neoliberalism of the 1980s, was concurrent with the decline of the intellectuals' influence. As in France, complaints are heard about their demise, as can be seen in Marc Henry Soulet's book *Le Silence des intellectuels* (1987).

The present recurrence of nationalism in Quebec can no longer be attributed to the ascendancy of the intellectuals, but rather to the action taken by politicians and the reaction of public opinion. During the most recent referendum campaign in the fall of 1995, a number of intellectuals tried to be heard as they had been in a similar campaign in 1980, but found that the rules of the game had changed. The movement did not succeed in rallying to its cause the massive open support it had formerly mustered from artists, actors, and authors. Many of them did commit themselves but not with the same intensity nor with the same enthusiasm. The arena tended to move from the world of artists to the circle of professors, especially social scientists and historians, where it became a debate between people acting as experts. On that occasion, political scientists trespassed the traditional rule of analytical distance in favour of dedicated comments for or against the independence of Quebec. The game unfolded largely among politicians, journalists, and academics whose fields of specialization could be associated with the Canadian crisis.

In English Canada, which was once predominantly Protestant, the Anglo-Saxon model has prevailed. Social scientists are frequently invited to sit on royal commissions, and economists are often consulted by private-sector advisory boards such as the C. D. Howe Institute, the Fraser Institute and the Conference Board.

Recently, one issue raised the collective concern of intellectuals in English Canada: the North American Free Trade Agreement (NAFTA). It was debated extensively during the Canadian election campaign of 1988. Opposed to NAFTA were people from the cultural field such as the Writers' Union, the Artists' Union, and the Alliance of Canadian Cinema, Television, and Radio Artists (ACTRA), all of whom believed that their professional activities were threatened. Counter-arguments were offered by other intellectuals who favoured the deal. Both camps paid for half-page advertisements in newspapers two days before election day. Companies and business organizations became involved to an unprecedented degree in the effort to persuade voters to support the Progressive Conservative party and its commitment to free trade. Full page advertisements in support of the deal appeared in the papers accompanied by lists of firms who favoured the agreement. The issue was a specific one that directly affected writers and artists, and their public involvement amounted to an isolated political intervention in defence of the artists' and writers' own collective interests. It was a far cry from the ideal of disinterestedness which is usually attached to the role of the intellectual.

With the worldwide trend toward liberalism, which in hindsight, is noticeable as early as the 1970s (Bélanger 1990), the intellectuals' audience has tended to shrink severely. Should this trend persist, it will likely mean their complete demise. Intellectuals usually attract audiences when they elaborate their opinions within the confines of large communitarian or collectivist ideologies. Liberalism offers a type of "disenchantment of the world" by giving moral and political responsibilities to individuals and (as intellectuals tend to think) by favouring their prosaic preferences. Some people might construe this last mutation as part of the total secularization process, whereby the liberal stage would be the ultimate stage. Total secularization would thus translate into the withering away of the intellectual. This is a question of interpretation which will not be discussed here.

This analysis is intended to establish and examine the relationship between a religious system of beliefs, Catholic ethics, and the emergence of a category of agents in the political representation of interests, the intellectuals. It was not intended to preclude identical or modified analyses of other religious systems and their relationships to other types of intellectuals. Protestantism, with its priesthood of the faithful, may be an exception among other religions. Furthermore, this discussion was not intended to compare the role of the clergy in Christianity with those played by spiritual leaders in other religions such as Judaism and Islam, or others. Nonetheless, one may infer, from the preceding argument, that it should be possible to estimate the sort of intellectuals that religious systems are likely to produce when secularization occurs. In other words, if we are familiar with the nature of the relationship between the clergy and the faithful, we should be able to outline the characteristics of the clergy's successors who will emerge with secularization.

The model remains an ideal type, which is an approximation of social reality. The model does not, however, offer any predictions about the actual influence of intellectuals, since this was not the purpose of my work. Such a question belongs more to an overall analysis of the representation of interests within systems of decision making. Some cultural systems, as we have seen, are more receptive than others to the self-appointed representative status of intellectuals. It remains to be seen how effectively intellectuals break through the barriers of the political system. In a wider perspective, the phenomenon of intellectualism raises questions about what types of social determinants render certain modes of political representation both legitimate and efficient.

APPENDIX

The Latin American Experience

Even though France has provided the best examples of the ideal intellectual, this does not exclude other countries. Indeed, the French experience is not more representative as such. It may be of greater interest because the process by which the intellectual was legitimized progressed autonomously over centuries, reaching the stage of complete secularization at the beginning of this century.

Thus, it is interesting to compare other Catholic societies with France. Latin American countries offer widely diversified experiences, as do some other European countries, though the latter usually took longer to adopt a purely secular approach to politics.

The model applies well to Latin American countries where the Catholic faith has enjoyed religious hegemony. It is generally agreed that intellectuals have been at the forefront of many political and social movements in Latin America (Crawford 1961, 3–11; Jorrin and Martz 1970, 3). Their presence is noticeable at all stages of the continent's history: at the start of its political emancipation, during the periods of independence and romantic liberalism; and later when positivist and idealist movements were followed by *Aprisma*, Marxism, and socialism. Whether from the right or the left of the political spectrum, *pensadores* have played a recognized role in the process of political change throughout the post-colonial history of Latin America.

As broad a term as "*philosophes*," "*pensadores*" refers to thinkers who are more often than not men of letters. They may also be poets, publicists, or social or political theorists. Some *pensadores* have also become politicians or bureaucrats. In general, the term refers to all those who, in one way or another, seek to interpret their own social reality, first within the borders of their own countries, and second within the confines of Latin America as a whole. Their works belong to an activist tradition and are deeply influenced by the political events of their own societies, which provide the immediate points of reference.

Whether in qualitative or quantitative terms, the ecclesiastical prerequisites for the intellectuals' actions in Latin America are present to a large degree. Great numbers of clerics took an active part in the establishment and operation of the colonies, whether for Spain or Portugal. The part played by religious orders is readily noticeable. The mendicant orders – the Franciscans, Dominicans, Augustinians, and Mercadorians – came first; then followed the Jesuits, who brought with them a more worldly but also a more general outlook.

Under the Spanish Habsburgs (who ruled until 1700), state and Church were closely linked through a patriarchal hierarchy (Graham 1972, 18–20). The Crown enjoyed patronage over the Church; the Crown was responsible for nominations and finances, since it was up to the monarch to collect the tithes and redistribute the sum. For its part, the clergy was highly politicized; it was granted economic and political authority over large plots of land. The Jesuits in particular secured both the material and educational development of whole areas. Members of the clergy could easily assume the functions of viceroy and archbishop at the same time. The extensive involvement of the clergy in politics served as a model of intellectual behaviour and contributed to the high number of lay intellectuals who would later take part in the governance of their respective countries.

With the advent of the French Bourbon dynasty in Spain (from 1700) came reforms inspired by the European Enlightenment: secular absolutism, neomercantilism, and Physiocracy (Rock 1985, 59). The Bourbons maintained the union of Church and state but were more sensitive to the desirability of maintaining the Church as a distinct institution.

At the end of the eighteenth century, Spanish America boasted over twenty universities across the continent, many of them in the hands of Jesuits or Dominicans. Founded in the sixteenth century, the University Saint Marcos of Lima and the Royal and Pontifical University of Mexico accounted for the two most active centres of learning in the Spanish colonies. Universities were entirely faithful to the traditional doctrine of strict obedience to the Church and the monarchy.

Before their expulsion from Brazil in 1759 and from the Spanish colonies in 1767, the Jesuits had built up an impressive network throughout the educational system, which enabled them in some areas to control recruitment for the colonial administration (Rock 1985, 49). They ran a large number of *colegios*, which they concentrated in urban areas such as Lima and Mexico City, just as they had previously done in Córdoba and Buenos Aires. The Jesuits also administered universities like the one in Córdoba that was founded in 1619, and that became a recognized intellectual centre.

Up to the time of their eviction, the Jesuits ensured the spiritual and intellectual cohesion of a whole continent. Because they had access to all levels of education, including university education, the Latin American Jesuits' contribution was both greater than and different from that of their French counterparts whose pedagogical influence was confined, on the whole, to the secondary level. University education, at the time, focused mainly on the training of the clergy in philosophy and theology.

In Latin America, certain features of Enlightenment thought were disseminated by the clergy, largely in the same manner that they had been spread in Spain. Whereas in France the Enlightenment was introduced with a spirit of defiance to the Church, in Latin America, it was managed in a fundamentally eclectic manner; so, for example, Aristotelian physics was criticized in the name of modernization of the science, but no direct implications for Christianity were drawn from these criticisms (Góngora 1975, 179; Stoetzer 1979). Modernizing philosophy meant replacing the monolithic approach of the Scholastics with the open-minded approach necessary for the understanding of history and knowledge in general.

The Jesuits established this new outlook in Latin America as well as in Spain. The Franciscans too, it seems, contributed to eclecticism (Schmitt 1959, 154). Clerical scholars would simultaneously invoke Bacon and Descartes whose perspectives are not readily compatible. The clerics' main concern was with the new experimental method and they would simply ignore or reject those aspects that were in too great contradiction with the Catholic doctrine.

The pro-scientific bent of the Enlightenment was not, in Latin America, interpreted as conveying any anti-religious content in itself. Scholars were more absorbed by the practical aspects of science than by its potential consequences for ideologies (Lockhart and Schwartz 1983, 344–5). One outcome of the teaching of science in Latin America was the rift it emphasized between the educated, who had access to "modernity," and the uneducated, who had none.

There is a certain irony in the expulsion of the Jesuits, since, at the time, they were the religious order that had been most receptive to the Enlightenment and had done the most to diffuse its principles (Góngora 1975, 186). Through their own reading of Enlightenment, the Jesuits bequeathed to their lay successors a mode of reasoning that facilitated the eclectic integration of dissimilar schools of thought. It is in this spirit of eclecticism that one must construe the liberal component found in the independence movement and in many ideological trends that followed.

It is generally agreed that independence, for all of Latin America, meant the substitution of the European aristocracy by a new aristocracy, which in Spanish America was made up of the Creole landowners, Creoles being American-born Spaniards. The new minority took exclusive control of lands and offices and exerted political power on the peasants and the workers, who formed the majority of the population; there was no room for a middle class. Lynch explains the Creoles' motives: "Situated as they were between the Spaniards and the masses, the Creoles wanted more than equality for themselves and less equality for their inferiors" (1973, 28).

The Creoles proved to be the only real beneficiaries of independence, since it granted them monopolistic control over economic and political matters. The situation in Brazil, which was ruled by Portugal, was more or less the same. There, the goal of independence was supported by those classes that desired to break the colonial link in order to free their commercial activities and ensure their administrative autonomy; otherwise, these classes wished to maintain the status quo (Viotti da Costa 1975, 88).

The event of independence that spanned the period from 1810 to 1824 in Latin America did not entail a revolutionary ideology; independence as such was quite conservative. Nevertheless, independence raised two questions that would command a great deal of reflection and consideration: what is the identity of the recently emancipated societies? And what type of legitimate political institutions should replace the former régime?

The Creole Jesuits in exile acted as precursor of the quest for identity that was to haunt Latin America for well over a century. Many thinkers, following the example of these Jesuits, would claim to be guides in the Latin American search for self-definition. As we shall see, such thinkers asserted their role as intellectuals in these nations' quests for national values. The Jesuits must be recognized for their contribution to the patriotic and nationalist movements which followed them, just as they must be acknowledged for their establishment of an eclectic approach that would be used to construe the liberal tradition being imported from Europe and the United States.

Liberalism, in the early stage of its existence in Latin America, served as an ideological instrument to legitimize independence and, for most, the republican institutions. It was a mixture of romantic idealism, utilitarianism, and common sense, though it also showed respect for certain traditional values.

The tradition derived from the teachings of Suarez, as it had been carried over into the eighteenth century, maintained that natural law was distinct from conscience, so that both society and its rulers, as well as individuals, were expected to abide by its precepts. The notion of contract was to be understood, not as the mere delegation of sovereign authority to the monarch, but as an absolute alienation of this authority to him, with provisions for reversal in specific cases bound by very strict rules and reservations. Suarez's works may not have been present in the minds of the liberals of the independence period, but the tradition of natural law was an obvious influence. Here, natural law assumed the form that it had taken for the thinkers of the French Enlightenment, it was considered to be a natural order, one that affected politics and its laws.

Argentine Creole intellectuals such as Mariano Moreno, Manuel Belgrano, and Bernardino Rivadavia believed in natural laws that governed economic and social affairs. They thought that scientific laws of economics existed that required corresponding political structures, and that these laws were part of the natural order of things. Collier's analysis of Chileans in the 1820s can be said to apply to these Argentine intellectuals: "At the back of many Chileans' minds there did exist a comforting feeling that there was a supreme law with which all human laws must, ultimately, be concordant" (1967, 135).

Liberalism in Latin America took different forms depending upon the authors and their regional traditions. To ascribe a single ideology to the entire continent would be an error. Nonetheless, the whole area felt through its thinkers the influence of French and Anglo-Saxon emancipating ideologies. The fascination of Hispanic-Americans with the political institutions of the United States led to constitutions that were closely modelled on the American one; these often included declarations of rights.

In Latin America the time was apparently ripe for liberalism. Many thinkers embraced the new ideology because they saw it as the road leading to modernity.

However, the reception of the liberal precepts and the acceptance of their legitimacy was eclectically selective and thus seldom complete. Adjustments were made which bespeak the attachment to former values. The views of Jeremy Bentham became popular but were also viewed with reservation. José Cecilio del Valle (1780–1834) had many affinities with Bentham but still adhered to the idea of natural law. The same was true of the Chilean (Venezuelan-born) Andrés Bello (1781–1865) who spent twenty years in England and became acquainted with Bentham and James Mill. People were ready to follow Bentham, but they still adhered to the notions of both natural law and the social contract.

The individualism borrowed from liberal thought related well to aristocratic conceptions of honour, pride, and patriotism, which might be termed a chivalrous liberalism. As the Chilean Francisco Bilbao wrote in *Sociabilidad Chilena* (1844), "We must educate (our people) in the theory of individualism and teach them their right to equality and honor" (From Zea 1968, 6).

The declarations of rights, in most constitutions, can be misleading. As in France, they were couched in general terms, and limitations were to be provided by law. It seems that they were designed to conform to and sustain the principles of natural law. The common good was still seen as the ultimate value (Dealy 1968). These constitutions usually provided a place for Catholicism as the state religion; religion, at the time, was not yet a contentious matter. They were more or less liberal, and, as Paz (1961, 116) writes, less rather than more, since they often served as cosmetics for the colonial system, which survived as oligarchies established in the name of freedom.

The ambiguities of this type of eclecticism were resolved by the advent of the *caudillos*, military chiefs who imposed authoritative rule in many countries, thus arresting the growth of the nascent liberalism. The period that followed was one where the vital importance of the intellectuals as a class was loudly proclaimed. Prodded by the pervasiveness of *caudillism* throughout the continent, Latin American thinkers began to develop solutions that went beyond the previous liberal optimism. Many of these intellectuals went into exile. Argentinian intellectuals such as Bartolomé Mitre, Domingo Sarmiento (both of whom would later become president), Juan Bautista Alberdi, and Esteban Echeverria all combated the "barbarism" of Caudillo Rosas' régime (1829–52) from other countries such as Chile or Uruguay. They often expressed themselves in more interventionist terms than their predecessors had done. Their goal was to bring about a complete change in the mentality of the people in order to achieve a new political organization within Argentina. Alberdi banked on massive immigration from Europe and the diffusion of the English language to cleanse the existing value system. Echeverria, who wrote *Dogma Socialista* in 1848, was more radical; he claimed a role for "collective reason," which belonged exclusively to the rational part of the collectivity (Burns 1979, 19). Intellectuals would later make the distinction between government *for* the people and government *by* the people.

Positivism stood as a response to the widespread *caudillism* on the continent. Opponents of the *caudillos* considered their rule anarchic and authoritarian, and they countered this vision with their own conception of a new order for society. The goal was to achieve social progress through order in accordance with Comte's positivist slogan which still today emblazons the Brazilian flag. The attempt to reform society through liberal institutions having failed, it was deemed advisable to adopt a more organic conception of society. Positivism offered the advantage of a scientific claim to modernity while simultaneously advocating a hierarchical model of social relations. The transition to modernity also meant a process of secularization to be administered by scholars; a process, therefore, that put them at the forefront of political action.

One of the great struggles in most Latin American countries at the time revolved around the separation of church and state. So much so, that the religious question served in the nineteenth century, as a means of differentiating so-called liberals from conservatives. The positivists advocated a double emancipation, emancipation from arbitrary rulers, and emancipation from the clergy.

The Mexican positivist Gabino Barreda (1820–80) used Comte's theory of three stages of society to sum up the situation: the first stage, the colonial period, corresponded to Comte's theological stage; the second stage, the war of independence against the European metropolis, to the metaphysical; the third stage, the victory of Benito Juárez over the foreigners, to the scientific. The events did not unfold at the same pace nor with the same intensity throughout Latin America. The brief summary which follows is intended only to outline the traits of the movement through which positivism attracted a great number of advocates. One should not conclude that positivism enjoyed the same popularity throughout the entire continent. In the middle of the nineteenth century, each country was quite ideologically autonomous and each of them encountered a specific intellectual experience. On the whole, though, the scientific pretensions of social thought affected most *pensadores*.

Speaking about positivism in Latin America is to make reference not only to Comte but also to Herbert Spencer. The ideas of the two thinkers were often made to seem compatible through the omission of Spencer's views on individualism and statelessness in industrial society. Latin American thinkers adopted Spencer's law of evolution and his exhaustive use of biology as a model for social theory. Many embraced Comte's conception of a hierarchical and organized society without necessarily accepting the positivist Church and priesthood. Here was eclecticism working at its best, especially as regards Spencer. Latin Americans selected from his thought those aspects that were compatible with their own intellectual culture, and discarded the features that contradicted their traditional values of public good and hierarchy. Just as Bentham's thought had been expurgated because of his radical individualism, so too was the thought of Spencer.

The Latin American advocates of positivism considered it to be fundamentally an operation that was carried out at all levels by intellectuals. Auguste Comte's writings arrived just at the time that the religious issue, the separation of church and state, was coming to the fore. Thus the writings served as a very useful instrument to legitimize a new class in the making. Comte's influence on the political arena in France was indirect, because the religious question came up decades after his death.

The goal of the Latin American positivists was to try to modify the popular mentality. To do so, intellectuals as an institutional body were expected to remodel the cultural structures of society as a whole. Many intellectuals reached the upper rungs of the political ladder, and assumed roles such as president or minister of education in their respective countries. The close association of intellectuals with the political class, if not at times, the actual fusion of the two, should not come as a surprise. This pattern had been set centuries earlier when members of both the clergy and the religious orders maintained close relationships with the government apparatuses, even assuming at times high political offices. The French model is typical of a system in which the clergy assumed a function more distinct from politics. The pattern that developed in France favoured intellectuals who *ideally* would refrain from direct involvement in politics. They were discouraged from becoming party militants, running in elections, or accepting ministerial nominations. In reality not all intellectuals did abstain from such involvement; André Malraux, for instance, became minister of culture under de Gaulle.

Mexico stands out as a place where positivism gained an important intellectual and political status. The triumph of positivism occurred during the long period that was dominated by the regime of Porfirio Díaz.[1] Benito Juárez, who preceded Díaz, had already initiated positivist reforms. Gabino Barreda is illustrative of the generation of "Los Cientificos" who thought of "scientific politics" as the best

---

1 On the Porfirian experience, one may wish to take note of Leopoldo Zea's well diffused interpretation to the effect that Mexican positivism was an ideological instrument of domination under the trappings of scientific parlance (1974, xiii). As follower of Karl Mannheim, he sees Comtean positivism as the expression of a social class, the *bourgeoisie*. (ibid., 130). This interpretation is tempered by Raat (1968).

method by which to govern. Barreda, who occupied a key position in education under Juárez (but was subsequently exiled by Díaz), believed that individual whims could easily ruin any educational system, whatever its qualities. He cited the example of the Jesuits' excellent system, which, he felt, had been marred by their lax system of discipline that allowed for individual interpretation. In a letter to his son Horacio he states that freedom of conscience is anachronistic and that it can lead only to chaos and anarchy (Zea 1974, 113, 208, 210). He believed in the notion of scientific truth in social and political matters and in the subordination of the individuals to the imperative interests of the nation. Barreda wished to revolutionize the educational system in order to mould the Mexican mind in accordance with the requirements of science.

Barreda's case is indicative of a trend that was fairly widespread, but one cannot conclude that all thinkers were as radical as Barreda. Nonetheless, some authors were ready to embrace the entire Comtean system. In Brazil, positivism came to be seen as virtually the official philosophy of the nation. Benjamín Constant, who became minister of education under the provisional government of 1890, adopted the Comtean Religion of Humanity (Cruz-Costa 1964, 87). In Chile, José Victorino Lastarria, who had studied under Andrés Bello, launched the positivist movement, though he maintained a commitment to individualism. But it did not take long for his successors like the Lagarrigue brothers (Juan Enrique, Jorge, and Luis), to advocate the creation of a positivist aristocracy, although such an aristocracy never materialized. Argentina was not immune from the spread of positivism. It was particularly influential at Domingo F. Sarmiento's Normal School at Paraña, which was created in 1870, and which acted as the centre for Comtean positivism in Argentina, even though its enthusiasm was tempered with a dose of individualism borrowed from Spencer. This sensitivity to individualism did not prevent Argentine thinkers from drifting from positivism to socialism and then advocating a mixture of the two. In Argentina, positivism served primarily as a polemical instrument with which intellectuals combated the influence of the Church. In Cuba, positivism took on different connotations since it was also employed as a means of achieving Independence from Spain in 1898. Zea sums up the diversity of positivism in Spanish American nations: "One can say there is a Hispanic American positivism, but it is just as accurate to say there is also a Mexican, Argentine, Uruguayan, Chilean, Peruvian, Bolivian or Cuban positivism" (1966, 29). Zea draws distinctions between the Brazilian and the Spanish American experiences of positivism. Brazil, he claims, tried to adapt positivism to its reality, whereas the Spanish American nations tried to adapt their realities to positivism (ibid., 27). Nonetheless, as he admits, positivism in Hispanic America enjoyed a popularity unlike that of any other philosophical movement, apart from the Scholasticism of the colonial era.

Though it was varied, the positivist experience expressed a deeply felt concern on the part of social thinkers to establish an *estado laico*, a joint elite comprised of intellectuals and statesmen. The means advocated to achieve this goal were diverse, but the intention or the ultimate goal remained to take over the clergy's former socializing and political functions. Social problems were expected to be solved first through intellectual and moral means, and then to be addressed by politicians. Since many intellectuals in Latin America gained ministerial positions in the government, they followed the exact route that clerics had done under colonial rule.

In response to the scientific pretensions, if not the sheer scientism of positivism, the generation of intellectuals during the early twentieth century adopted an idealist conception of politics that relied on intuition. Needless to say, the exercise and expression of intuition were again restricted to the happy few who were sufficiently cultured to make judicious use of it. The famous *Ariel* (1900) by the Uruguayan José Enrique Rodó is usually considered prototypical of Latin American antipositivism. It was widely read and was highly influential; in the book, Rodó advocated arielism, a doctrine which attracted a fair bit of attention in Latin America. *Ariel* calls for a return to classical spiritual and humanist values as opposed to those of materialism and utilitarianism which Rodó observed in his own society. Like the Jesuits, he opposes egalitarianism in favour of some type of selection of leaders; he proposes the creation of a cultured elite who would be able to counter the vulgarity of the masses.

The Argentine writer José Ingenieros was more immersed in the scholarly tradition. At the turn of the century, he had promoted scientism in the study of morality, but in *El hombre mediocre* (1913), he takes a different stance. There he calls for a true moral idealism that is neither metaphysical nor theological but is grounded on the solidarity of human social experience and is, therefore, subject to the laws of evolution. In *Hacia una moral sin dogmas* (1917), Ingenieros proposes that ideals are "natural formations" which "appear when the thought process reaches such a state of development that the imagination can anticipate experience" (In Stabb 1967, 55). Thus, for Ingenieros, idealism is the ability of imagination to foresee the course taken by "humanity," based on and justified by experience. Like Rodó, Ingenieros also believed that the problems of his society stemmed from the masses' refusal to pay heed to the superior ideals of their true leaders (ibid., 56).

The intellectual climate of this period in Latin America also reflected a quest for identity (to borrow the title of Martin S. Stabb's book). The move towards *indigenismo* was obvious in the aspirations voiced by promoters of *Mexicanidad, Perunidad,* and *Argentinidad,* who vied for the rediscovery of America in messianic terms.

In Mexico two major figures stand out, Antonio Caso (1883–1946) and José Vasconcelos (1882–1959). Both belonged to the *Ateneo de la juventud* (Athenaeum of Youth), a group which was founded in 1908 with the purpose of countering the still pervasive positivism of the time. They were part of the generation that accompanied the Revolution of 1910. Writing against positivism, Caso advocates a spiritual conception of ethics, which is based on justice and solidarity, the two elements that constitute the moral unity of persons, though not, significantly, individuals as distinct agents. Caso saw in the Mexican condition a moral problem that could be resolved only by a renewed national conscience. Vasconcelos, who was also reacting strongly against positivism, relied on intuition and even emotion to establish a new humanism based upon a spiritual reality which is beyond the reach of pure reason. He believed that America had a mission that should lead to a spirit of universalism supported by love. The Indian, African, and European components from which the Mexican identity was comprised should have led to a type of mysticism, but this mysticism was derailed by the importation of certain French and English ideas. Vasconcelos associated Protestantism with capitalism; therefore, he attributed to South America a role distinct from that assumed by North America. He openly advocated an aristocracy of the mind that would devote itself to the promotion of the good and the beautiful.

These are several examples of the intense search for the rediscovery and redefinition of Latin America which followed the positivist era. This idealist trend was strong until at least the Second World War. If some authors such as Caso leaned toward the right, others, such as the Mexican Samuel Ramos turned to the left and tried to introduce elements of psychoanalysis and even Marxism into their thought.

Politically speaking, the *Aprista* movement translated the desires for a truly Latin American identity into a political platform. APRA, the *Alianza popular revolucionaria americana,* was founded by writer Raúl Haya de la Torre in Peru in 1924. Ideologically comprised of a mixture of socialism and *indigenismo* (the latter being a way of reintegrating the Indian presence in a number of Latin American cultures), it soon spread to other countries. It promoted the unification of Latin America, denounced the imperialism of the United States, and advocated a program of nationalization of land and industry. Furthermore, it proclaimed solidarity with the oppressed peoples of the world. Sympathy for Marxism was emerging at the time. APRA later laid the foundations for the school of the dependency and would enable intellectuals to assume positions at the forefront of social and political debates.

Pécaut's study (1986) of Brazilian intellectuals sums up a process which is not dissimilar to other Latin American countries. The intellectuals in Brazil saw themselves as carriers of the national identity who also knew the laws of historical development. Like the positivists, these intellectuals established a connection between knowledge and social action. From 1925 to 1940, the Brazilian intellectuals were mostly concerned with constructing a national culture that was not subject to foreign influences. Because they conceived of society and authority as integrated, they saw themselves as privileged representatives. Liberalism was scoffed at and was considered an imported product ill-adapted to Brazil (Pécaut 1986, 23). Later on, between 1954 and 1964, intellectuals became more sensitive to Marxism and tended to combine Marxism with nationalism. As spokespersons for the masses in a class-divided society, Brazilian intellectuals took it upon themselves to raise consciousness in order to prepare for the revolution to come. Pécaut notices that, in 1975, liberal democracy was received as if it were a new idea, and that since 1985, intellectuals have come to realize that political liberalism plants the seeds of division in their ranks (ibid., 283, 473). This rediscovery, if not *the* discovery, of liberalism parallels the trend we observed in France, where it was also followed by lamentations for the intellectuals' fading influence.

The very sketchy profile I have just drawn is intended to suggest two related points: that there is a Latin American tradition of intellectualism, but that it is far from uniform in its expressions. The influence of Catholicism and its ethics on this tradition is indubitable, but there have also been many other cultural influences. Argentina, which is the most European of the Latin American nations, has received large numbers of Italian immigrants as well as a fair number of English and German immigrants; moreover, it has boasted a significant Jewish community. On the other hand, Peru, Bolivia, Ecuador, Mexico, and Guatemala have a high number of Indians in their ethnic composition. And though Brazil is Latin, it is a former Portuguese colony, which makes it distinct from the others. These factors, together with many others, contribute to making up a diversified continent. For a long time the Latin American countries have had a propensity to remain culturally isolated one from one another, thus accentuating their respective distinctiveness.

The purpose of this brief overview of intellectualism in Latin

America is to suggest the relevancy of my model to this continent of Catholic tradition, and to also take into consideration the differences between Latin America and France. The cleric's role in Latin America was not the same as it was in France; thus, neither has been the intellectual's role. The quest for a specific cultural identity, itself a consequence of the colonial past, added a dimension to Latin American intellectualism which was virtually non-existent in France. The nationalism advocated by Maurice Barrès in France, for example, was one of cultural pride and self-defence, not one of soul searching. These variations account for differences in the ways in which intellectuals are socialized and in the cultural challenges they choose to confront. Through this diversity emerges nonetheless a *corps d'élite* whose function is to set means and goals for society as a whole.

The Latin American countries are interesting to examine because, like France, they satisfy the two conditions I have laid down; the nations of Latin America are the inheritors of a Catholic tradition, and they possess totally secularized modes of social authority.

Bibliography

Aaron, Daniel. 1969 (1961). *Writers on the Left.* New York: Avon Books.
Aaron, Richard I. 1971 (1937). *John Locke.* Oxford: Clarendon Press.
Adair, Douglass. 1974. *Fame and the Founding Fathers.* Trevor Colbourn (ed.). New York: W.W. Norton & Co.
Adam, Antoine. 1964. *Les Libertins au xviie Siècle.* Paris: Buchet-Chastel.
– 1967. *Le mouvement philosophique dans la première moitié du xviiie Siècle.* Paris: Société d'édition d'enseignement supérieur.
Adams, R.G. 1958 (1922). *Political Ideas of the American Revolution.* New York: Barnes & Noble.
Adams, Willi Paul. 1980 (1973). *The First American Constitutions.* Chapel Hill: University of North Carolina Press.
Agulhon, Maurice. 1973. *1848 ou l'apprentissage de la République.* Paris: Seuil.
Aldridge, A. Owen. 1971. *The Ibero-American Enlightenment.* Urbana: University of Illinois Press.
Alembert, Jean le Rond d'. 1965 (1805 edit., 1759). *Essai sur les éléments de philosophie.* Hildesheim: Georg Olms.
Allen, Peter. 1985. "S.T. Coleridge's *Church and State* and the Idea of an Intellectual Establishment." *Journal of the History of Ideas* 49, No. 1, (Jan.–Mar.): 89–106.
Alquié, Ferdinand. 1974. *Le Cartésianisme de Malebranche.* Paris: Vrin.
Althusser, Louis. 1971 (1970). "Ideology and Ideological State Apparatuses" in *Lenin and Philosophy.* London: New Left Books.
Altwegg, Jürg. 1989 (1986). *Querelles de Français.* Paris: Grasset.
Anderson, Thomas C. 1979. *The Foundation and Structure of Sartrean Ethics.* Lawrence: Regents Press of Kansas.

Anderson, William. 1955. "The Intention of the Framers: A note on Constitutional Interpretation." *American Political Science Review* 49, No. 2 (June): 340–52.
Andrew, Edward. 1988. *Shylock's Rights*. Toronto: University of Toronto Press.
Annan, N.G. 1955. "The Intellectual Aristocracy." In J.H. Plumb, *Studies in Social History*, 243–87. London: Longmans, Green & Co.
– 1990. *Our Age*. New York: Random House.
Aquinas, Thomas. 1947. *Summa Theologica*. New York: Benziger Brothers.
– 1954. *Selected Political Writings*. A.P. d'Entrèves (ed.). Oxford: Basil Blackwell.
– 1955. *On the Truth of the Catholic Faith. Summa Contra Gentiles*. A.C. Pegis (transl.). Garden City, NY: Hanover House.
Ardal, P.S. 1966. *Passion and Value in Hume's Treatise*. Edinburgh: Edinburgh University Press.
Ardao, Arturo. 1963. "Assimilation and Transformation of Positivism in Latin America." *Journal of the History of Ideas* 24, No. 4, (Oct.–Dec.): 515–22.
Arieli, Yehoshua. 1964. *Individualism and Nationalism in American Ideology*. Cambridge, MA.: Harvard University Press.
Aristotle. 1975. *The Nicomachean Ethics*. Dordrecht: D. Reidel.
Armstrong, R.A. 1966. *Primary and Secondary Precepts in Thomistic Natural Law Teaching*. The Hague: Martinus Nijhoff.
Aron, Raymond. 1962 (1955). *The Opium of the Intellectuals*. New York: W.W. Norton.
– 1983. *Mémoires*. Paris: Julliard.
Aronson, Ronald. 1975–76. "Sartre and the Radical Intellectual's Role." *Science & Society* 39, No. 4. (Winter): 436–49.
Auden, W.H. et al. 1937. *Authors Take Sides on the Spanish War*. London: Left Review.
Aulard, F.A. 1892. *Le Culte de la Raison et le culte de l'Etre suprême*. Paris: Félix Alcan.
Aulotte, Robert. 1979. *Montaigne. Apologie de Raimond Sebond*. Paris: Société d'édition d'enseignement supérieur.
Azevedo, Fernando de. 1950. *Brazilian Culture*. New York: Macmillan.
Badinter, Elizabeth, and Robert Badinter. 1988. *Condorcet*. Paris: Fayard.
Bagge, Dominique. 1952. *Les Idées politiques en France sous la Restauration*. Paris: Presses Universitaires de France.
Bailyn, Bernard (ed.). 1965. *Pamphlets of the American Revolution 1750–1776*. Cambridge, MA: Harvard University Press.
– 1967. *The Ideological Origins of the American Revolution*. Cambridge, MA: Harvard University Press.
Bainton, Roland H. 1956. *The Age of Reformation*. Princeton, NJ: D. Van Nostrand.
– 1964. *Studies on the Reformation*. London: Hodder and Stoughton.

Baker, Keith M. 1975. *Condorcet*. Chicago, IL: University of Chicago Press.
- (ed.). 1987. *The French Revolution and the Creation of Modern Political Culture*. vol. 1. Oxford: Pergamon Press.
Baldwin, Alice M. 1958 (1928). *New England Clergy and the American Revolution*. New York: Frederick Ungar.
Barante, Prosper de. 1878 (1851). *La Vie politique de Royer-Collard*. 2 vols. Paris: Didier et Cie.
Barko, Ivan P. 1961. *L'Esthétique littéraire de Charles Maurras*. Genève: E. Droz.
Barni, Jules. 1970 (1873). *Les Moralistes français au dix-huitième Siècle*. Genève: Slatkine Reprints.
Barral, Pierre (ed.). 1968. *Les Fondateurs de la Troisième République*. Paris: Armand Colin.
Barrès, Maurice. 1902. *Scènes et doctrines du nationalisme*. Paris: Félix Juven.
- 1966 (1917). *Les Diverses familles spirituelles de la France*. In *Oeuvres*, vol. 8. Paris: Club de l'Honnête Homme.
Barret-Kriegel, Blandine. 1989. *Les Droits de l'homme et le droit naturel*. Paris: Presses Universitaires de France.
Barrett, William. 1983. *The Truants*. Garden City, NY: Anchor Books.
Barthélemy-Saint Hilaire, J. 1895. *M. Victor Cousin, sa vie et sa correspondance*. 3 vols. Paris: Félix Alcan & Hachette.
Barthes, Roland. 1970 (1957). *Mythologies*. Paris: Seuil.
- 1978. *Leçon*. Paris: Seuil.
Bastid, Paul. 1966. *Benjamin Constant et sa doctrine*. 2 vols. Paris: Armand Colin.
- 1970. *Sieyès et sa pensée*. Paris: Hachette.
Bauman, Zygmunt. 1987. *Legislators and Interpreters*. Ithaca, NY: Cornell University Press.
Baumgold, Deborah. 1988. *Hobbes's Political Theory*. Cambridge: Cambridge University Press.
Bayet, Alfred, and François Albert. 1917. *Les Ecrivains politiques du XVIIIe Siècle*. Paris: Armand Colin.
Bayle, Pierre. 1968. *Oeuvres diverses*. Hildesheim: George Olms.
Beauvoir, Simone de. 1948 (1947). *Ethics of Ambiguity*. New York: Philosophical Library.
- 1955. *Privilèges*. Paris: Gallimard.
- 1984 (1981). *Adieux: A Farewell to Sartre*. New York: Pantheon Books.
Becker, Carl. 1915. "The Dilemma of Diderot." *Philosophical Review* 24, No. 1: 54–71.
- 1932. *The Heavenly City of the Eighteenth Century Philosophers*. New Haven, Conn.: Yale University Press.
- 1953 (1922). *The Declaration of Independence*. New York: Alfred A. Knopf.
Bélanger, André-J. 1977. *Ruptures et constantes*. Montreal: Hurtubise HMH.
- 1985. *Framework for a Political Sociology*. Toronto: University of Toronto Press.

- 1990. "Political Science: *Die Frau ohne Schatten*, or the Challenges of Liberalism and Nationalism." *Canadian Journal of Political Science* 23, No. 4 (Dec.): 643–52.
Belaunde, Victor Andrés. 1938. *Bolivar and the Political Thought of the Spanish American Revolution*. Baltimore, MD: Johns Hopkins University Press.
Belin, J.-P. 1913. *Le Mouvement philosophique de 1748 à 1789*. Paris: Belin frères.
Bell, Daniel. 1980. *The Winding Passage*. Cambridge, MA: Abt Books.
Bellah, Robert N., Richard Madsen, William M. Sullivan, Ann Swidler, and Steven M. Tipton. 1985. *Habits of the Heart*. Berkeley: University of California Press.
Belot, Gustave. 1921 (1907). *Études de morale positive*. 2 vols. Paris: Félix Alcan.
Benda, Julien. 1928a (1927). *The Great Betrayal*. London: George Routeledge & Sons.
- 1928b. *La Fin de l'éternel*. Paris: Gallimard.
- 1937. *Précision (1930–1937)*. Paris: Gallimard.
- 1968 (1937). *La Jeunesse d'un clerc*. Paris: Gallimard.
Bénéton, Philippe. 1983. *Le Fléau du bien*. Paris: Robert Laffont.
Bénichou, Paul. 1971. *Man and Ethics*. Garden City, NY: Doubleday.
- 1973. *Le Sacre de l'écrivain 1750–1830*. Paris: José Corti.
- 1977. *Le Temps des prophètes*. Paris: Gallimard.
- 1988. *Les Mages romantiques*. Paris: Gallimard.
Benrubi, Isaac. 1926. *Contemporary Thought of France*. London: Williams and Norgate.
Bentham, Jeremy. 1843. *The Works of Jeremy Bentham*. J. Bowring (ed.). vol.1. Edinburgh: William Tait.
- 1948 (1776, 1789). *Fragment of Government and an Introduction to the Principles of Morals and Legislation*. Oxford: Basil Blackwell.
- 1951. *The Theory of Fictions*. In C.K. Ogden, *Bentham's Theory of Fictions*. London: Routledge & Kegan Paul.
Berger, Fred R. 1984. *Happiness, Justice and Freedom: the Moral and Political Philosophy of J. S. Mill*. Berkeley: University of California Press.
Berger, Peter L. 1967. *The Sacred Canopy*. Garden City, NY: Doubleday.
- 1969. *The Social Reality of Religion*. London: Faber & Faber.
Bernauer, James, and David Rasmussen. 1988. *The Final Foucault*. Cambridge, MA: MIT Press.
Bernoville, Gaétan. 1934. *Les Jésuites*. Paris: Bernard Grasset.
Berns, Walter. 1987. *Taking the Constitution Seriously*. New York: Simon & Schuster.
Berr, Henri. 1960. *Du Scepticisme de Gassendi*. Paris: Albin Michel.
Berth, Edouard. 1914. *Les Méfaits des intellectuels*. Paris: Marcel Rivière.
Bertman, Martin A. 1981. *Hobbes: The Natural and the Artifacted Good*. Bern: Peter Lang.

Besterman, Theodore. 1976. *Voltaire*. Oxford: Basil Blackwell.
Bierck, Harold A. (ed.). 1967. *Latin American Civilization*. Boston, MA: Allyn & Bacon.
Blackstone, William T. 1965. *Francis Hutcheson and Contemporary Ethical Theory*. Athens: University of Georgia Press.
Blanchot, Maurice. 1984. "Les intellectuels en question." *Le Débat*, No 29 (Mar.): 3–28.
Bloom, Alexander. 1986. *Prodigal Sons*. New York: Oxford University Press.
Boas, George. 1964. *French Philosophies of the Romantic Period*. New York: Russell & Russell.
Bobbio, Norberto. 1993. *Thomas Hobbes and the Natural Law Tradition*. Chicago, IL: University of Chicago Press.
Bodin, Louis. 1962. *Les Intellectuels*. Paris: Presses Universitaires de France.
Bodin, Louis, and Jean Touchard. 1959. "Les Intellectuels dans la société française contemporaine." *Revue française de Science politique* 9, No. 4 (Dec): 835–59.
– 1961. *Front populaire 1936*. Paris: Armand Colin.
Boehmer, H. 1910. *Les Jésuites*. Paris: Armand Colin.
Boesche, Roger. 1987. *The Strange Liberalism of Alexis de Tocqueville*. Ithaca, NY.: Cornell University Press.
Boggs, Carl. 1993. *Intellectuals and the Crisis of Modernity*. New York: State University of New York Press.
Bon, Frédéric, and M.-A. Burnier. 1971 (1966). *Les Nouveaux intellectuels*. Paris: Seuil.
Bonilla, Frank. 1967. "Cultural Elites." In S.M. Lipset and A. Solari (eds.), *Elites in Latin America*, 233–55. New York: Oxford University Press.
Bonnaud-Lamotte, D., and J.-L. Rispail (eds.). 1989. *Intellectuel(s) des années trente*. Paris: Centre national de la recherche scientifique.
Boorstin, Daniel J. 1953. *The Genius of American Politics*. Chicago, Ill.: University of Chicago Press.
Bossuet, Jacques Bénigne. 1818 (1679). *Politique tirée des propres paroles de l'Écriture sainte*. In *Oeuvres*, vol. 36. Versailles: J.A. Lebel.
Boudon, Raymond. 1981. "L'Intellectuel et ses publics: les singularités françaises." In J.-D. Reynaud and Y. Grafmeyer, *Français, qui êtes-vous?* Paris: Documentation française.
– 1990. "Les Intellectuels et le second marché." *Revue européenne des sciences sociales* 28, No. 87: 89–103.
Bouglé, Célestin. 1907. *Le Solidarisme*. Paris: V. Giard & E Brière.
Bourdieu, Pierre, and J.C. Passeron. 1977 (1970). *Reproduction in Education, Society and Culture*. London: Sage.
– 1980. *Questions de sociologie*. Paris: Minuit.
– 1984. *Homo Academicus*. Paris: Minuit.
– 1989. *La Noblesse d'Etat*. Paris: Minuit.

Bourgeois, Léon. 1906 (1896). *Solidarité*. Paris: Armand Colin.
Bourgin, Hubert. 1970 (1938). *De Jaurès à Léon Blum, l'École normale et la politique*. Paris: Gordon & Breach.
Bourke, Vernon J. 1974. "Is Aquinas a Natural Law Ethicist?" *The Monist* 58, No. 1 (Jan.): 52–66.
Bourricaud, François. 1980. *Le Bricolage idéologique*. Paris: Presses Universitaires de France.
Boutmy, Emile. 1907. *Etudes politiques*. Paris: Armand Colin.
Boutroux, Emile. 1927. *Nouvelles études d'histoire de la philosophie*. Paris: Félix Alcan.
Bové, Paul A. 1986. *Intellectuals in Power*. New York: Columbia University Press.
Brandes, Georg. 1934 (1930). *Voltaire*. New York: Tudor Publishing.
Bréal, Michel. 1881 (1872). *Quelques mots sur l'instruction publique en France*. Paris: Hachette.
Bredin, Jean-Denis. 1983. *L'Affaire*. Paris: Julliard.
Bremond, Henri. 1923–33. *Histoire littéraire du sentiment religieux en France*. Paris: Bloud et Gay.
Brogan, Denis. 1966 "The Intellectual in Great Britain." In H. Malcolm Macdonald (ed.), *The Intellectual in Politics*, 60–73. Austin: University of Texas.
Brooks, Stephen, and Alain G. Gagnon. 1988. *Social Scientists and Politics in Canada*. Kingston & Montreal: McGill-Queen's University Press.
– 1990. *Social Scientists, Policy, and the State*. New York: Praeger.
Brouillard, R. 1941. "Suarez-Théologie pratique." *Dictionnaire théologique catholique* 14, pt 2, 2 691–728. Paris: Letouzey & Ané.
Brown, Oscar J. 1981. *Natural Rectitude and Divine Law in Aquinas*. Toronto: Pontifical Institute of Mediaeval Studies.
Brumfitt, J.H. 1972. *The French Enlightenment*. London: Macmillan.
Brym, Robert J. 1980. *Intellectuals and Politics*. London: George Allen & Unwin.
Bryson, Gladys. 1945. *Man and Society: The Scottish Inquiring of the Eighteenth Century*. Princeton, NJ: Princeton University Press.
Burnier, Michel-Antoine. 1966. *Les Existentialistes et la politique*. Paris: Gallimard.
– 1982. *Le Testament de Sartre*. Paris: Olivier Orban
Burns, E. Bradford. 1979. "Cultures in Conflict: The Implication of Modernization in Nineteenth-Century Latin America." In Richard Bernhard (ed.), *Elites, Masses, and Modernization in Latin America*, 11–77. Austin, TX: University of Texas Press.
Bushnell, David, and Neill Macaulay. 1988. *The Emergence of Latin America in the Nineteenth Century*. New York: Oxford University Press.
Busson, Henri. 1922. *Les Sources et le développement du rationalisme dans la littérature française de la Renaissance*. Paris: Letouzé et Ané.

- 1933. *La Pensée religieuse française de Charron à Pascal.* Paris: Vrin.
- 1957. *Le Rationalisme dans la littérature française de la Renaissance.* Paris: Vrin.
Camp, Roderic A.. 1985. *Intellectuals and the State in Twentieth-Century Mexico.* Austin: University of Texas Press.
Calvert, Susan, and Peter Calvert. 1989. *Argentina: Political Culture and Instability.* Houndmills: Macmillan.
Capaldi, Nicholas. 1989. *Hume's Place in Moral Philosophy.* New York: Peter Lang.
Capitan Peter, Colette. 1972. *Charles Maurras et l'idéologie d'Action française.* Paris: Seuil.
Carey, George W. 1989. *The Federalist.* Urbana: University of Illinois Press.
Cassirer, Ernst. 1953 (1932). *The Platonic Renaissance in England.* Edinburgh: Nelson.
- 1961 (1932, 1951) *The Philosophy of the Enlightenment.* Boston, MA: Beacon Press.
Caute, David. 1964. *Communism and the French Intellectuals.* New York: Macmillan.
Chadwick, Owen. 1968 (1964). *The Reformation.* Harmondsworth: Penguin.
- 1975. *The Secularization of the European Mind in the Nineteenth Century.* Cambridge: Cambridge University Press
Charle, Christophe. 1990. *Naissance des "intellectuels."* Paris: Minuit.
Charlton, D.G. 1959. *Positivist Thought in France during The Second Empire.* Oxford: Clarendon Press.
- 1963. *Secular Religions in France 1815–1870.* London: Oxford University Press.
Charmot, F. (S.J.). 1951. *La Pédagogie des Jésuites.* Paris: Spes.
Charron, Pierre. 1970 (1635). *Oeuvres,* vol. 1. Geneva: Slatkine Reprints.
Chartier, Roger. 1991. *The Cultural Origins of the French Revolution.* Durham NC: Duke University Press.
Chaudhuri, J. (ed.). 1977. *The Non-Lockean Roots of American Democratic Thought.* Tucson: University of Arizona Press.
Chebel d'Appollonia, Ariane. 1991. *Histoire politique des intellectuels en France (1944–54).* 2 vols. Paris: Complexe.
Childress, James F., and David B. Harned (eds.). 1970. *Secularization and the Protestant Prospect.* Philadelphia, PA: Westminster Press.
Chinard, Gilbert. 1979 (1931). *The Correspondence of Jefferson and Du Pont de Nemours.* New York: Arno Press.
Chitnis, A.C. 1976. *The Scottish Enlightenment: A Social History.* London: Croom Helem.
Chomsky, Noam. 1969. *American Power and the New Mandarins.* New York: Pantheon Books.
- 1974. *Peace in the Middle East.* New York: Pantheon Books.

- 1982. *Towards a New Cold War.* New York: Pantheon Books.
- 1983. *The Fatefull Triangle.* Boston, MA: South End Press.
- 1987. *Turning the Tide.* Montreal: Black Rose.
Chomsky, Noam, and Edward S. Hermans. 1979. *The Political Economy of Human Rights.* 2 vols. Boston, MA: South End Press.
Clark, Priscilla P. 1979. "Literary Culture in France and the United States." *American Journal of Sociology* 84, No 5: 1057–77.
Clark, Ronald W. 1976. *The Life of Bertrand Russell.* New York: Knopf.
Clissold, Stephen. 1965. *Latin America, A Cultural Outline.* New York: Harper & Row.
Cohen, Lester H. 1978. "The American Revolution and Natural Law Theory." *Journal of the History of Ideas* 39, No 3 (July–Sept.): 491–502.
Cole, Margaret 1961. *The Story of Fabian Socialism.* Stanford, CA: Stanford University Press.
Coleman, Frank M. 1977. *Hobbes and America.* Toronto: University of Toronto Press.
Coleridge, Samuel Taylor. 1976 (1830). *On the Constitution of the Church and State.* Princeton NJ: Princeton University Press.
Collier, Simon. 1967. *Ideas and Politics of Chilean Independence 1808–1833.* Cambridge: Cambridge University Press.
Colman, John. 1983. *John Locke's Moral Philosophy.* Edinburgh: Edinburgh University Press.
Colombel, Jeannette 1981. *Sartre ou le parti de vivre.* Paris: Grasset.
Compayré, Gabriel. 1880. *Histoire critique des doctrines de l'éducation en France.* 2 vols. Paris: Hachette.
Comte, Auguste. 1854a. *Système de philosophie positive.* 4 vols. Paris: Carilian-Goeury & V. Dalmont.
- 1854b, *Appendice général du système de philosophe positive.* Paris: n.p.
- 1908 (1830). *Cours de philosophie positive.* 6 vols. Paris: Schleicher Frères.
Condorcet, Caritat Marquis de. 1791. *Bibliothèque de l'homme public.* 2nd year, vol 1. Paris: Buisson.
- 1933 (1794). *Esquisse d'un tableau historique des progrès de l'esprit humain.* Paris: Boivin & Cie.
- 1968. *Oeuvres.* O'Connor and Arago (eds.) (1847–49). Stuttgart-Bad Cannstatt: Friedrich Frommann.
Constant, Benjamin. 1957. *Oeuvres.* Paris: Gallimard.
Cooney, Terry A. 1986. *The Rise of the New York Intellectuals.* Madison, WI: University of Wisconsin Press.
Coser, Lewis A. 1965. *Men of Ideas.* New York: Free Press.
- 1973. "The Intellectual as Celebrity." *Dissent* 20, No 1 (Winter): 46–56.
Coste, Brigitte. 1975. *Mably, pour une utopie du bon sens.* Paris: C. Klincksieck.
Cousin, Victor. 1836. *Cours de philosophie sur le fondement des idées absolues du vrai, du beau et du bien.* Paris: Librairie classique et élémentaire de L. Hachette.

- 1850. *Oeuvres de Victor Cousin, Instruction publique.* Paris: Paguerre.
- 1851. *Oeuvres de M. Victor Cousin: Discours politiques.* Paris: Didier.
- 1857. *Philosophie écossaise.* 3e ed. Paris: Librairie nouvelle.
- 1866a. *Fragments philosophiques.* Paris: Didier et Cie.
- 1866b. *Philosophie sensualiste au XVIIIe siècle.* Paris: Didier et Cie.
- 1873 (1829). *Philosophie de Locke.* Paris: Didier et Cie.
- 1895. *Du Bien.* Paris: Librairie académique Didier, Perrin et Cie.

Cousins, Mark, and Athar Hussain. 1984. *Michel Foucault.* New York: St Martin's Press.

Cowling, Maurice. 1963. *Mill and Liberalism.* Cambridge: Cambridge University Press.

Crawford, William R. 1961. *A Century of Latin American Thought.* Cambridge, MA: Harvard University Press.

Crick, Bernard. 1980. *George Orwell.* Boston, MA: Little, Brown & Co.

Crimmins, James E. 1983. "John Brown and the Theological Tradition of Utilitarian Ethics." *History of Political Thought* 4, No. 3 (Winter): 523–50.

Crimmins, James E. (ed.) 1990. *Religion, Secularization and Political Thought.* London: Routledge

Cristiani, L. 1948. *L'Eglise à l'époque du Concile de Trente.* Paris: Blond & Gay.

Crocker, Lester G. 1963. *Nature and Culture: Ethical Thought in the French Enlightenment.* Baltimore, MD: Johns Hopkins Press.

Crocker, Lester G. 1974. *Diderot's Chaotic Order.* Princeton, NJ: Princeton University Press.

Crowley, Francis J. 1938. *Voltaire's Poème sur la loi naturelle.* Berkeley, CA: University of California Press.

Crozier, Michel. 1964. *The Bureaucratic Phenomenon.* Chicago, IL: University of Chicago Press.

Cruz Costa, Joao. 1964 (1956). *A History of Ideas in Brazil.* Berkeley: University of California Press.

Cueva, Mario de la, Miguel Leon-Portillo, and Edmund O'Gorman, et al. (eds). 1966. *Major Trends in Mexican Philosophy.* Notre Dame, IN: Notre Dame Press.

Dahl, Robert A. 1956. *A Preface to Democratic Theory.* Chicago IL: University of Chicago Press.

Dainville, François de (S.J.). 1940. *La Naissance de l'humanisme moderne.* Paris: Beauchesne.

- 1978. *L'Education des Jésuites.* Paris: Editions de Minuit.

Darnton, Robert. 1979. *The Business of Enlightenment.* Cambridge, MA: Harvard University Press.

Davidow, Robert P. (ed). 1986. *Natural Rights and Natural Law.* Fairfax, VA: George Mason University Press.

Davies, Howard. 1987. *Sartre and 'les Temps modernes'.* Cambridge: Cambridge University Press.

Davis, Harold E. 1968. "The History of Ideas in Latin America." *Latin*

American Research Review 3, No. 4: 23–44.
- 1972. *Latin American Thought.* Baton Rouge: Louisiana State University Press.
Dealy, Glen C. 1968. "Prolegomena on the Spanish American Political Tradition." *The Hispanic American Historical Review* 48, No. 1 (Feb.): 37–58.
- 1977. *The Public Man.* Amherst: University of Massachusetts Press.
Debray, Régis. 1980. *Le Scribe.* Paris: Bernard Grasset.
- 1981 (1979). *Teachers, Writers, Celebrities.* London: Verso.
Delbos, Victor. 1924. *Étude de la philosophie de Malebranche.* Paris: Blond & Gay.
Delesalle, Jacques. 1975. *La Morale de Descartes.* 2 vols. Service de reproduction des thèses. Lille: Université de Lille III.
Deleuze, Gilles, and Félix Guattari. 1972. *Capitalisme et Schizophrénie: l'anti-Oedipe.* Paris: Minuit.
- 1977. *Politique et psychanalyse.* Alençon: Des Mots perdus.
Delisle de Sales, J.-B.-C. 1770. *De la Philosophie de la nature.* vol. 1. Amsterdam: Arsklée.
Delumeau, Jean. 1971. *Le Catholicisme entre Luther et Voltaire.* Paris: Presses Universitaires de France.
- 1973. *Naissance et affirmation de la Réforme.* Paris: Presses Universitaires de France.
Derathé, Robert. 1950. *Jean-Jacques Rousseau et la science politique de son temps.* Paris: Presses Universitaires de France.
Derrida, Jacques. 1972. *Marges de la philosophie.* Paris: Minuit.
Descartes, René. 1958 (1953). *Oeuvres et lettres.* Paris: Gallimard.
- 1967. *The Philosophical Works of Descartes.* 2 vols. Cambridge: Cambridge University Press.
Diamond, Martin. 1959."Democracy and the Federalist: a Reconsideration of the Framers' Intent." *American Political Science Review* 53, no.1 (March): 52–68.
- 1977. "Ethics and Politics: The American way." In Robert H. Horwitz, (ed.), *The Moral Foundation of the American Republic,* 39–72. Charlottesville, VA: University Press of Virginia.
Dickens, A.G. 1967 (1959). *The English Reformation.* NY Schocken Books.
- 1966. *Reformation and Society in Sixteenth Century Europe.* London: Thames and Hudson.
Diderot, Denis. 1773. *Collection complète des oeuvres philosophiques, littéraires et dramatiques.* 7 vols. London. no pub.
- 1961. *Pensées philosophiques.* Paul Vernière (ed.). Paris: Garnier.
- 1963. *Oeuvres politiques.* Paul Vernière (ed.) Paris: Garnier.
- 1986. *Oeuvres complètes.* 25 vols. Paris: Hermann.
Dieckmann, Herbert. 1948. *Le Philosophe.* Saint Louis, MS: Washington University Studies.

Dietze, Gottfried. 1965 (1960). *The Federalist.* Baltimore, MD: Johns Hopkins Press.
Diggins, John P. 1984. *The Lost Soul of American Politics.* New York: Basic Books.
Dodge, Guy Howard. 1980. *Benjamin Constant's Philosophy of Liberalism.* Chapel Hill: University of North Carolina Press.
Domenach, Jean-Marie. 1989. "L'Intellectuel aujourd'hui." *Mesure,* no. 2 (Oct.): 105–11.
Donnelly, Francis P. 1934. *Principles of Jesuit Education in Practice.* New York: P.J. Kennedy & Sons.
Donohue, John W. 1963. *Jesuit Education.* New York: Fordham University Press.
Doren, Carl van. (1948) 1969. *The Great Rehearsal,* New York: Viking Press.
Douglass, Elisha P. (1955) 1965. *Rebels and Democrats.* Chicago, IL: Quadrangle Books.
Draper, Theodore. 1984. "Intellectuals in American Politics: Past and Present." In Nissan Oren (ed.), *Intellectuals in Politics,* 15–42. Jerusalem: Magnes Press.
Drescher, Seymour, 1968. *Dilemmas of Democracy, Tocqueville and Modernization.* Pittsburgh, PA: University of Pittsburgh Press.
Dreyfus, Hubert L., and Paul Rabinow. 1983 (1982). *Michel Foucault: Beyond Structuralism and Hermeneutics.* Chicago, IL: University of Chicago Press.
Dunn, John. 1968. "Justice and the Interpretation of Locke's Political Theory." *Political Studies* 16, no. 1: 68–87.
– 1969a. "The Politics of Locke in England and America in the Eighteenth Century." In John W. Yolton (ed.), *John Locke: Problems and Perspectives,* 45–80. Cambridge: Cambridge University Press.
– 1969b. *The Political Thought of John Locke.* London: Cambridge University Press.
– 1984. *Locke.* Oxford: Oxford University Press.
– 1985. *Rethinking Modern Political Theory.* Cambridge: Cambridge University Press.
Du Pont de Nemours, P.S. 1910 (1768). *De l'Origine et des progrès d'une science nouvelle.* Paris: Librairie Paul Geuthner.
Durkheim, Emile. 1938. *L'Évolution pédagogique en France.* Paris: Presses Universitaires de France.
– 1973. *On Morality and Society.* Chicago, IL: University of Chicago Press.
Dworetz, Steven M. 1990. *The Unvarnished Doctrine.* Durham, NC: Duke University Press.
Easton, David. 1965. *A Systems Analysis of Political Life.* New York: John Wiley & Sons.
Ehrard, Jean. 1963. *L'Idée de nature en France dans la première moitié du XVIII Siècle.* 2 vols. Paris: SEVPEN.

Einaudi, Mario. 1938. *The Physiocratic Doctrine of Judicial Control*. Cambridge, MA: Harvard University Press.

Eisenstadt, Abraham S. (ed.). 1988. *Reconsidering Tocqueville's Democracy in America*. New Brunswick, NJ: Rutgers University Press.

Eisenstadt, S.N. 1968. *The Protestant Ethic and Modernization*. New York: Basic Books.

– 1972. "Intellectuals and Tradition." *Daedalus* 101, no. 2 (Spring): 1–19.

Eisenstein, Elizabeth L. 1980 (1979). *The Printing Press as an Agent of Change*. Cambridge: Cambridge University Press.

Encrevé, André. 1985. *Les Protestants en France*. Paris: Stock.

Encrevé, André, and Michel Richard. 1979. *Les Protestants dans les débuts de la III ème République*. Paris: Société de l'Histoire du Protestantisme français.

Epstein, David F. 1984. *The Political Theory of "The Federalist."* Chicago: University of Chicago Press.

Eribon, Didier. 1989. *Michel Foucault*. 2 vols. Paris: Flammarion.

Espinas, Alfred. 1925. *Descartes et la morale*. Paris: Brossard.

Etzioni-Halevy, Eva. 1985. *The Knowledge Elite and the Future of Prophecy*. London: George Allen & Unwin.

Evennett, H.O. 1968. *The Spirit of the Counter-Reformation*. Cambridge: Cambridge University Press.

Fabiani, Jean-Louis. 1988. *Les Philosophes de la République*. Paris: Minuit.

Faguet, Emile. 1891–1903. *Politiques et moralistes du Dix-neuvième Siècle*. 3 vols. Paris: Société française d'imprimerie et de librairie.

Farman, Christopher. 1972. *The General Strike*. London: Rupert Hart-Davis.

Farrell, Allan P. (S.J.). 1938. *The Jesuit Code of Liberal Education*. Milwaukee, WI: Bruce Publishing Co.

Fauré, Christine (ed.). 1988. *Les Déclarations des droits de l'homme de 1789*. Paris: Payot.

Ferrand, Max (ed.). 1966 (1911). *The Records of the Federal Convention of 1787*. 4 vols. New Haven, CT: Yale University Press.

Ferrari, Joseph. 1983 (1849). *Les Philosophes salariés*. Paris: Payot.

Ferry, Luc, and Alain Renaut. 1985. *La Pensée 68*. Paris: Gallimard.

– 1987. *68–86 Itinéraire de l'individu*. Paris: Gallimard.

Figgis, John N. 1956 (1907). *Studies of Political Thought from Gerson to Grotius*. Cambridge: Cambridge University Press.

Finkielkraut, Alain. 1987. *La Défaite de la pensée*. Paris: Gallimard.

Finnis, John. 1980. *Natural Law and Natural Rights*. Oxford: Clarendon Press.

Flynn, Thomas R. 1984. *Sartre and Marxist Existentialism*. Chicago, IL: University of Chicago Press.

Ford, Hugh D. 1965. *A Poets' War*. Philadelphia: University of Pennsylvania Press.

Forsyth, Murray. 1987. *Reason and Revolution*. New York: Holmes & Meier.

Foucault, Michel. 1971 *L'Ordre du discours.* Paris: Gallimard.
- (ed.) 1973. *Moi, Pierre Rivière, ayant égorgé ma mère, ma soeur et mon frère.* Paris: Gallimard-Julliard.
- 1977a. *Discipline and Punish.* London: Allen Lane.
- 1977b. *Language, Counter-Memory, Practice.* Ithaca, NY: Cornell University Press.
- 1980. *Power/Knowledge.* Brighton: Harvester Press.
- 1988. *Politics, Philosophy, Culture.* L.D. Kritzman (ed). New York: Routledge.
Foucault, Michel, and Gilles Deleuze. 1972. "Les Intellectuels et le pouvoir." *L'Arc* 49: 3–10.
Fouillée, Alfred. 1880. *La Science sociale contemporaine.* Paris: Hachette.
- 1896b. *Le Mouvement idéaliste et la réaction contre la science positive.* Paris: Félix Alcan.
- 1899. *Critique des systèmes de morale contemporains.* 4th ed. Paris: Félix Alcan.
- 1900. *La France au point de vue moral.* Paris: Félix Alcan.
Fox-Genovese, Elizabeth. 1976. *The Origins of Physiocracy.* Ithaca, NY: Cornell University Press.
Furtwangler, Albert. 1984. *The Authority of Publius.* Ithaca, NY: Cornell University Press.
Gabaude, Jean-Marc. 1970. *Liberté et raison.* Toulouse: Publications de la Faculté des lettres et sciences humaines de Toulouse.
Galtung, Johan. 1981. "Structure, Culture, and Intellectual Style: an Essay Comparing Saxonic, Teutonic, Gallic, and Nipponic Approaches." *Social Science Information* 20, no. 6: 817–56.
Gandal, Keith. 1986. "Michel Foucault: Intellectual Work and Politics." *Telos,* no. 67 (Spring): 121–34.
Gassendi, Pierre. 1972. *Selected Works of Pierre Gassendi.* Craig Brush (transl. and ed.). New York: Johnson Reprint Co.
Gauchet, Marcel. 1985. *Le Désenchantement du monde.* Paris: Gallimard.
- 1989. *La Révolution des droits de l'homme.* Paris: Gallimard.
Gauthier, David P. 1969. *The Logic of Leviathan.* Oxford: Clarendon Press.
Gavi, Ph., J.-P. Sartre,, and P. Victor. 1974. *On a raison de se révolter.* Paris: Gallimard.
Gay, Peter. 1959. *Voltaire's Politics.* Princeton, NJ: Princeton University Press.
- 1966–1969. *The Enlightenment.* 2 vols. New York: Alfred A. Knopf.
Gella, Aleksander. 1976. *The Intelligentsia and the Intellectuals.* Beverly Hills, CA: Sage.
George, Charles H., and Katherine George. 1961. *The Protestant Mind of the English Reformation, 1570–1640.* Princeton, NJ: Princeton University Press.
George, Robert P. (ed.). 1992. *Natural Law Theory.* Oxford: Clarendon Press.
Gerassi, John. 1989. *Jean-Paul Sartre.* vol. 1. Chicago, IL: University of Chicago Press.
Gierke, Otto 1958 (1913, 1934). *Natural Law and the Theory of Society 1500 to*

1800. Cambridge: Cambridge University Press.
Gillie, Christopher. 1975. *Movements in English Literature 1900–1940*. Cambridge: Cambridge University Press.
Girard, Louis. 1985. *Les Libéraux français 1814–1875*. Paris: Aubier.
Glasner, Peter E. 1977. *The Sociology of Secularisation*. London: Routeledge & Kegan Paul.
Glucksmann, André. 1975. *La Cuisinière et le mangeur d'hommes*. Paris: Seuil.
– 1985. *La Bêtise*. Paris: Seuil.
Godechot, Jacques. 1985 (1951). *Les Institutions de la France sous la Révolution et l'Empire*. Paris: Presses Universitaires de France.
Goerner, E.A. 1979. "On Thomistic Natural Law: the Bad Man's View of Thomistic Natural Right." *Political Theory* 7, No. 1 (Feb.): 101–22.
– 1983. "Thomistic Natural Right: the Good Man's View of Thomistic Natural Law." *Political Theory* 11, No. 3 (Aug.): 393–418.
Góngora, Mario. 1975. *Studies in the Colonial History of Spanish America*. Cambridge: Cambridge University Press.
Gooch, G.P. 1954 (1898). *English Democratic Ideas in the Seventeenth Century*. Cambridge: Cambridge University Press.
Gough, John. 1973 (1950). *John Locke's Political Philosophy*. Oxford: Clarendon Press.
Gouhier, Henri. 1926. *La Philosophie de Malebranche et son expérience religieuse*. Paris: Vrin.
– 1962. *La Pensée métaphysique de Descartes*. Paris: Vrin.
– 1972 (1924). *La Pensée religieuse de Descartes*. Paris: Vrin.
Gouldner, Alvin W. 1979. *The Future of Intellectuals and the Rise of the New Class*. New York: Seabury Press.
Goyard-Fabre, Simone. 1972. *La Philosophie des lumières en France*. Paris: Librairie C. Klincksieck.
– 1973. *La Philosophie du droit de Montesquieu*. Paris: Klincksieck.
Gracia, Jorge J.E. 1986. *Latin American Philosophy*. Buffalo, NY: Prometheus Books.
Graham, Richard. 1972. *Independence in Latin America*. New York: Alfred A. Knopf.
Graham, Richard, and Peter H. Smith (Eds.) 1974. *New Approaches of Latin American History*. Austin: University of Texas Press.
GRAL. 1979. *Intellectuels et Etat au Mexique au XXe siècle*. Paris: Conseil national de la recherche scientifique.
Gray, John. 1983. *Mill on Liberty: A Defence*. London: Routledge & Kegan Paul.
Grean, Stanley. 1967. *Shaftesbury's Philosophy of Religion and Ethics*. Athens: Ohio University Press.
Greene, Jack P. (ed.). 1979 (1968). *The Reinterpretation of the American Revolution 1763–1789*. Westport, CT: Greenwood Press.
Gueroult, Martial. 1955–59. *Malebranche*. 3 vols. Paris: Aubier.
Guerrier, W. 1971 (1886). *L'Abbé de Mably*. Geneva: Slatkine Reprints.

Guillermou, Alain. 1961. *Les Jésuites*. Paris: Presses Universitaires de France.

Guizot, François. 1864–68. *Méditations sur l'essence de la religion chrétienne*. 3 vols. Paris: Michel Lévy et frères.

– 1869. *Mélanges politiques et historiques*. Paris: Michel Lévy et frères.

– 1882 (1851). *Méditations et études morales*. Paris: Didier & Cie.

Gunn, J. Alexander. 1922. *Modern French Philosophy*. London: T. Fisher Unwin.

Gusdorf, Georges. 1988. "La France, pays des droits de l'homme." *Droits*, no. 8: 23–31.

Haakonssen, Knud. 1988. "Moral Philosophy and Natural Law: From the Cambridge Platonists to the Scottish Enlightenment." *Political Science* 10, No. 1 (July): 97–100.

– 1996. *Natural Law and Moral Philosophy*. Cambridge: Cambridge University Press.

Hale, Charles A. 1968. *Mexican Liberalism in the Age of Mora*. New Haven, CT: Yale University Press.

– 1989. *The Transformation of Liberalism in Late Nineteenth-Century Mexico*. Princeton, NJ: Princeton University Press.

Halévy, Elie. 1972 (1901–4). *The Growth of Philosophic Radicalism*. Clifton, NJ: Augustus M. Kelley.

Hall, John A. 1979. "The Curious Case of the English Intelligentsia." *British Journal of Sociology* 30, no 3 (Sept.): 291–306.

Halls, W.D. 1976. *Education, Culture and Politics in Modern France*. Oxford: Pergamon Press.

Halperin-Donghi, Tulio. 1973. *The Aftermath of Revolution in Latin America*. New York: Harper & Row.

Hamburger, Joseph. 1965. *Intellectuals in Politics*. New Haven, NJ: Yale University Press.

Hamilton, A., J. Jay, and J. Madison (1787). *The Federalist*. New York: Modern Library.

Hamilton, Bernice. 1963. *Political Thought in Sixteenth Century Spain*. Oxford: Clarendon Press.

Hamon, Hervé, and Patrick Rotman. 1981. *Les Intellocrates*. Paris: Ramsay.

– 1987–88. *Génération*. 2 vols. Paris: Seuil.

Hancock, Ralph C. 1989. *Calvin and the Foundations of Modern Politics*. Ithaca, NJ: Cornell University Press.

Harris, Louis K., and Victor Alba. 1974. *The Political Culture and Behavior of Latin America*. Kent, OH: Kent State University Press.

Harrison, Jonathan. 1976. *Hume's Moral Epistemology*. Oxford: Clarendon Press.

Hartz, Louis. 1955. *The Liberal Tradition in America*. New York: Harcourt Brace & Co.

– (ed). 1964. *The Founding of New Societies*. New York: Harcourt, Brace and World.

Hawkins, Richmond L. 1936. *Positivism in the United States (1853–61)*.

Cambridge, MA: Harvard University Press.
Hawthorn, Geoffrey. 1987 (1976). *Enlightenment and Despair.* Cambridge: Cambridge University Press.
Hayward, J.E.S. 1961. "The Official Social Philosophy of the French Third Republic: Léon Bourgeois and Solidarism." *International Review of Social History* 61: 19–48.
Hazard, Paul. 1953 (1935). *The European Mind 1680–1715.* New Haven, CT: Yale University Press.
– 1954 (1946). *European Thought in the Eighteenth Century.* New Haven, Conn.: Yale University Press.
Head, Brian, and James Walter (Eds). 1988. *Intellectual Movements and Australian Society.* Oxford: Oxford University Press.
Heath, Dwight B., and R.N. Adams (eds). 1965. *Contemporary Cultures and Societies of Latin America.* New York: Random House.
Heidegger, Martin. 1976. *Basic Writings.* New York: Harper & Row.
Heimert, Alan. 1966. *Religion and the American Mind.* Cambridge, MA: Harvard University Press.
Helvétius, Claude Adrien. 1967–69 (1795). *Oeuvres complètes.* 14 vols. Hildesheim: Georg Olms.
Herbert, Gary B. 1989. *Thomas Hobbes, The Unity of Scientific and Moral Wisdom.* Vancouver: University of British Columbia Press.
Herr, Richard. 1958. *The Eighteenth-Century Revolution in Spain.* Princeton NJ: Princeton University Press.
Higham, John, and Paul K. Conkin (eds). 1979. *New Directions in American Intellectual History.* Baltimore, MD: Johns Hopkins University Press.
Hill, Christopher. 1975. *Change and Continuity in Seventeenth Century England.* Cambridge, MA: Harvard University Press.
Himmelfarb, Gertrude. 1968. *Victorian Minds.* London: Weidenfeld and Nicolson.
– 1974. *On Liberty and Liberalism.* New York: Knopf.
Hirschman, Albert O. 1977. *The Passions and the Interests.* Princeton NJ: Princeton University Press.
Hobbes, Thomas. 1965 (1651). *Leviathan.* Oxford: Clarendon Press.
Hoberman, Louisa S. 1980. "Hispanic American Political Theory as a Distinct Tradition." *Journal of the History of Ideas* 41, no. 2 (Apr.–June): 199–218.
Hofstadter, Richard. 1957 (1948). *The American Political Tradition and the Men Who Made It.* New York: Alfred A. Knopf.
– 1963 (1962). *Anti-intellectualism in American Life.* New York: Vintage Books.
– 1969. "A Constitution against Parties: Madisonian Pluralism and the Anti-Party Tradition." *Government and Opposition* 4, no. 3 (Summer): 345–66.
Holbach, Paul-Henri Thiry d'. 1967 (1776). *Ethocratie.* Paris: Editions d'Histoire sociale.

- 1969 (1773). *Système social.* 3 vols. Hildesheim: Georg Olms.
- 1970 (1776). *La Morale universelle.* 3 vols. Stuttgart-Bad Cannstatt: Friedrich Frommann.
- 1971 (1773). *La Politique naturelle.* 2 vols. Hildesheim: Georg Olms.

Hollander, Paul. 1981. *Political Pilgrims.* New York: Oxford University Press.

Holmes, Stephen. 1984. *Benjamin Constant and the Making of Modern Liberalism.* New Haven, CT: Yale University Press.

Hont, I, and M. Ignatieff (eds). 1983. *Wealth and Virtue.* Cambridge: Cambridge University Press.

Hood, F.C. 1964. *The Divine Politics of Thomas Hobbes.* Oxford: Clarendon Press.

Hooker, Richard. 1977 (1888). *The Works.* vol. 1. Hidelsheim: Georg Olms.

Howe, Daniel W. 1987. "The Political Psychology of *The Federalist.*" *The William and Mary Quarterly.* (3rd) 14; no. 3 (July): 485–509.

Howe, Irving. 1968. "The New York Intellectuals, a Chronicle and a Critique." *Commentary* 46, no.4 (Oct.): 29–51.

Huber, J. 1875. *Les Jésuites.* 2 vols. Paris: Sandoz & Fischerbacher.

Hume, David. n.d. *Essays Literary, Moral and Political* Including "An Enquiry concerning the Principles of Morals." London: George Routeledge & Sons.
- 1896 (1739). *A Treatise of Human Nature.* Oxford: Clarendon Press.

Humphreys, R.A. 1976 (1937). "The rule of Law and the American Revolution." In John R. Howe, *The Role of Ideology in the American Revolution,* 20–27. New York: Holt, Rinehardt and Winston.

Humphreys, R.A., and J. Lynch. 1965. *The Origins of the Latin American Revolutions.* New York: Alfred A. Knopf.

Hunt, Lynn. 1984. *Politics, Culture, and Class in the French Revolution.* Berkeley: University of California Press.

Huyler, Jerome. 1995. *Locke in America.* Lawrence: University of Kansas Press.

Hynes, Samuel. 1976. *The Auden Generation.* London: Bodley Head.

Isambert-Jamati, Viviane. 1970. *Crises de la société crise de l'enseignement.* Paris: Presses Universitaires de France.

Jacoby, Russell 1983. "Graying of the Intellectuals." *Dissent* 30, no. 2 (Spring): 234–37
- 1987. *The Last Intellectuals.* New York: Basic Books.

Jarlot, Georges. 1949. "Les Idées politiques de Suarez et le pouvoir absolu." *Archives de Philosophie* 18: 64–107.

Jaume, Lucien. 1989. *Le Discours jacobin et la démocratie.* Paris: Fayard.

Jeanson, Francis. 1980 (1947). *Sartre and the Problem of Morality.* Bloomington, IN: Indiana University Press.

Jefferson, Thomas. 1944. *The Life and Selected Writings of Thomas Jefferson.* Adrienne Koch and William Peden (eds.). New York: Modern Library.

Jellinek, George. 1902. *La Déclaration des droits de l'homme et du citoyen.* Paris:

Albert Fontemoing.

Jenkins, J.J. 1967. "Locke and Natural Rights." *Philosophy* 42, 160 (April): 149–54.

Jette, Marie Henri. 1958 (1956). *France religieuse du XVIIIme Siècle*. Paris: Casterman.

Johnson, J.J., P.J. Bakewell, and M.D. Dodge (eds.) 1985. *Readings in Latin American History* vol. 2. Durham: Duke University Press.

Johnstone, J.K. 1954. *The Bloomsbury Group*. London: Secker & Warburg.

Jorrin, Miguel, and John D. Martz. 1970. *Latin-American Political Thought* Chapel Hill, NC: University of North Carolina Press.

Jouffroy, Théodore. 1876 (1833–34). *Cours de Droit naturel*. 5th ed. 2 vols. Paris: Hachette.

– 1886 (1833). *Mélanges philosophiques*. Paris: Hachette.

Judt, Tony. 1992. *Past Imperfect: French Intellectuals, 1944–56*. Berkeley, CA: University of California Press.

Jouvenel, Bertrand de. 1947. "Essai sur la politique de Rousseau." In J.J. Rousseau, *Du Contrat Social*. Geneva: Cheval ailé.

Kadushin, Charles. 1974. *The American Intellectual Elite*. Boston, MA: Little, Brown & Co.

Kandel, I.L. 1924. *The Reform of Secondary Education in France*. New York: Teachers College, Columbia University.

Kantor, Harry. 1966. *The Ideology and Program of the Peruvian Aprista Movement*. New York: Octagon.

Kavka, Gregory S. 1986. *Hobbesian Moral and Political Theory*. Princeton NJ: Princeton University Press.

Kelly, George Armstrong. 1987. "Parnassian Liberalism in Nineteenth-Century France. Tocqueville, Renan, Flaubert." *History of Political Thought* 8, no. 3 (Winter): 476–503.

Kemp, J. 1970. *Ethical Naturalism: Hobbes and Hume*. London: Macmillan.

Kenyon, Cecelia M. 1955. "Men of Little Faith: The Anti-Federalists on the Nature of Representative Government." *The William and Mary Quarterly* (3rd) 12, no. 1: 3–43.

– 1966. *The Antifederalists*. Indianapolis, IN: Bobbs-Merrill.

Keohane, Nannerl O. 1980. *Philosophy and the State in France*. Princeton NJ: Princeton University Press.

Khilnani, Sunil. 1993. *Arguing Revolution: the Intellectual Left in Postwar France*. New Haven, CT: Yale University Press.

Knight, Isabel F. 1968. *The Geometric Spirit*. New Haven, CT: Yale University Press.

Knights, Ben. 1978. *The Idea of the Clerisy in the Nineteenth Century*. Cambridge: Cambridge University Press.

Koch, Adrienne. 1943. *The Philosophy of Thomas Jefferson*. New York: Columbia University Press.

Kogel, Renée. 1972. *Pierre Charron*. Genève: Librairie Droz.
Konrad, George and Istvan Szelenyi. 1979. *Intellectuals on the Road to Class Power*. New York: Harcourt, Brace & Jovanovich.
Kornhauser, William. 1959. *The Politics of Mass Society*. Glencoe, IL: Free Press.
Kors, Alan Charles. 1976. *D'Holbach's Coterie*. Princeton NJ: Princeton University Press.
Kors, A.C., and P.J. Korshin. 1987. *Anticipations of the Enlightenment in England, France and Germany*. Philadelphia: University of Pennsylvania Press.
Kramnick, Isaac. 1968. *Bolingbrooke and his Circle*. Cambridge, MA: Harvard University Press.
– 1988. "The Great National Decision: the Discourse of Politics in 1787." *The William and Mary Quarterly* (3rd) 45, no. 1.(Jan.): 3–32.
– 1990. *Republicanism and Bourgeois Radicalism*. Ithaca, NY: Cornell University Press.
Krieger, Leonard. 1965. *The Politics of Discretion*. Chicago, IL: University of Chicago Press.
– 1975. *An Essay on the Theory of Enlightened Despotism*. Chicago IL: University of Chicago Press.
Kurland, Philip B., and R. Lerner (eds). 1987. *The Founders' Constitution*. 5 vols. Chicago, IL: University of Chicago Press.
Laboulaye, Edouard. 1869 (1863). *Le Parti libéral, son programme et son avenir*. 7th ed. Paris: Charpentier.
Labrousse, Roger. 1938. *Essai sur la philosophie de l'ancienne Espagne*. Paris: Sirey.
Ladd, Everett C., Jr. 1962. "Helvétius and d'Holbach: "La moralisation de la politique."*Journal of the History of Ideas* 23, no. 1 (Jan.–Mar.): 221–38.
– 1969. "Professors and Political Petitions." *Science* 163, no. 3874 (28 Mar.): 1425.
Lagarde, Georges de. 1926. *Recherches sur l'esprit politique de la Réforme*. Paris: Auguste Picard.
Lamberti, Jean-Claude. 1970. *La Notion d'individualisme chez Tocqueville*. Paris: Presses Universitaires de France.
– 1989 (1983). *Tocqueville and the Two Democracies*. Cambridge, MA: Harvard University Press.
La Mettrie, Julien Offray de. 1970. *Oeuvres philosophiques*. 2 vols. Hildesheim: Georg Olms.
– 1981 (1750). *Discours préliminaire*. In Ann Thomson, *Materialism and Society in the Mid-Eighteenth Century: La Mettrie's Discourse préliminaire*. Genève: Droz.
Lamont, Michèle. 1987a. "The Production of Culture in France and the United States Since World War II." In Alain G. Gagnon, *Intellectuals in Liberal Democracies*, 167–78. New York: Praeger.

– 1987b. "How to Become a Dominant French Philosopher: The Case of Jacques Derrida." *American Journal of Sociology* 93, no. 3 (Nov.): 584–622.

Lanfrey, P. 1857. *L'Église et les philosophes au XVIII ème Siècle*. Paris: Pagnerre.

Lanning, John Tate. 1940. *Academic Culture in the Spanish Colonies*. London: Oxford University Press.

Laporte, Jean. 1959 (1945). *Le Rationalisme de Descartes*. Paris: Presses Universitaires de France.

Lasch, Christopher. 1965. *The New Radicalism in America*. New York: Alfred A. Knopf.

Laski, Harold J. 1936. *The Rise of European Liberalism*. London: George Allen & Unwin.

Laslett, Peter. 1967 (1960). "Introduction." In John Locke, *Two Treatises of Government*. Cambridge: Cambridge University Press.

Latreille, A., E. Delaruelle, and J.R. Palanque. *Histoire du catholicisme en France*. 2 vols. Paris: Spes.

Laval-Reviglio, Marie-Claire. 1987. "Les Conceptions politiques des physiocrates." *Revue française de science politique* 37, no. 2 (April): 181–213.

Le Goff, Jacques, and René Rémond (eds). 1988. *Histoire de la France religieuse* vol. 2. Paris: Seuil.

Lehmann, Hartmut, and Guenther Roth (eds.). 1993. *Weber's Protestant Ethic*. Washington DC: Cambridge University Press.

Legrand, Louis. 1961. *L'Influence du positivisme dans l'oeuvre scolaire de Jules Ferry*. Paris: Marcel Rivière et Cie.

Lemée, Pierre. 1954. *Julien Offray de la Mettrie*. Mortain: Imprimerie du Mortainais.

LeMercier de la Rivière, Paul-Pierre. 1910 (1767). *L'Ordre naturel et essentiel des sociétés politiques*. Paris: Librairie Paul Geuthner.

Lemert, Charles C. 1981a. "Literary Politics and the *Champ* of French Sociology." *Theory and Society* 10, no. 5 (Sept.): 645–69.

– 1981b. *French Sociology*. New York: Columbia University Press.

– 1991. *Intellectuals and Politics*. Newsbury Park, CA: Sage.

Lempérière, Annick. 1992. *Intellectuels, État et société au Mexique*. Paris: L'Harmattan.

Leroux, Pierre. 1846. *D'une Religion nationale, ou du culte*. Paris: A. Boussac.

Leroy, Géraldi. 1983. *Les Écrivains et l'Affaire Dreyfus*. Paris: Presses Universitaires de France.

Leroy, Géraldi, and Anne Roche. 1986. *Les Écrivains et le Front populaire*. Paris: Presses de la Fondation nationale des sciences politiques.

Leroy, Maxime. 1962. *Histoire des idées sociales en France*. Paris: Gallimard.

Le Trosne, Guillaume François. 1980 (1777). *De L'Ordre social*. München: Kraus Reprint.

Lévy, Bernard-Henri. 1977. *La Barbarie à visage humain*. Paris: Grasset.

– 1987. *Éloge des intellectuels*. Paris: Grasset.

– 1991. *Les Aventures de la liberté.* Paris: Grasset.
Levy, Leonard W. 1988. *Original Intent and the Framers' Constitution.* New York: Macmillan.
Lévy-Bruhl, Lucien. 1899a. *History of Modern Phisosophy in France.* Chicago: Open Court Publishing Co.
– 1899b. *Lettres inédites de John Stuart Mill à Auguste Comte.* Paris: Félix Alcan.
– 1913. *La Philosophie d'Auguste Comte.* Paris: Félix Alcan.
– 1937 (1903). *La Morale et la science des moeurs.* Paris: Félix Alcan.
Leyden, W. von. 1954. "Introduction." In John Locke, *Essays on the Law of Nature,* 1–92. Oxford: Clarendon Press.
– 1956. "John Locke and Natural Law." *Philosophy* 31, No. 116 (Jan.): 23–35.
Lindenberg, Daniel, 1990. *Les Années souterraines.* Paris: La Découverte.
Lipovetsky, Gilles. 1983. *L'Ère du vide.* Paris: Gallimard.
Lipp, Solomon. 1969. *Three Argentine Thinkers.* New York: Philosophical Library.
Lipset, Seymour M. 1959. "American Intellectuals: Their Politics and Status." *Daedalus* 88, no. 3 (Summer): 460–86.
– 1963 (1959). *Political Man.* Garden City, NY: Doubleday.
– 1964 (1963). *The First New Nation.* London: Heinemann.
Lipset, S.M., and A. Basu. 1975. "Intellectual Types and Political Roles." In L.A. Coser (ed.), *The Idea of Social Structure,* 433–70. New York: Harcourt Brace Jovanovich.
Lipset, S.M., and R.B. Dobson. 1972. "The Intellectual as Critic and Rebel: with Special Reference to the United States and the Soviet Union." *Daedalus* 101, no. 3 (Summer): 137–98.
Littré, Émile. 1866. *Auguste Comte et Stuart Mill.* Paris: G. Baillière.
– 1876. *Fragments de philosophie positive.* Paris: Bureaux de la philosophie positive.
– 1877. *Auguste Comte et la philosophie positive.* 3rd ed. Paris: Bureaux de la philosophie positive.
Lively, Jack. 1962. *The Social and Political Thought of Alexis de Tocqueville* Oxford: Clarendon Press.
Locke, John. 1948 (1690). *The Second Treatise of Civil Government* and *A Letter concerning Toleration.* Oxford: Basil Blackwell.
– 1954 (1676). *Essays on the Law of Nature.* Oxford: Clarendon Press.
– 1963 (1689). *Essay Concerning Human Understanding in Works.* vols. 1–3. Darmstadt: Scientia Verlag Aalen.
Lockhart, James, and Stuart B. Schwartz. 1983. *Early Latin America.* Cambridge: Cambridge University Press.
Loeb, Louis E. 1988. "Was Descartes Sincere in his Appeal to the Natural Light?" *Journal of the History of Philosophy* 26, no. 3 (July): 377–406.
Longstaff, S.A. 1976. "The New York Family." *Queen's Quarterly* 83, no.4 (Winter): 556–73.

Lottin, Dom Odon. 1931. *Le Droit naturel chez Saint Thomas d'Aquin*. Bruges: Charles Beyaert.
– 1950. "La Valeur des formules de Saint Thomas d'Aquin concernant la loi naturelle." In *Mélanges Joseph Maréchal*, 345–77. vol 2. Paris: Desclée de Brouwer.
Loubet del Bayle. 1969. *Les Non-conformistes des années 30*. Paris: Seuil.
Lottman, Herbert. 1982. *The Left Bank*. Boston, MA: Houghton Mifflin.
Lough, John. 1975. "Who were the *Philosophes?*" In J.H. Fox, M.H. Waddicor, and D.A. Watts (eds.), *Studies in the Eighteenth-Century French Literature presented to Robert Niklaus*, 139–49. Exeter: University of Exeter.
– 1982. *The Philosophes and Post-Revolutionary France*. Oxford: Clarendon Press.
Lourau, René. 1981. *Le Lapsus des intellectuels*. Paris: Privat.
Lynch, John. 1973. *The Spanish American Revolutions 1808–1826*. New York: W.W. Norton.
Lynd, Staughton. 1968. *Intellectual Origins of American Radicalism*. New York: Pantheon Books.
Lyons, David. 1973. *In the Interest of the Governed*. Oxford: Clarendon Press.
Lyotard, Jean-François. 1973. *Dérive à partir de Marx et Freud*. Paris: 10/18.
– 1984. *Tombeau de l'intellectuel et autres papiers*. Paris: Editions Galilée.
Mably, Abbé de. 1789. *Oeuvres complètes*. 12 vols. London: no publ.
– 1821. *Oeuvres complètes*. "Oeuvres posthumes." vols. 13–15. Paris: Guillaume et Cie.
Mace, George. 1979. *Locke, Hobbes, and the Federalist Papers*. Carbondale, IL: Southern Illinois University Press.
Mackie, J. L. 1980. *Hume's Moral Theory*. London: Routeledge & Kegan Paul.
MacLachlan, 1988. *Spain's Empire in the New World* Berkeley, CA.: University of California Press.
Maclean, Ian, Alan Montefiore, and Peter Winch (eds). 1990. *The Political Responsibility of Intellectuals*. Cambridge: Cambridge University Press.
Macpherson, C.B. 1962. *The Political Theory of Possessive Individualism*. London: Oxford University Press.
Madison, James. 1953. *The Complete Madison*. Saul K. Padover (ed.). New York: Harper and Row.
Maier, Joseph, and Richard W. Weatherhand. 1979. *The Latin American University*. Albuquerque: University of New Mexico Press.
Maistre, Joseph de. n.d. (1821). *Les Soirées de Saint-Pétersbourg*. Paris: Garnier Frères.
– 1988 (1797). *Considérations sur la France*. Paris: Complexe.
Malebranche, Nicolas. 1879 (1712). *De la Recherche de la vérité*. 2 vols. Paris: Garnier.
– 1939 (1707). *Traité de morale*. Paris: Vrin.
Manent, Pierre. 1982. *Tocqueville et la nature de la démocratie*. Paris: Julliard.

Marshall, Gordon 1982. *In Search of the Spirit of Capitalism.* New York: Columbia University Press.
Martin, David. 1978. *A General Theory of Secularization.* New York: Harper & Row.
Martin, Kingsley. 1954 (1929). *French Liberal Thought in the Eighteenth Century.* London: Turnstile Press.
– 1980. *The Rise of French Liberal Thought.* Princeton NJ: Princeton University Press.
Martz, John D. 1971 (1966). "Characteristics of Latin American Political Thought." In *Dynamics of Change in Latin American Politics.* Englewood Cliffs, NJ: Prentice Hall.
Mason, John H. 1982. *The Irresistible Diderot.* London: Quartet Books.
Mason, Sheila M. 1975. *Montesquieu's Idea of Justice.* The Hague: Martinus Nijhoff.
Matthews, Richard K. 1984. *The Radical Politics of Thomas Jefferson.* Lawrence, KS: University Press of Kansas.
Maurras, Charles. 1905. *L'Avenir de l'intelligence.* Paris: Albert Fontemoing.
– 1912a (1898). *Trois Idées politiques.* Paris: Honoré & Edouard Champion.
– 1912b. *La Politique religieuse.* Paris: Nouvelle Librairie nationale.
– 1937. *Mes Idées politiques.* Paris: Arthème Fayard.
– 1972. *De la Politique naturelle au nationalisme intégral.* Paris: Vrin.
May, Henry F. 1976. *The Enlightenment in America.* New York: Oxford University Press.
Mayer, Jacob. P. 1942. *Political Thought in France from Sieyès to Sorel.* London: Faber and Faber.
McCloskey, H.J.M. 1971. *John Stuart Mill: A Critical Study.* London: Macmillan.
McDonald, Forrest. 1985. *Novus Ordo Seclorum: The Intellectual Origins of the Constitution.* Lawrence: University Press of Kansas.
McGucken, William J. (S.J.). 1932. *The Jesuits and Education.* New York: Bruce Publishing Co.
McNeilly, F.S. 1968. *The Anatomy of Leviathan.* London: Macmillan.
Mehl, Roger. 1970. *Ethique catholique et éthique protestante.* Neuchatel: Delachaux et Niestlé.
– 1970. *The Sociology of Protestantism.* Philadelphia: Westminster Press.
Mesnard, Pierre. 1936. *Essai sur la morale de Descartes.* Paris: Boivin & Cie.
– 1969 (1935). *L'Essor de la philosophie politique.* Paris: Vrin.
– 1972. La "Pédagogie des Jésuites." In Jean Chateau (ed.), *Les Grands pédagogues,* 57–119. Paris: Presses Universitaires de France.
Michel Foucault philosophe. (Collection) 1989. Paris: Seuil.
Michelet, Jules. 1965 (1846). *Le Peuple.* Paris: Julliard.
Mill, John Stuart. 1963–89. *Collected Works.* 31 vols. Toronto: University of Toronto Press.

Mirabeau, Victor de Riqueti 1972 (1769). *Les Économiques*. Darmstadt: Scientia Verlag Aalen.
Mohan, Raj P. (ed).1987. *The Mythmakers*. New York: Greenwood Press
Molnar, Thomas. 1961. *The Decline of the Intellectual*. Cleveland, Ohio: Meridian Books.
Montaigne, Michel de. 1962. *Oeuvres complètes*. Paris: Gallimard.
Montesquieu, Charles-Louis de Secondat. 1900 (1748). *The Spirit of the Laws*. T. Nugent(transl.) 2 vols. New York: Colonial Press.
– 1949, 1951. *Oeuvres complètes*. 2 vols. Paris: Gallimard.
Morange, Jean. 1988. *La Déclaration des droits de l'homme et du citoyen*. Paris: Presses Universitaires de France.
Morelly. 1950 (1755). *Code de la nature*. G. Chinard (ed.). Abbeville: Imprimerie F. Paillart.
Moreno, Rafael. 1966. "Modern Philosophy in New Spain" In Mario de la Cueva, *Major Trends in Mexican Philosophy*, 130–183. Notre Dame, IN: Notre Dame Press.
Morgan, Edmund S. 1976. *The Challenge of the American Revolution*. New York: W.W. Norton.
Morgan, Robert. 1974. "Madison's Theory of Representation in the Tenth Federalist." *Journal of Politics* 36, no. 4 (Nov.): 852-85.
Mornet, Daniel. 1933. *Les Origines intellectuelles de la Révolution française*. Paris: Armand Colin.
Mourant, John Arthur. 1943. *The Physiocratic Conception of Natural Law*. Chicago, IL: University of Chicago Press.
Mueller, Iris W. 1956. *John Stuart Mill and French Thought*. Urbana: University of Illinois Press.
Murdoch, Iris. 1961 (1953). *Sartre Romantic Rationalist*. New Haven, CT: Yale University Press.
Nettl, J.P. 1970. "Ideas, Intellectuals, and Structures of Dissent." In Philip Rieff (ed.), *On Intellectuals*, 53–122. Garden City, NY: Anchor Books.
Nichols, Ray. 1978. *Treason, Tradition and the Intellectual*. Lawrence: Regents Press of Kansas.
Nicolet, Claude. 1982. *L'Idée républicaine en France*. Paris: Gallimard.
Niebuhr, H. Richard. 1961. "The Protestant Movement and Democracy in the United States." In James W. Smith and A.L. Jamison (eds.), *The Shaping of American Religion*. Princeton NJ: Princeton University Press.
Nisbet, Robert A. 1965. "What is an Intellectual." *Commentary*, 40, no. 6 (Dec.): 93–101.
Nizan Paul. 1974 (1932). *Les Chiens de garde*. Paris: François Maspero.
Nora, Pierre. 1980. "Que peuvent les intellectuels?" *Le Débat*, no. 1 (May): 3–19.
Norton, David F. 1966. *From Moral Sense to Common Sense*. San Diego: Univ. of California Ph.D. Thesis.

- 1982. *David Hume*. Princeton, NJ: Princeton University Press.
Oakeshott, Michael. n.d. "Introduction." In Thomas Hobbes, *Leviathan*. London: Basil Blackwell.
- 1974 (1962). *Rationalism in Politics*. London: Methuen.
O'Brien, Conor C., and William D. Vanech (eds). 1969. *Power and Consciousness*. London: University of London Press.
O'Connor, D.J. 1967. *Aquinas and Natural Law*. London: Macmillan.
Orwell, George. 1940. *Inside the Whale*. London: Victor Gollancz.
- 1955 (1952). *Homage to Catalona*. Boston: Beacon Press.
Ory, Pascal (ed.). 1990. *Dernières questions aux intellectuels*. Paris: Olivier Orban.
Ory, Pascal, and J.-F. Sirinelli. 1986. *Les Intellectuels en France, de l'Affaire Dreyfus à nos jours*. Paris: Armand Colin.
Paine, Thomas. 1880 (1791). *Rights of Man*. Chicago, IL: Belford, Clarke & Co.
Palmer, R.R. 1961 (1939). *Catholics and Unbelievers in Eighteenth Century France*. New York: Cooper Square Publ.
Pangle, Thomas L. 1973. *Montesquieu's Philosophy of Liberalism*. Chicago IL: Chicago University Press.
- 1988. *The Spirit of Modern Republicanism*. Chicago: University of Chicago Press.
Parodi, D. 1925. *La Philosophie contemporaine en France*. Paris: Félix Alcan.
Pascal, Blaise 1960 (1670). *Pensées*. Brunschvicg ed. Paris: Garnier.
Passerin d'Entrèves, A. 1951. *Natural Law*. London: Hutchinson's House.
Payne, Harry C. 1976. *The Philosophes and the People*. New Haven, Conn.: Yale University Press.
Paz, Octavio. 1961. *The Labyrinth of Solitude*. New York: Grove Press.
Pécaut, Daniel. 1986. *Le Rôle politique des intellectuels en Amérique latine*. Paris: Centre d'étude des mouvements sociaux.
- 1989. *Entre le peuple et la nation*. Paris: Maison des sciences de l'homme.
Perrens, F.T. 1896. *Les Libertins en France au Dix-septième Siècle*. Paris: Léon Chailley
Perry, Ralph B. 1944. *Puritanism and Democracy*. New York: Vanguard Press.
Phillips, William. 1983. *A Partisan View*. New York: Stein & Day.
Picon-Salas, Mariano. 1962 (1944). *A Cultural History of Spanish America from Conquest to Independence*. Berkeley: University of California Press.
Pierce, Roy. 1966. *Contemporary French Political Thought*. London: Oxford University Press.
Pike, Frederick B. 1964. *The Conflict Between Church and State in Latin America*. New York: Alfred A. Knopf.
Pintard, René. 1943. *Le Libertinage érudit*. Paris: Boivin & Cie.
Pinto, Louis. 1984a. *L'Intelligence en action: Le Nouvel Observateur*. Paris: A.M. Métailié.

– 1984b. "La Vocation de l'Universel." *Actes de la recherche en sciences sociales.* No. 55, November.
Piobetta, J.B. 1937. *Le Baccalauréat.* Paris: J.B. Baillière & Fils.
Plamenatz, John. 1949. *The English Utilitarians.* Oxford: Basil Blackwell.
– 1963. *Man and Society.* 2 vols. London: Longmans.
Pocock, J.G.A. 1975. *The Machiavellian Moment.* Princeton, NJ: Princeton University Press.
– 1985. *Virtue, Commerce and History.* Cambridge: Cambridge University Press.
Poggi, Gianfranco. 1983. *Calvinism and the Capitalist Spirit.* Amherst: University of Massachusetts Press.
Poinsenet, M.D. 1958 (1952). *France du XVIIe Siècle.* Paris: Casterman.
Pomeau, René. 1956. *La Religion de Voltaire.* Paris: Librairie Nizet.
– 1963. *Politique de Voltaire.* Paris: Armand Colin.
– 1966. *L'Europe des Lumières.* Paris: Stock.
– 1994. *On a voulu l'enterrer: 1770–1791.* Oxford: Voltaire Foundation.
Ponteil, Félix. 1966. *Histoire de l'enseignement en France.* Paris: Sirey.
Popkin, Richard H. 1979. *The History of Scepticism from Erasmus to Spinoza.* Berkeley, CA: University of California Press.
Poster, Mark. 1984. *Foucault, Marxism and History.* Cambridge: Polity Press.
Prochasson, Christophe. 1991. *Les Années électriques 1880–1910.* Paris: La Découverte
– 1993. *Les Intellectuels, le socialisme et la guerre.* Paris: Seuil.
Prost, Antoine, 1968. *L'Histoire de l'enseignement en France. 1800–1967.* Paris: Armand Colin.
Proust, Jacques. 1967. *Diderot et l'Encyclopédie.* Paris: Armand Colin.
Prunel, Louis. 1921. *La Renaissance catholique en France au XVIIème Siècle.* Paris: Desclée, De Brouwer.
Quesnay, François. 1958 (1765). "Le Droit naturel." In *François Quesnay et la physiocratie* (no authors). Paris: Institut national d'études démographiques.
Raat, William D. 1968. "Leopoldo Zea and Mexican Positivism: a Reappraisal." *The Hispanic American Historical Review* 48, no 1 (Feb.): 1–18.
Ramos, Samuel. 1962 (1934). *Profile of Man and Culture in Mexico.* Austin: University of Texas Press.
Rangel, Carlos. 1976. *Du Bon sauvage au bon révolutionnaire.* Paris: Robert Laffont.
Raphael, D.D. 1947. *The Moral Sense.* London: Oxford University Press.
– 1967. *Political Theory and the Rights of Man.* Bloomington, IN: Indiana University Press.
– 1969. *British Moralists 1650–1880.* 2 vols. Oxford: Clarendon Press.
– 1977. *Hobbes, Morals and Politics.* London: George Allen and Unwin.
Ratio atque institutio studiorum. 1850. (1599) Paris: Firmin Didot.
Rauh, Frédéric. 1903. *L'Expérience morale.* Paris: Félix Alcan.
Ravaisson, Félix. 1904 (1867). *La Philosophie en France au XIXème Siècle.* Paris: Hachette.

Raynal, Abbé de. 1777. *Histoire philosophique et politique des établissements et du commerce des Européens dans les deux Indes.* 7 vols. Maestricht: Jean Edme Dufour et Philippe Roux.

Raynaud, Philippe. 1985. "Des Droits de l'homme à l'État de droit." *Droits,* Presses Universitaires de France, no. 2: 61–73.

Redier, Antoine. 1925. *Comme disait Monsieur de Tocqueville.* Paris: Perrin et Cie.

Rees, John. 1977. "The Thesis of the Two Mills." *Political Studies* 25 (Sept.): 369–82.

Rémond, Gabriel. 1933. *Royer-Collard.* Paris: Sirey.

Rémond, René. 1959. "Les Intellectuels et la politique." *Revue française de science politique* 9, no. 4 (Dec.): 860–80.

– 1982. *Les Droites en France.* Paris: Aubier.

Renan, Ernest. 1947. *Oeuvres complètes.* Paris: Calmann-Lévy.

Rendall, Jane. 1978. *The Origins of the Scottish Enlightenment, 1707–1776.* London: Macmillan Press.

Renouvier, Charles. 1867. *Science de la morale.* Paris: Librairie philosophique de Ladrange.

Rials, Stéphane. 1988. *La Déclaration des droits de l'homme et du citoyen.* Paris: Hachette.

Ribot, Alexandre. 1900. *La Réforme de l'enseignement secondaire.* Paris: Armand Colin.

Rieffel, Rémy. 1993. *La Tribu des clercs.* Paris: Calmann-Lévy, CNRS.

Rioux, J.-P., and J.-F. Sirinelli. 1991. *La Guerre d'Algérie et les intellectuels français.* Paris: Complexe

Ritaine, Evelyne. 1983. *Les Stratèges de la culture.* Paris: Presses de la Fondation nationale des sciences politiques.

Robbins, Bruce (ed.) 1990. *Intellectuals, Aesthetics, Politics Academics.* Minneapolis, MN: University of Minnesota Press.

Robespierre, Maximilien. 1967. *Oeuvres* vol. 10. Paris: Presses Universitaires de France.

Robinet, Jean-Baptiste. 1766. *De la Nature.* 5 vols. Amsterdam: E. Van Harrevelt.

Roche, Daniel. 1988. *Les Républicains des lettres.* Paris: Fayard.

Rock, David. 1985. *Argentina 1516–1982.* Berkeley: University of California Press.

Rodis-Lewis, Geneviève. 1957. *La Morale de Descartes.* Paris: Presses Universitaires de France.

Rogers, G.A.J., and Alan Ryan. 1988. *Perspectives on Thomas Hobbes.* Oxford: Clarendon Press

Romanell, Patrick. 1967 (1952). *The Making of the Mexican Mind.* Lincoln, Ne.: University of Nebraska Press.

Romero, José Luis. 1963 (1946). *A History of Argentine Political Thought.* Stanford. Calif.: Stanford University Press.

Rosanvallon, Pierre. 1985. *Le Moment Guizot*. Paris: Gallimard.
Ross, George. 1987. "The Decline of the Left Intellectual in France." In Alain Gagnon (ed.), *Intellectuals in Liberal Democracies*. New York: Praeger.
– 1991. "French Intellectuals from Sartre to Soft Ideology." In Charles C. Lemert, *Intellectuals and Politics*. Newbury Park, CA: Sage.
Rossiter, Clinton. 1963 (1953). *The Political Thought of the American Revolution*, (part 3 of *Seedtime of the Republic*). New York: Harvest Book.
Rubenstein, Diane. 1990. *What's Left? The École Normale Supérieure and the Right*. Madison, WI: University of Wisconsin Press.
Ruggiero, Guido de. 1959 (1927). *The History of European Liberalism*. Boston: Beacon Press.
Rutland, Robert A. 1955. *Birth of the Bill of Rights 1776–1791*. Chapel Hill, N.C.: University of North Carolina Press.
Ryan, Alan. 1988. *Bertrand Russell*. New York: Hill and Wang.
Sabrié, J.B. 1913. *De l'Humanisme au rationalisme*. Paris: Félix Alcan.
Sadri, Ahmad. 1992. *Max Weber's Sociology of Intellectuals*. New York: Oxford University Press.
Saint-Simon, Claude-Henri de. 1925 (1803). *Lettres d'un habitant de Genève à ses contemporains*. Paris: Félix Alcan.
– 1966 (1869). *Oeuvres*, 6 vols. Paris: Anthropos.
Samuels, Stuart. 1969. "English Intellectuals and Politics in the 1930s." In Philip Rieff (ed.), *On Intellectuals*, 196–247. Garden City, NY: Anchor Books.
Sarrailh, Jean. 1964. *L'Espagne éclairée de la seconde moitié du XVIIIe siècle*. Paris: C. Klincksieck.
Sartre. 1977. Film réalisé par A. Astruc & M. Contat. Paris: Gallimard.
Sartre, Jean-Paul. 1948. *Situations* II. Paris: Gallimard.
– 1956 (1943). *Being and Nothingness*. New York: Philosophical Library.
– 1960. "Avant-propos." Paul Nizan, *Aden-Arabie*, Paris: François Maspero.
– 1964 (1963). *The Words*. London: Hamish Hamilton.
– 1971. "Sartre accuses the Intellectuals of Bad Faith." Interview with J. Gerassi, *New York Times Magazine*, 17 Oct., 38–9,116–18.
– 1972. *Situations* VIII. Paris: Gallimard.
– 1973. "Élections, piège à cons." *Temps modernes*, no. 318 (Jan.): 1099–1108.
– 1974. *Between Existentialism and Marxism*. London: NLB.
– 1976 (1960). *Critique of Dialectical Reason*. London: NLB.
– 1983. *Cahiers pour une morale*. Paris: Gallimard.
Scanlan, James P. 1959. "*The Federalist* and Human Nature." *Review of Politics* 21, No. 4 (Oct.): 657–77.
Schalk, David L. 1979. *The Spectrum of Political Engagement*. Princeton NJ: Princeton University Press.
Schapiro, J. Salwyn. 1934. *Condorcet and the Rise of Liberalism*. New York: Harcourt, Brace and Co.
Schleifer, James T. 1980. *The Making of Tocqueville's Democracy in America*. Chapel Hill, NC: University of North Carolina Press.

Schmitt, Karl. 1971 (1959). "The Clergy and the Enlightenment." In Richard E. Greenleaf, *The Roman Catholic Church in Colonial Latin America*, 151–63. New York: Alfred A. Knopf.

Schouls, Peter A. 1989. *Descartes and Enlightenment*. Kingston: McGill-Queen's University Press.

Schumpeter, Joseph A. 1975 (1942). *Capitalism, Socialism and Democracy*. New York: Harper Colophon.

Scott, John A. 1951. *Republican Ideas and the Liberal Trend in France 1870–1914*. New York: Columbia University Press.

Sée, Henri. 1925. *L'Évolution de la pensée politique en France au XVIIIème siècle*. Paris: Marcel Giard.

Selby-Bigge, L.A.. 1964 (1987). *British Moralists*. 2 vols. Indianapolis, IN: Bobbs-Merrill.

Seliger, M. 1968. *The Liberal Politics of John Locke*. London: George Allen & Unwin.

Sertillanges, A.-D. 1922. *La Philosophie morale de Saint Thomas d'Aquin*. Paris: Félix Alcan.

Shackleton, Robert. 1961. *Montesquieu*. Oxford: Oxford University Press.

Sher, Richard B., and Jeffrey R. Smitten. 1990. *Scotland and America in the Age of the Enlightenment*. Edinburgh: Edinburgh University Press.

Sheridan, Alan. 1980. *Michel Foucault: The Will to Truth*. London: Tavistock.

Shils, Edward, 1970. *Selected Essays*. Chicago IL: Center for Social Organization Studies, University of Chicago.

– 1972. *The Intellectuals and the Powers*. Chicago, IL: University of Chicago Press.

– 1973. "Intellectuals, Tradition and the Traditions of Intellectuals: Some Preliminary Considerations." In S.N. Eisenstadt and S.R. Graubard, *Intellectuals and Tradition*, 1–19. New York: Humanities Press.

Shklar, Judith N. 1969. *Men and Citizens*. Cambridge: Cambridge University Press.

Shumway, Nicolas. 1991. *The Invention of Argentina*. Berkeley: University of California Press.

Sidgwick, Henry. 1962 (1886). *Outlines of the History of Ethics*. London: Macmillan.

Sieyès, Abbé Emmanuel. 1789. *Préliminaire de la Constitution*. In Christine Fauré (ed.), (1988), *Les Déclarations des droits et de l'homme de 1789*, 91–107. Paris: Payot.

– 1963 (1789). *What is the Third Estate?* London: Pall Mall Press.

– 1985. *Écrits politiques*. Paris: Archives contemporaines.

– 1988. "Manuscrit inédit de Sieyès sur les Déclarations des droits de l'homme." In Christine Fauré (ed.), *Les Déclarations des droits et de l'homme de 1789*, 319-24. Paris: Payot. (dated year III of the Republic by Forsyth (1987, 110)).

Simmons, A. John. 1992. *The Lockean Theory of Rights*. Princeton, NJ: Princeton University Press.

Simon, Jules. 1867. *La Liberté politique.* 3rd ed. Paris: Hachette.
Simon, W. M. 1963. *European Positivism in the Nineteenth Century.* Ithaca, NY: Cornell University Press.
– 1972. *French Liberalism 1789–1848.* New York: John Wiley & Sons.
Simon, Yves R. 1967 (1965). *The Tradition of Natural Law.* New York: Fordham University Press.
Sinkin, Richard N. 1979. *The Mexican Reform, 1855–1876.* Austin: University of Texas Press.
Sirinelli, Jean-François. 1988. *Génération intellectuelle.* Paris: Fayard.
– 1990. *Intellectuels et passions françaises.* Paris: Fayard.
Skinner, Quentin. 1978. *The Foundations of Modern Political Thought.* 2 vols. Cambridge: Cambridge University Press.
Smith, David C. 1986. *H.G. Wells.* New Haven: Yale University Press.
Smith, David G. 1965. *The Convention and the Constitution.* New York: St Martin's Press.
Smith, James Allen. 1991. *The Idea Brokers.* New York: Free Press.
Smith, James W., and A.L. Jamison. 1961. *The Shaping of American Revolution.* Princeton, NJ: Princeton University Press.
Smith, Robert J. 1982. *The École Normale Supérieure and the Third Republic.* Albany: State University of New York Press.
Snyder, David C. 1986. "Faith and Reason in Locke's *Essay*" *Journal of the History of Ideas* 47, no. 2 (Apr.–June): 197–205.
Snyders, Georges. 1965. *La Pédagogie en France aux XVIIe et XVIIIe Siècle.* Paris: Presses Universitaires de France.
Sorum, Paul C. 1977. *Intellectuals and Decolonization in France.* Chapel Hill: University of North Carolina Press.
Soulet, Marc Henry. 1987. *Le Silence des intellectuels.* Montreal: Editions Saint-Martin.
Spender, Stephen. 1937. *Forward From Liberalism.* London: Victor Gollancz.
Spink, J.S. 1960. *French Free-Thought from Gassendi to Voltaire.* London: Athlone Press.
Spire, Antoine. 1985. "Les intellectuels, le pouvoir et les médias." *Raison présente,* no. 73: 5–14.
Stabb, Martin S. 1967. *In Quest of Identity.* Chapel Hill: University of North Carolina Press.
State, S.A. 1991. *Thomas Hobbes and the Debate over Natural Law and Religion.* New York: Garland.
Stephen, Leslie. 1900. *The English Utilitarians.* 3 vols. London: Duckworth & Co.
– 1962 (1876,1902). *History of English Thought in The Eighteenth Century.* 2 vols. New York: Harcourt, Brace & World.
Sternhell, Zeev. 1985 (1972). *Maurice Barrès et le Nationalisme français.* Paris: Complexe.

– 1987 (1983). *Ni gauche ni droite.* Paris: Complexe.
Sternhell, Zeev, M. Sznajder, and M. Asheri. 1989. *Naissance de l'idéologie fasciste.* Paris: Fayard.
Stewart, John B. 1963. *The Moral and Political Philosophy of David Hume.* New York: Colombia University Press.
Stoekl, Allan. 1992. *Agonies of the Intellectual.* Lincoln: University of Nebraska Press.
Stoetzer, O. Carlos. 1979. *The Scholastic Roots of the Spanish American Revolution.* New York: Fordham University Press.
Storing, Herbert J. 1981. *What The Anti-Federalists Were For.* Chicago IL: University of Chicago Press.
Strauss, Leo. 1953. *Natural Right and History.* Chicago IL: University of Chicago Press.
Strugnell, Anthony. 1973. *Diderot's Politics.* The Hague: Martinus Nijhoff.
Sutton, Michael. 1982. *Nationalism, Positivism and Catholicism.* Cambridge: Cambridge University Press.
Swingewood, Alan W. 1987. "Intellectuals and the Construction of Consensus in Postwar England." In Alain Gagnon (ed.), *Intellectuals in Liberal Democracies,* 87–100. New York: Praeger.
Symons, Julian. 1957. *The General Strike.* London: Cresset Press.
Taine, Hippolyte. 1901. *Les Origines de la France Contemporaine.* (vol. XI, *Le Régime moderne*). vol. 3. Paris: Hachette.
– (1905). *Les philosophes classiques.* Paris: Hachette.
Tawney, R.H. 1975 (1926). *Religion and the Rise of Capitalism.* Harmondsworth: Penguin Books.
Taylor, A.E. 1965. "The Ethical Doctrine of Hobbes." In Keith C. Brown, *Hobbes Studies,* 35–55. Cambridge, MA: Harvard University Press.
Thibaudet, Alfred. 1927. *La République des professeurs.* Paris: Grasset.
Thomas, P.-Félix. 1967 (1889). *La Philosophie de Gassendi.* New York: Burt Franklin.
Thomson, Ann. 1981. *Materialism and Society in the Mid-Eighteenth Century: La Mettrie's Discours préliminaire.* Genève: Droz.
Tocqueville, Alexis de. (1951–83). *Oeuvres complètes.* 18 vols. Paris: Gallimard.
– 1864–66 *Oeuvres complètes* 9 vols. Paris: Michel Levy.
Topazio, Virgil. 1956. *D'Holbach's Moral Philosophy.* Geneva: Institut et Musée Voltaire.
Torrey, Norman L. 1930. *Voltaire and the English Deists.* New Haven, Conn.: Yale University Press.
Touraine, Alain. 1974a. *Pour la Sociologie.* Paris: Seuil.
– 1974b. *Lettres à une étudiante.* Paris: Seuil.
Tourneux, Maurice. 1970 (1899). *Diderot et Catherine II.* Geneva: Slatkine Reprints.

Troeltsch, Ernst. 1912. *Protestantism and Progress*. London: Williams & Norgate.
- 1931 (1912). *The Social Teaching of the Christian Churches*. 2 vols. London: George Allen & Unwin.
Tuck, Richard. 1979. *Natural Rights Theories*. Cambridge: Cambridge University Press.
Tully, James. 1980. *A Discourse on Property*. Cambridge: Cambridge University Press.
- 1993. *An Approach to Political Philosophy: Locke in Contexts*. Cambridge: Cambridge University Press.
Turk, Christopher 1988. *Coleridge and Mill*. Aldershot: Avebury.
Vacherot, Étienne. 1860. *La Démocratie*. 2ème ed. Brussels: A. Lacroix, Van Meenen & Co.
- 1864. *Essais de philosophie critique*. Paris: F. Chamerot.
Vartanian, Aram. 1953. *Diderot and Descartes*. Princeton NJ: Princeton University Press.
Vedel, Georges. 1992. "Abrégé de l'histoire des droits de l'homme en France depuis 1789." I. *Commentaire*, no 59: 639–46.
Venturi, Franco. 1971. *Utopia and Reform in the Enlightenment*. Cambridge: Cambridge University Press.
Verneaux, Roger. 1945. *Renouvier disciple et critique de Kant*. Paris: Vrin.
Vial, Francisque. 1936. *Trois siècles d'histoire de l'enseignement secondaire*. Paris: Delagrave.
Viotti da Costa, Émilia. 1975. "The Political Emancipation of Brazil." In A.J.R. Russell-Wood (ed.), *From Colony to Nation*, 43–88. Baltimore, MD: John Hopkins University Press.
Volney, Constantin-François. 1837. *Oeuvres complètes*. Paris: Firmin Didot.
Voltaire. 1785. *Oeuvres* 70 vols. Paris: De l'Imprimerie de la Société littéraire typographique.
- 1901. *Works*. W.F. Fleming (transl.). 43 vols. New York: St Hubert Guild.
- 1938 (1756). *Poème sur la loi naturelle*. Berkeley: University of California Press.
- 1953–65. *Correspondence*. 107 vols. Geneva: Les Délices.
- 1955 (1751–77). *Dialogues et anecdotes philosophiques*. Paris: Garnier.
Waddicor, Mark H. 1970. *Montesquieu and the Philosophy of Natural Law*. The Hague: Martinus Nijhoff.
Wade, Ira O. 1971. *The Intellectual Origins of the French Enlightenment*. Princeton NJ: Princeton University Press.
- 1977. *The Structure and Form of the French Enlightenment*. 2 vols. Princeton, NJ: Princeton University Press.
Wald, Alan M. 1987. *The New York Intellectuals*. Chapel Hill: University of North Carolina Press.
Walton, C., and P.J. Johnson (eds.). 1987. *Hobbes's "Science of Natural Justice."* Dordrecht: Martinus Nijhoff.
Walzer, Michael. 1965. *The Revolution of the Saints*. Cambridge, MA: Harvard

University Press.
Warrender, Howard. 1957. *Political Philosophy of Hobbes*. Oxford: Clarendon Press.
Watkins, J.W.N. 1965. *Hobbes's System of Ideas*. London: Hutchinson University Library.
Watson, George. 1977. *Politics and Literature in Modern Britain*. Totowa, NJ: Rowman and Littlefield.
Weaver, R. Kent. 1989. "The Changing World of Think Tanks." *P.S.: Political Science & Politics* 22, no. 3 (Sept.): 563–78.
Webb, Beatrice. 1985. *The Diary of Beatrice Webb*. vol. 4 (1924–43). Cambridge, MA: Belknap Press.
Weber, Eugen. 1962. *Action française*. Stanford, CA: Stanford University Press.
– 1968. *The Nationalist Revival in France 1905–1914*. Berkeley, CA: University of California Press.
Weber, Max. 1952 (1904–5). *The Protestant Ethic and the Spirit of Capitalism*. New York: Charles Scribner's Sons.
– 1968. *Economy and Society*. 3 vols. New York: Bedminster Press.
Weill, Georges. 1921. *Histoire de l'enseignement secondaire en France*. Paris: Payot.
– 1929. *Histoire de l'idée laïque en France au XIXème Siècle*. Paris: Félix Alcan.
Weinstein, Michael A. 1976. *The Polarity of Mexican Thought*. University Park, PA: Pennsylvania State University Press.
Weintraub, Stanley. 1968. *The Last Great Cause*. New York: Weybright & Talley.
Weulersse, Georges. 1910. *Le Mouvement physiocratique en France*. 2 vols. Paris: Félix Alcan.
Whelan, Frederick G. 1985. *Order and Artifice in Hume's Political Philosophy*. Princeton, NJ: Princeton University Press.
Whitaker, Arthur P. 1961 (1942). *Latin America and the Enlightenment*. Ithaca, NY: Cornell University Press.
White, Morton. 1978. *The Philosophy of the American Revolution*. New York: Oxford University Press.
– 1987. *Philosophy, The Federalist, and the Constitution*. New York: Oxford University Press.
White, R.J. 1970. *The Anti-Philosophers*. London: Macmillan.
Wiarda, Howard J. (ed). 1982. *Politics and Social Change in Latin America*. Amherst: University of Massachusetts Press.
Wilenius, Reijo. 1963. *The Social and Political Theory of Francisco Suarez*. Acta Philosophica Fennica XV. Helsinki. no publisher.
Willaert, Léopold (S.J.). 1960. *Après le Concile de Trente*. Paris: Bloud et Gay.
Willey, Basil. 1964. *The English Moralists*. London: Chatto & Windus.
Williams, Edward J. 1973. "Secularization, Integration and Rationalization: Some Perspectives from Latin American Thought." *Journal of Latin American Studies* 5, pt 2 (Nov.): 199–216.
Wills, Garry. 1978. *Inventing America*. New York: Doubleday.

– 1981. *Explaining America: The Federalist*. New York: Doubleday.
Wilson, Stephen. 1969. "The "Action française" in French Intellectual Life." *The Historical Journal* 12, no. 2: 328–50.
Winock, Michel. 1975. *Histoire politique de la revue "Esprit" 1930–1950*. Paris: Seuil.
– 1990. *Nationalisme, antisémitisme et fascisme*. Paris: Seuil.
– 1993. *Histoire de l'extrême droite*. Paris: Seuil.
Wolin, Sheldon S. 1960. *Politics and Vision*. Boston: Little, Brown & Co.
Wood, Gordon S. 1969. *The Creation of the American Republic*. Chapel Hill, N.C.: University of North Carolina Press.
– 1992. *The Radicalism of the American Revolution*. New York: Alfred A. Knopf.
Woodward, Ralph Lee Jr., (ed). 1971. *Positivism in Latin America, 1850–1900*. Lexington, MA: D.C. Heath.
Woolf, Cecil, and John Bagguley. 1967. *Authors Take Sides on Vietnam*. London: Peter Owen.
Woolf, Leonard. 1967. *Downhill all the way*. London: Hogarth.
Woolf, Virginia. 1980. *The Diary of Virginia Woolf*. vol. 3 (1925–30). London: Hogarth Press.
Wortman, Miles L. 1982. *Government and Society in Central America 1680–1840*. New York: Columbia University Press.
Wright, Benjamin F. 1962 (1931). *American Interpretations of Natural Law*. New York: Russell & Russell.
Wrong, Dennis H. 1970. "The Case of the "New York Review." *Commentary* 50, no. 5 (Nov.): 49–63.
Yolton, John W. 1956. *John Locke and the Way of Ideas*. London: Oxford University Press.
– 1988. "Locke and Materialism: The French Connection." *Revue internationale de philosophie* 42, no. 165: 229–53.
Zea, Leopoldo. 1966 (1963). *The Latin American Mind*. Norman, OK: University of Oklahoma Press.
– 1968. "Philosophy and Thought in Latin America." *Latin American Research Review* 3, no. 2: 3–16.
– 1974 (1943). *Positivism in Mexico*. Austin, Texas: University of Texas Press.
Zuckert, Michael P. 1994. *Natural Rights and the New Republicanism*. Princeton, NJ: Princeton University Press.

Index

Aaron, R., 36
Action française, 161–4
Adair, D., 54
Agrippa, 57
Alberdi, J.B., 194
Allen, Woody, 184–5
Althusser, L., 176
Annan, N.G., 68
Anti-Federalists, 56–7
Aprisma, 189, 199
Aquinas, T., 20–6;
    Suarez, 27; Locke, 35;
    Cambridge Platonists,
    39; Shaftesbury, 42,
    Bentham, 48; British
    Enlightenment, 48–9;
    Madison, 55; United
    States founders, 58;
    Council of Trent, 75;
    Descartes, 93; Voltaire,
    106; Physiocrats, 118;
    Maurras, 163
Aragon, L., 66
Aristotle, 23, 24, 49, 88,
    89, 90
Aron, R., 82, 171
Auden, W.H., 66
Augustine, 20, 94

Bachelard, G., 172

Bacon, F., 33, 191
Bagguley, J., 66
Bainville, J., 162
Baker, K., 119, 120
Balguy, J., 40
Barker, E., 51
Barbeyrac, J., 32n
Barko, I., 162
Barreda, G., 195, 196–7
Barrès, M., 160–1, 162,
    163n, 165, 201
Barthes, R., 172, 175,
    176–7
Bastid, P., 127
Basu, A., 5
Baudelot, C., 179
Bayle, P., 98–9
Beauvoir, S. de, 8, 169,
    170, 171
Belgrano, M., 193
Bell, V. and C., 65
Bello, A., 193–4, 197
Belot, G., 152n
Benda, J., 6, 165–6
Bénichou, P., 136, 143
Benrubi, I., 152n
Bentham, J., 45, 47–8,
    113, 121, 193, 196
Bergson, H., 161, 167
Berns, W., 57

Berth, E., 161
Besterman, T., 107
Bilbao, F., 194
Blackstone, W., 51
Blanchot, M., 6
Boehmer, H., 79
Boesche, R., 141
Boltansky, L., 179
Bonald, L. de, 133, 159,
    163
Bossuet, J.B., 131–2, 135,
    142
Boudon, R., 179
Bourdieu, P., 81, 158,
    172, 173
Bourgeois, L., 155–6
Bréal, M., 80
Bredin, J.D., 158
Brown, J., 48
Brym, R., 5
Buisson, F., 153, 157
Burke, E., 60, 159
Burlamaqui, J.J., 32n,
    50–1
Butler, J., 42–3, 44

Calvinism: calling, 10;
    Calvin, 31; contribu-
    tion, 31, 180; laicism,
    32; Mill, 63; Véron,

85; reaction to, 86;
Rousseau, 99; Guizot,
136; Mill and Comte,
149. *See also* individualism; Protestantism
Cambridge Platonists,
39–40
Capitan Peter, C., 163
Carré de Malberg, 127,
130
Caso, A., 199
Cassirer, E., 39
Catholicism: mediation by elite, 9, 12, 20; ethics, 9, 85, 91; secularization, 9, 11, 83, 106, 120, 152, 181, 195; as opposed to Protestantism, 9–12, 19, 32, 49, 60, 62–4, 76, 79, 83–4, 90, 125, 137, 146–7, 149; Clarke, 39; Bentham, 47; Mill, 62–3; Montaigne, 87; Descartes, 93–4; Comte, 145, 146–8; persistence, 156; Benda, 165–6; and intellectuals, 180–1; and press, 182–3; and Latin America, 189. *See also* Aquinas; Council of Trent; elite; Jesuits; justice (objective); natural law; Suarez
Charron, P., 87–8
Chateaubriand, F.R. de, 144
Chomsky, N., 71
Churchill, W., 65
Clarke, S., 39, 40, 120
clerisy, 59–60
"Co-Efficients, " 65
Coleridge, S., 59–60, 62–4
Collier, S., 193
Colman, J., 36
Comte, A., 52, 63–4, 136, 145–50, 154, 155, 161–3 *passim*, 195, 196
Condorcet, C., de, 118–20, 122

conscience, 98–9; Butler, 42; Reid, 48. *See also* moral sense
Constant Benjamin, 133–4, 137
Constant, Benjamín, 197
Cooke, S., 53
Cornford, J., 66
Coser, L.A., 5
Council of Trent, 9, 29, 75–6, 82
Cousin, V., 134–6, 144, 153, 155, 158
Cowling, M., 61
Crawford, W.R., 189
Crocker, L., 98, 102, 110
Crozier, M., 81
Cudworth, R., 39

Dahl, R., 56
Dealy, G., 194
Déclaration des droits, 124–30
Deleuze, G., 173, 174
Delisle de Sales, J., 121
Delumeau, J., 75
Derathé, R., 129n
Descartes, R., 92–4, 96, 191; and Hobbes, 33; and Locke, 38; and *philosophes*, 98, 122; and Condorcet, 119
Dewey, J., 69n
Diderot, D., 107–9, 113, 121, 122
Dieckmann, H., 97–8
Dobson, R.B., 70
Doctorow, E.L., 184
doctrinaires, 134–7
Duguit, L., 130
Dunn, J., 36, 37, 38, 129
Du Pont de Nemours, P., 117
Durkheim, E., 152n, 157, 176
Dworetz, S., 50

Easton, D., 140
Echeverria, E., 194
Einstein, A., 69
elite: Aquinas, 23–4; Locke, 35; Jefferson, 52; Madison, 55, American tradition, 58; Protestantism, 58; British Enlightenment, 59; clerisy, Coleridge, 59–60; Mill, 60–4; Fabian Society, 64–5; Jesuits, 79; Council of Trent, 82–3; Descartes, 94; Malebranche, 96; Voltaire, 103–6; Diderot, 108–9; Helvétius and d'Holbach, 111; La Mettrie, 112–3; Raynal, 113; Mably, 114; Morelly, 114; Physiocrats, 117; Condorcet, 119; *philosophes*, 120–3; Cousin, 135–6; Royer-Collard, 136; *doctrinaires*, 136–7; Michelet, 144; Saint-Simon and Comte, 147–50; Renan, 150–1; Renouvier, 153; Fouillée, 155; Barrès, 160; Maurras, 163; Sartre, 170; in Latin America, 197–8, 199
Encyclopedists, 81, 102, 108, 113, 161
Epicurus, 89
Esmein, E., 127
Etzioni-Halevy, E., 5

Fabian Society, 64, 68
Ferry, J., 156
Ferry, L., 175
Figgis, J., 28
Flaubert, G., 168
Fonda, J., 7
Forster, E.M., 65, 67
Forsyth, M., 127n
Foucault, M., 173–5
Fouillée, A., 154–5
Freud, S., 171
Fry, R., 65

Galileo, 33
Gassendi, P., 88–9, 121
Gauchet, M., 128
Gauthier, D., 34, 35
Gaxotte, P., 162

239 Index

Gay, J., 48
George, C. and K., 31n
Ginsberg, A., 184
Glucksmann, A., 177, 179
Godechot, J., 130
Goerner, E.A., 23n
Góngora, M., 191
Gooch, G.P., 182
Gough, J., 36, 37, 129
Gouldner, A.W., 5
Gramsci, A., 5
Grant, D., 65
Grotius, H., 32n, 37
Guattari, F., 174
Guillermou, A., 79
Guizot, F., 136–7, 158

Hamilton, B., 28
Hartz, L., 50
Hauriou, M., 127, 130
Hayward, J.E.S., 155
Hegel, F., 8, 169
Heidegger, M., 168
Helvétius, C.A., 109–11, 112, 113
Henry, P., 56
Hichborn, B., 56
Hobbes, T., 33–5, 39–40, 46, 54, 55, 131
Hofstadter, R., 69–70
Holbach T. d', 109–12, 113, 121
Hooker, R., 33
Hugo, V., 143, 144
Hume, D., 40, 43, 44, 45–7, 54, 59, 121
Hunt, L., 130
Hutcheson, F., 40, 43–4, 52, 121
Huxley, A., 67

ideal type, 187
IEA, 68
individualism, 12, 180–2; Aquinas, 23, 24–5, 26, 49; Suarez, 28; Dominicans, 29; Protestantism, 31–2, 38–9, 49, 63–4, 106, 135, 182; divisiveness, 125, 142; Calvinism, 31; Hobbes, 33–5 passim; Locke, 37, 38, 128–9; Shaftesbury, 41, 42; Butler, 42–3; Hutcheson, 43; Hume, 46, 47; Bentham, 47–8; Smith, 48; Reid, 48; Puritanism, 50; Jefferson, 53; United States, founders, 53–4, 58; Madison, 57; Coleridge, 60; Mill, 60, 61, 63; Jesuits, 77, 82; Voltaire, 103, 106; Diderot, 107, 108; Helvétius and d'Holbach, 109–11, 112; Raynal, 113; Morelly, 114; Mably, 114; Physiocrats, 115–7; Condorcet, 119; *philosophes*, 122–3; revolutionaries. 124, 125; Sieyès, 126–7; 128; *Déclaration des droits*, 128, 129; Robespierre and Jacobins, 131, 132; Constant, 133, 134; Cousin, 134–5; Tocqueville, 138–9, 140, 141, 142; Laboulaye, 142; Vacherot, 143; Comte, 147; Renan, 150; Belot and Rauh, 152n; Renouvier, 154; Fouillée, 155; Bourgeois, L., 155; Ferry, J., 156; republicans, 156–7; Maurras, 162–3; Sartre, 167, 169; Foucault, 174; and liberalism, 178; intellectuals, 178, 186; Lipovetsky, 178; in Latin America, 194–7 *passim. See also* rights; society
Ingenieros, J. 198
intellectual: self-appointed representative, 4–5; definition, 5–9; sacred zone, 5–6; *intellectuel engagé*, 6; usurpation of competence, 7; individual conscience, 9; product of secularization, 11–2; plurality of determinants, 13; clerisy, 59–60; in Great Britain, 65–9; in United States, 69–71; in New York, 70; Jewish, 70; ideal type, 83, 187; Voltaire, 105–6, 107; Helvétius and d'Holbach, 111; Tocqueville, 142; in nineteenth-century politics, 144; Saint-Simon and Comte, 148, 150; Dreyfus Affair, 157–9; right-wing, 160–4; Sartre, 167–71, 178; Aron, 171; Bourdieu, 172–3; Touraine, 172–3; Foucault, 174–6; Barthes, 176–7; Lyotard, 177; Lamont, 178; Ross, 178; academics, 178–9; and liberalism, 178, 179, 181, 185, 186, 200; summary of, 180–2; in Canada, 186–7; influence of, 187; in Latin America, 189, 193–4, 195, 196, 198, 200 interests. *See* representation of interests

Jacobins, 124, 126, 128, 130–2, 133, 134, 165–6
Jacoby, R., 71
Jansenism, 90, 91
Jarlot, G., 27, 28
Jaume, L., 130, 131
Jefferson, T., 52–3
Jesuits, 85, 90; Suarez, 26–9; pedagogy, 76–82, 83, 94, 158–9, 161, 165–6, 170, 171; in Latin America, 190–2, 197, 198
Jorrin, M., 189
Jouffroy, T., 135
Jouvenel, B. de, 129n
Juárez, B., 196

240 Index

justice (objective) 10, 39, 60, 83; Aquinas, 24; Suarez, 28; Hume, 47; British Enlightenment, 48; Malebranche, 94–6; Voltaire, 102; Diderot, 107; Helvétius and d'Holbach, 110; Physiocrats, 115–6, 117; Condorcet, 118–9; *philosophes*, 120–2 *passim*; Robespierre, 131; Cousin, 135; Tocqueville, 140–1, 142; Comte, 147; Sartre, 170; and intellectuals, 180. *See also* natural law

Kadushin, C., 71
Kant, I., 153
Kenyon, C., 56, 57
Keynes, J.M., 65
Kornhauser, W., 138

La Mettrie, J. de, 112–3
Laboulaye, É., 142
Lafayette, M.J. de, 53
Lagarrigue brothers, 197
Lamartine, A., 144
Lamennais, F. de, 144
Lamont, M., 71, 178
Lanfrey, P., 107
Laski, H., 31
Lastarria, J.V., 197
Le Mercier de la Rivière, P.P., 115–6, 117
Le Trosne, G., 115, 117
Lévy, B.H., 177, 179
Lévy-Bruhl, L., 152n, 157
Lipovetsky, G., 178
Lipset, S.M., 5
Litré, E., 149n, 150
Locke, J., 35–8, 39, 50, 52, 53, 55, 120, 128–9
Lockhart, J., 191
Lough, J., 97–8, 105
Luther, M., 9, 30–1
Lynch, J., 192
Lyotard, J.F., 6, 177

Mably, A. de, 113–4
Macpherson, C.B., 33

Madison, J., 54–6, 57, 58
Maistre, J. de, 133, 159, 160, 163
Malebranche, N., 94–6, 122, 135
Malraux, A., 7, 196
Mandeville, B., 43
Mannheim, K., 196n
Marshall, G., 10
Martin, K., 67
Martz, J.M., 189
Marx, K., 168, 171, 173, 199, 200
Mason, G., 53
Maurras, C., 161–4, 165
mediation, 3–4, 14, 83. *See also* representation of interests
Michelet, J., 144
Mill, J., 194
Mill, J.S., 45, 60–4, 138, 149, 150
Mitre, B., 194
Molnar, T., 71
Montaigne, M. de, 86–7, 88
Montand, Y., 7
Montesquieu, 99–101, 113, 119, 137, 140
Moore, H., 67
moral sense, 42, 43–4, 47, 52, 121. *See also* conscience
Morelly, 113–4
Moreno, M., 193
Morgenthau, H., 71
Mounier, E., 166

Natural law, 10; Aquinas, 21, 23–5; Suarez, 26–9; Hobbes, 33–4; Locke, 35–6; Hume and Bentham, 47; in United States, 50–2, 58; Jefferson, 52; Coleridge, 60; Catholic tradition, 83; Montaigne, 87; Jansenists, 90; Pascal, 91; *philosophes*, 98, 122; Montesquieu, 99–110; Voltaire, 103; Diderot, 109; Helvétius and d'Holbach, 110–11; Physiocrats, 116; Delisle de Sales, 121; *Déclaration des droits*, 125; Sieyès, 126; Jouffroy, 135; Bourgeois, L., 156; Maurras, 163; in Latin America, 192, 194, 197. *See also* justice (objective)

Nettl, J.P., 5
Newton, I., 39
Nicolet, C., 156
Nietzsche, F., 161, 171, 174
Nizan, P., 168, 170
Norton, D.F., 43, 44

Oakeshott, M., 33, 34–5
Occam, W. of, 28, 39
Orwell, G., 67
Ory, P., 158
"Other Club," 65

Paley, W., 48
Pangle, T., 50, 129
Pascal, B., 91
Passerin d'Entrèves, A., 24, 25
Passeron, J.C., 81, 172
Paz, O., 194
Pécaut, D., 200
Pécaut, F., 153
pensadores, 189–90, 195
philosophes, 97–8, 111–3 *passim*, 126n, 133, 136, 159, 169, 170; Voltaire, 101, 104–6; Diderot, 108, Condorcet, 118–24 *passim*; Tocqueville, 141
Physiocrats, 113, 115–8, 120n
Plamenatz, J., 34
Plato, 24, 90, 94, 154; Cambridge Platonists, 39–40
Poggi, G., 10
Popkin, R.H., 86
Polsby, N.W., 8
positivism: in Latin

America, 194–8. *See also* Comte; Renan
Pound, E., 67
press and religious tradition, 182–3
Pressensé, E. de, 157
Price, R., 40
Prost, A., 80
Protestantism: Bible, 9, 30–2, 38–9, 40; subjective ethics, 9, 10; secularization, 9, 11, 12, 40; individual conscience, 9–11, 32, 60, 146, 184; onslaught, 30–3; Calvin, 31; priesthood of believers, 31, 90, 182, 186; evolution, 58; Coleridge, 60; Mill, 62; Fabians, 65; in United States, 70; Jesuits, 79, 83; Sieyès, 125; Constant, 133–4; Cousin, 135; Guizot, 136–7; Tocqueville, 142; Renouvier, 153; Pécaut and Buisson, 153; Benda, 165; and intellectuals, 180–2, 184; and press, 182–3. *See also* Calvinism; individualism
Proust, M., 168
Pufendorf, S., 32n, 37
Puritanism, 50

Quesnay, F., 115

Raat, W., 196n
Ramos, S., 199
Raphael, D.D., 34
rationalism. *See* reason, rationalism
Rauh, F., 152n
Raynal, A. de, 113
Reagan, R., 7
reason, rationalism: Aquinas, 20–3, 25; Suarez, 28, 29; Hobbes, 33–4; Locke, 35–7; Cambridge Platonists, 39–40; Shaftesbury,
41–2; Hutcheson, 43–4; Hume, 45–6; Bentham, 47; Reid, 48; British Enlightenment, 48–9; Jefferson, 52; Madison, 55; Jesuits, 79–80; Montaigne, 87; Gassendi, 89; Pascal, 91; Descartes, 92–4; Malebranche, 95–6; *philosophes*, 98, 121, 122; Montesquieu, 100; Voltaire, 102, 104, 106; Diderot, 108, 109; Helvétius and d'Holbach, 110; de Raynal, 113; Morelly and Mably, 114; Physiocrats, 116; Condorcet, 118–9, 120; revolutionaries, 124; Robespierre, 131; Royer-Collard, 134; Cousin, 134; *doctrinaires*, 136–7; Tocqueville, 137, 140; Vacherot, 143; Comte, 147, 148, 150; Renan, 150; Renouvier, 153; Bourgeois, L., 156; French right wing, 159, 161; Maurras, 162–3, 164; and intellectuals, 180
Redier, A., 142
Reid, T. 48, 134
Rémond, R., 158
Renan, E., 150–1, 163
Renaut, A., 175
Renouvier, C., 152n, 153–4
representation of interests, 57, 129, 187. *See also* mediation
Ricoeur, P., 171, 179
Rieffel, R., 6
right(s), individual: Aquinas, 24–5; Hobbes, 33–4; Locke, 36, 38; Grotius and Pufendorf, 37; Bentham, 48; in American tradition, 50–2, 58; Jefferson, 52–3; Blackstone, 53;
Madison, 55–6; Anti-Federalists, 57; Quesnay, 115; Physiocrats, 115–6; Condorcet, 118–9; *Déclaration des droits*, 124–5, 128; Sieyès, 126; Robespierre, 130–1; Laboulaye, 142; Vacherot, 143; in Latin America, 194
Rivadavia, B., 193
Robespierre, M. de, 130–2
Robinet, J.B., 121
Rodó, J.E., 198
Rosanvallon, P., 136, 179
Ross, G., 178
Rossiter, C., 50, 51
Rousseau, J.J., 8, 98–9, 113, 119, 127–9 *passim*, 150
Royer-Collard, P., 134–6
Russell, B., 65, 68–9

Saint-Simon, C.H. de, 63, 145–6, 148, 154
Sarmiento, D., 194, 197
Sartre, J.P., 6–8 *passim*, 14, 69, 82, 166, 172, 173, 182; conception of the intellectual, 159, 167–71, 181
Schapiro, J.S., 119
Scheurer-Kestner, A., 157
Schmitt, K., 191
Schwartz, S.B., 191
Schwartzenberg, L., 179
secularization: British moralists, 40; Hutcheson, 44; in United States, 51, 58; in France, 157, 158, 160. *See also* Catholicism; Protestantism
Sée, H., 117
Shackleton, R., 99
Shaftesbury, Lord A., 41–2, 43, 121
Shaw, G.B., 65
Shils, E., 5
Shklar, J., 129n
Sieyès, E., 124, 125–8
Simmons, A., 37–8

Sirinelli, J.F., 158
Skinner, Q., 27, 29
Smith, C., 65
Snow, C.P., 67
Snyders, G., 78
society: collectivity prior to individuals, 150, 155, 163; holism 181
solidarism, 153–6
Sorel, G., 161
Soulet, M.H., 185
"Souls" group, 65
Spencer, H., 195–7 *passim*
Spender, S., 66
Staël, G. de, 133, 137
Stephen, L., 32, 35, 39, 43, 46
Stoekl, A., 184
Stoetzer, O.C., 191
Storing, 57
Suarez, 26–9, 39, 193
Swingewood, A.W., 68

Taine, H., 153
Tawney, R.H., 65
Taylor, A.E., 34
Thibaudet, A., 158
think-tanks, 184
Tocqueville, A. de, 137–42, 143
Torre, R.H. de la, 199
Touraine, A., 82, 172, 173, 179
Troeltsch, E., 30, 31
Tuck, R., 25n
Tully, J., 37

Vacherot, É., 143, 153
Vair, G. du, 87
Valle, J.C. del, 193
Vasconcelos, J., 199
Vasquez, F., 26
Vidal-Naquet, P., 179
Vigny, A., 144
Viotti da Costa, E., 192
Vitoria, F. de, 26
Vlady, M., 179
Voltaire, 101–7, 108, 109, 118, 157, 165–8 *passim*, 171

Vovelle, M., 179

Waddicor, M., 99
Walzer, M., 31–2
Warrender, H., 34
Watkins, J.W.N., 34
Waugh, E., 67
Webb, B., 64–5, 66
Webb, S. 64–5
Weber, M., 10–11, 31, 180
Wells, H.G., 65
White, M., 54, 55
Willey, B., 42
Wills, G., 52
Wilson, S., 161
Winthrop, J., 57
Wood, G., 53, 56
Woolf, C., 66
Woolf, L., 65, 67
Woolf, V., 65

Zea, L., 196n, 197–8
Zola, É., 14, 157, 165, 167, 168
Zuckert, M., 50